JOY LARKCOM

Joy Larkcom has had wide experience of both growing vegetables and writing about them. She spent many years experimenting with different techniques before embarking on a year's tour around Europe, studying traditional and modern intensive systems of vegetable growing. In Belgium, Holland, France, Italy, Spain, Portugal, Hungary and Yugoslavia she collected varieties of seeds and studied local methods, returning to England with a wealth of ideas which she soon put into practice, and which provided the background for this book.

Author of *Vegetables from Small Gardens*, and of numerous articles published in many well-known gardening periodicals, Joy Larkcom is currently under contract to write a regular feature for the Royal Horticultural Society's journal, *The Garden*. From her home in East Anglia she runs a business producing organically grown vegetables – mainly salad plants – for the wholefood market.

SALADS
THE YEAR
ROUND

JOY LARKCOM

Illustrated by Elizabeth Winson

Hamlyn Paperbacks

SALADS THE YEAR ROUND
ISBN 0 600 38381 4

First published in Great Britain 1980
by Hamlyn Paperbacks
Copyright © 1980 by Joy Larkcom

Hamlyn Paperbacks are published by
The Hamlyn Publishing Group Ltd,
Astronaut House,
Feltham,
Middlesex, England

Typeset, printed and bound in Great Britain by
Hazell Watson & Viney Ltd, Aylesbury, Bucks

To my very dear Dad

CONTENTS

ACKNOWLEDGEMENTS

First I would like to thank all those people we met on our 'Grand Vegetable Tour' who either passed on their salad wisdom to us, or put us in touch with other knowledgeable people in the salad field. In Belgium Mme Jelena de Belder, and the late Jean and Mieke Collet; in France M. Jean Berrard, the Pozzer family, and M. Gaston Houriez, M. and Mme Bonnome, and fellow members of the Cheminot. In Northern Italy thank you to Prof. Garofalo, Heidi Munscheid, Guy Gagnon, Ursula Arese, Dott. Giuseppe Bellia, Sig. Terzolo of Olter Seeds, Anna Laura Fanelli, Sergio Gorrino and Signora Stefano – and Trevor Sykes for directing us there. In Sardinia my thanks to Isabella Pugioni and Dott. Milia; in Naples to Mario Mennella and his family; in Bari to Dott. V. Bianco and the Rosario family; in Andria the D'Avanzo family; in Chioggia Achille Perini; in Portugal Chris Shinn – and everywhere the seedsmen, market gardeners, market traders, gardeners and ordinary people, many of whose names we never knew, who each added something to our knowledge. I would also like to thank Allan Jackson, for stimulating, or provoking us (from the cosiness of his Welsh fireside), to go on our 'expedition', and the Stanley Smith Horticultural Trust for helping to finance it.

Back at home, thank you to Rosemary Verey, for her generous invitation to browse through her library – which opened up a whole new, or rather old, world to me.

On the technical side my thanks to the following for samples of their products: Corruplast Limited (Correx sheeting), Fisons Limited (Blockaid and Levington blocking compost), the manufacturers of the Devon, Westray and Essex cloches respectively, and Tangent Marketing (Sproutakit).

For up-to-date information on fennel, I am indebted to Philip Hollowell, on bush tomato varieties to Mr A. J. George, and for professional advice on nutritional aspects of seed sprouting to Michael Nelson.

Thank you also to Ken Toyé for his enthusiastic and expert advice on recipes; to John and Caroline Stevens for much advice and for reading through the chapters on herbs, flowers and wild plants; and to Dr P. J. Salter, who bore the brunt of reading through the manuscript and made so many helpful and thoughtful comments, which I am sure have resulted in a far better book.

A special thank you to Elizabeth Winson for her painstaking and enthusiastic work on the illustrations. Another special thank you to my husband Don, not only for carrying out most of the theoretical and practical 'research' on the recipes, but for running the house and garden during the final months. Thanks also to my children Brendan and Kirsten for being remarkably understanding. You can have the pop radio on now as loud as you like!

Thank you also to Joanna Jellinek for her helpful opinions on what to eliminate (!), to Carole Williams for typing with such willingness, and to Bob Pearson and the publishers for their continual encouragement and help.

And finally, no rural writer could do without the postmen. Thank you, Tony, George, Alan and Michael, for overcoming the alleged deficiencies of the Post Office with an unsurpassable personal service. So what if you were bribed with Little Gem and bewildered by 'saladini'!

Montrose Farm
Hepworth
Diss
Norfolk

LIST OF ILLUSTRATIONS

Introduction:
A Personal Saga

I feel I should start by confessing that I am a vegetable klepto-maniac – more precisely, a *raw* vegetable kleptomaniac. I find it almost impossible to walk around a kitchen garden without nibbling a leaf here, snapping off a pea pod there, savouring a fragment of parsley or chervil. I can only suppose it is this habit which has led to my appreciation of the wonderful variety of flavours and textures which can be produced in an English garden, and above all, to a passionate interest in salads.

For years I had a limited, conventional view of salads. They came with summer (how one longed for the first fresh salad of the year), and they were mainly of lettuce, with radish, spring onion, cucumber and tomato in supporting roles. Only gradually did I realize that it is perfectly feasible to pick salads from your garden all the year round and, moreover, that an almost infinite number of plants can be used in salads: cultivated and wild plants; roots, leaves, seed pods and flowers; sprouted seeds and seedlings.

Looking back, it seems to me that the somewhat meandering road to these discoveries was marked with several milestones. It began about ten years ago when we moved to our present home in East Anglia. With little money, plenty of space, and a family on the way, there was every incentive to grow vegetables. I started systematically to try out the 'unusual' vegetables in seed cata-logues, and found that a great many of them were salads; in particular, salads which could be used in late autumn, winter and early spring, when it is so hard to grow a good lettuce. Within a few years I had discovered celeriac, land cress and corn salad, the enormous long red Chinese winter radish, Welsh onions which stay green all winter, Chinese cabbage for a quick autumn crop, succulent Sugar Loaf chicory and endive.

Winter salads became one of the specialities of the house. I loved to go out into the apparently bare garden in winter to collect a salad, digging up roots protected with straw, and wheedling corn salad out from a covering of bracken. The leaves of land cress and corn salad would be used whole, the Chinese cabbage (which survived until heavy frost) and the various chicories would be chopped up, while the celeriac and radish would be grated: the end result was a lovely blend of fresh flavours, doubly welcome in midwinter. I wallowed unashamedly in visitors' praise, and surprise: 'Not all from the garden at *this* time of year? – but what's this? – and this?'

The next milestone was being commissioned to write a book on growing vegetables in small gardens, during one of those periods of economic crisis when people were digging up their lawns to plant potatoes and the queues for allotments were lengthening. I began experimenting with intensive techniques such as intercropping and undercropping and growing dwarf varieties. But the most fascinating idea I came upon was the 'cut-and-come-again' technique. I knew that you could chop off an old cabbage, cut a cross in the stalk, and with luck get four or five more young cabbages growing from the cut; but I did not realize you could cut off lettuce, turnip tops, kale and spinach at different stages of growth and that they would resprout once, twice or even three times.

On a visit to some allotments in Manchester 'the Italian's' was pointed out to me. He was not there, unfortunately, but his fellow allotment holders told me that he grew many unusual vegetables and in most unusual ways – including 'cut-and-come-again'. My curiosity was aroused. At about the same time I heard of experiments that the National Vegetable Research Station were doing with what they called 'leaf lettuce': growing cos lettuce plants very close together, and close cropping them several times in the season before the plants reached maturity. By using this method a small patch of ground could yield more than twice the normal weight of lettuce in one season.

By now I had a hunch that there was a lot to be learned about both vegetables and techniques from the Continent, particularly from the peasant farmers. I was also becoming interested in the need to collect and preserve the seed of old and local varieties which, under modern pressure for conformity and economy, were being squeezed out of use and were in danger of disappearing for ever. Apart from their intrinsic interest and value, these old and local varieties often prove of value to plant breeders, harbouring useful genetic characteristics such as hardiness, resistance to disease, and adaptation to particular climatic conditions.

These ideas gave my husband and me an excuse to realize a long-cherished dream, to take a year off and travel. He gave up his job, we let the house, bought a second-hand van and caravan and with our two children, then aged five and seven, set off on a year's wandering around Europe to investigate vegetable growing. We called it The Grand Vegetable Tour, and were fortunate enough to get a grant towards the cost from the Stanley Smith Horticultural Trust. Before our departure we had collected a mass of advice, names of people to contact, requests to look for certain species and varieties and so on. But perhaps ringing loudest in my ears as we left were the words: 'Don't forget to look out for those lovely red Italian chicories.'

As far as knowledge of salads was concerned, what a milestone that year proved to be. The first influx of new ideas came from Belgium, where in the remarkable kitchen garden attached to the de Belders' arboretum at Kalmhout I first saw little patches of gold-leaved purslane, rocket, ordinary cress, chervil and the oak-leaved Salad Bowl lettuce – all grown for salads. Sometimes no more than a square metre each, resown and cut over several times during the year to keep a large household in supply. From Mme de Belder, who is Yugoslav, we first learnt of the Yugoslavian 'bottoms-up' phenomenon – the countryside in spring full of people, heads down, bottoms up, collecting the first young leaves of dandelion and other wild plants for salads. We were soon to come across this ourselves in Northern Italy, in fact we were soon to be doing it ourselves!

In the trial grounds of the Belgian seed firm Gonthier I came across what to me was a completely new salad plant, *Claytonia perfoliata*, or winter purslane. I have since found it to be amongst the hardiest of salad plants, surviving even severe winters unprotected, with its heart-shaped succulent leaves and dainty white flowers bursting into vigorous growth early in spring. It is naturalized in many parts of Britain and considered to be a weed, but what a useful one.

It was a cold and wet late summer before we reached France. Camping in the Cheminot, the French Railway Workers' gardens (perhaps the nearest equivalent to our allotments), I was introduced to a whole range of curled and broad-leaved endives, the latter all colours – reddish brown, green, yellow, striped, grown for autumn and winter, and later blanched.

It was also in France, on the seed firm Clause's trial grounds, that I got my first glimpse into the world of Italian chicories. Being early autumn the red varieties had still not acquired the intense red colouring which comes with the cold weather, but I was astounded at the variety: coarse serrated-leaved wild chicories, closely resembling and closely related to dandelion; the sweet Sugar Loaf and Milan types, sometimes eaten when seedlings, sometimes when they have developed crisp hearts; the round and loose-headed coloured types; the green ground-hugging rosettes of the 'grumolos' and the blade-leaved 'spadonas'; and the curious asparagus Catalogna chicories, with bitter leaves but throwing up delicious asparagus-like shoots, the *puntarelle*, in spring.

Five months later we had worked our way, via Portugal and Spain, to Italy. It was mid-March and on the advice of a knowledgeable friend we immediately headed north to catch the tail end of the winter salads. Our first stop, due to nightfall overtaking us, was Cuneo in the Piedmontese plain. Shopping the next morning in a local store, we encountered our first crate of mixed Italian salad, and bought half a kilo. What a salad that was – both for the eye and for the palate! It was a mixture like my salads at home, but almost all the ingredients were unfamiliar. There was crinkly red-leaved lettuce of the Salad Bowl type, beautiful red, green and variegated chicories, a miniature lettuce (the exceptionally hardy Parella), the contrasting lime and dark-green rosettes of different varieties of Grumolo chicory, mild-flavoured lamb's lettuce and pungent rocket.

The next two weeks were undoubtedly our Salad Days. From Turin, we visited wholesale and local markets, market gardens and amateur gardens, seed stalls and seed houses in an attempt to unravel and identify this host of new salad plants. The task of identifying them was complicated by the fact that the common names used can vary, literally, from village to village. In those two weeks I discovered nine local names for Grumolo chicory alone!

Apart from the immense variety of cultivated plants, the markets were full of baskets of wild plants and herbs, gathered from the countryside by the peasants. Among them were dandelion, rocket, valerianella, chicory, poppy, thistle, sorrel – and others I never identified. Yet another category were the 'saladini', tiny seedling leaves and thinnings, mainly chicories and lettuce, for mixing into salads. At home, these would have been thrown away. We also learnt something about the growing techniques: in many cases they were broadcast on to long narrow beds and thinned out in stages, the thinnings being sold. There was a great deal of clever intercropping, every spare piece of ground being used intensively.

On one peasant farm we came across an interesting system of intercropping chicory, clover and wheat. The farmer's wife had a market stall where she sold mostly wild salad plants, and I had asked if she would show us how she gathered them. She willingly agreed, and we wandered with her across the field, as with her razor-like knife she cut young growths of poppies, thistles, dandelions, saying as she went 'This one you can eat' – 'this one is bitter' – and so on. There was a great deal of the by now familiar Grumolo chicory growing among the grass and this, she explained, had been sown the previous spring. They mixed the chicory seed with clover seed, and broadcast the two together between the rows of young wheat. First the wheat was harvested, then the clover matured and was cut and fed to livestock, and finally the chicory, unharmed by the summer cutting, struggled through the surrounding weeds to be cut in its turn in spring, two or three times. The more you cut it, said the farmer's wife, the more it grows!

We returned from our Grand Vegetable Tour in late August, armed with ideas and packets of foreign seed, all of which we were longing to try in British conditions. Our own neglected kitchen garden, apart from the inevitable weeds, was almost bare of vegetables. Not quite bare, however, for some of the Sugar Loaf chicories, endive and corn salad left in the ground the previous year had gone to seed and sown themselves. And this brought home to me another of the merits of these old, rustic, salad crops. They have been grown for centuries simply because they are so endurable, and so easy to raise from seed.

I learnt something else from our homecoming. There were little cresslike seedlings all over the garden, and mistaking them for land cress, I transplanted them into orderly rows in useful places. But they did not behave like land cress; they were indeed the wild hairy bitter cress, and what a useful little plant it is. It disappears in hot weather but reappears in early autumn, continuing to grow in any mild spells in winter and spring, fresh and green long before even the first aconites appear. The tiny leaves can be cut off with scissors and are a lovely addition to a salad.

In the testing, long winter of 1978/79 we tried out many varieties of red chicory and found that several were truly hardy. Some we left unprotected; some we covered with straw. In midwinter I absentmindedly put a miniature plastic cloche over one of the plants, and one bleak day in February found snuggled in the straw beneath a beautiful rose-red nugget of a red chicory – what a cheering sight in that miserable winter!

We started growing our own version of the Italian mixed salads to sell to wholefood shops, blending together fifteen or twenty ingredients which varied with the seasons. We called them, nostalgically, and a little inappropriately, 'saladini'. The main ingredient was Little Gem lettuce; to add the colour, so essential in a mixed salad, we used edible flowers: elderflowers, borage, cucumber, nasturtium and rose petals. We incorporated finely-shredded white and red cabbage, oriental vegetables such as chop suey greens and the serrated-leaved Japanese greens, Mizuna – another very hardy species. We also tried various edible weeds and found chickweed, when grown in the shade, to be wonderfully succulent. I began to cultivate little patches of it, not least because, like hairy bitter cress, it is at its best late and early in the year. For further variety we would add a few finely-chopped herbs. I must admit I was proud of our saladini. They looked and tasted lovely. I thought we were doing something really original, which brings me to the last of the milestones.

1979 was the 'Year of the Garden', and as part of the celebrations, the Victoria and Albert Museum mounted an historical exhibition, 'The Garden', covering ten centuries of British gardening. I was invited to suggest material for the vegetable section. It was a daunting task; what did I know of vegetable growing in the past ten centuries? The answer was very little, but in attempting to discover more, I delved for the first time into the works of the great classical writers: John Parkinson, John Evelyn, Leonard Meager and J. Worlidge of the 17th century; Stephen Switzer, Richard Bradley and Batty Langley of the 18th. And to my amazement I discovered that during these two centuries salads were of immense importance and the art of growing them highly developed.

An astonishing range of plants, many of which have since gone out of common usage, were grown for salads. They also used wild plants, weeds, garden flowers, seeds and seedlings, and cooked roots. Some of their lists of salads could have been our own lists of saladini! For example, Batty Langley's 'Raw Sallets for July, August and September' from *New Principles of Gardening* (1728), included: 'borage flowers, chervil, corn sallet, garden cresses, cucumber, lettice, mustard, melons, nasturtium flowers, young onions, purslane, horse radish, sorrel, tarragon'. Almost all of these had, at one time or another, gone into our saladini. We were not, it seemed, doing anything original after all; we had merely stumbled upon forgotten skills of the past. But there was no reason why we should not learn from the past and transplant some of their ideas to our 20th-century garden; and this we have tried to do. Indeed, through following suggestions in these old books, my seed order this year contained a number of new items which I hope to grow in the future: skirret, violets, primroses and Jenny stonecrop, for example.

One of the most authoritative of the early writers was the diarist John Evelyn, who devoted an entire book to the subject: *Acetaria, a Discourse on Salads*. He summarized his gardening ideas in 1669 in a short book of directions for his gardener at Sayes Court, which is a mine of information on the cultivation and use of salad herbs, as they were then known, in the 17th century. First he lists those salads which were blanched, in other words kept in the dark or grown with light excluded to render them sweeter and whiter. He goes on to describe the many plants which could be used green, stating precisely the stage at which the leaves should be picked: another sphere in which we can learn from the past, for with our modern tendency to stress size in vegetables, we overlook the fact that it is often the young leaves which are the tastiest, the most tender, and often the most nutritious.

Here are a few examples from Evelyn's *Directions*: with lettuce use leaves 'of a fine middling size'; with the broad- and curled-leaved cresses and spinach use 'just the leaves next the seed leaves and the next to them'; with sorrel 'take only the first young leaves of spring'; with sweet chervil, burnet, Spanish rocket and parsley 'the young leaves after the seed leaves'.

He then advises his gardener to select the flowers and flower buds of nasturtium; the tender young leaves of shallot, chives and young onion; the seed leaves and young tops of rampion and Trip Madam (the stonecrop *Sedum reflexum*); seed leaves of turnip, mustard, and the weed scurvy grass; the young tender leaves and shoots of sampier (or samphire, collected from cliffs), balm and red sage ... and so on. Evelyn even suggests using the first seedling leaves of oranges and lemons. Growing these exotic fruits was the height of fashion in his day!

The early gardening writers took pains to advise the cook, and one often encounters suggestions that salads 'should be judiciously mixed'. Perhaps to help the less experienced they would break down the salads into 'the hot and biting' and 'the more cool and insipid'. Batty Langley graded his plants by degrees: onion almost in the 4th degree, garden rocket 3rd degree, broom buds (a common favourite) 2nd degree. To me this was yet another link with saladini. In preparing it I would often have a bucket of mixed 'mild' plants and another of 'strong', to give balance to the final mixture.

Research into the past also shows how salads have gone in and out of fashion in England over the centuries. It seems that it was the Romans who first introduced them. In Rome they were known as 'vinegar diets' and were highly valued, not least because they needed no cooking, so economized on fuel. Pliny remarked that 'They were found to be easy of digestion, by no means apt to overload the senses, and to create but little craving for bread as an accompaniment.' This was of economic significance, for wheat was imported from North Africa, and the price of bread was normally subsidized to bring down the cost of living.

The Romans may well have been the earliest to force salads. Emperor Tiberius, who lived from 42 BC to AD 37, was advised for medical reasons to eat cucumber all the year round. So he devised a system of making cucumber beds on frames, mounted on wheels. These could be moved out into the sun in summer and brought indoors in winter, to be protected under frames glazed with the mica *Lapis specularia*.

So when the Romans invaded Britain, they brought with them the art of cultivating lettuce, endive, radish, cucumber and many other salad plants. As far as we can tell from the scant records which remain, most of these died out of cultivation in the centuries following the Roman withdrawal, in many cases not to be revived until Tudor times. In spite of our amenable climate, we were remarkably uninterested in the use of any vegetables other than for their medicinal properties, for seasoning or for soups. When Catherine of Aragon wanted a salad she had, says Holinshed, to despatch a messenger to Flanders to procure it !

The Renaissance on the continent of Europe was accompanied by a revival of interest in vegetable growing, which eventually spread to Britain, so by the 17th and 18th centuries appreciation of salads was at its peak in this country. It apparently ebbed away slowly in favour of more substantial cooked vegetables in the middle of the 19th century. For some reason, as we discovered while touring Europe, interest in and knowledge of the diversity of European salad plants was never lost on the Continent.

There has, of course, always been a minority in this country who enjoy the delights of fresh salad, for preference grown only a few paces from the kitchen. That minority is currently being swollen by the ever-increasing numbers of people concerned with health, weight, vegetarianism and the 'organic' movement – even perhaps by the many travellers to the Continent who return with their food horizons widened and curiosity aroused.

I hope this book will act as a springboard for all those who, for whatever motive, want to grow their own salads all the year round. And I hope they will get as much fun and pleasure from it as I have – both in the garden and where it all ends, at table. *Bon appétit!*

Part I
Basic Principles

In the following nine chapters many of the basic principles and practices of vegetable growing are discussed, largely with the ever-growing army of 'new' gardeners in mind. For experienced gardeners much of the material will, no doubt, be familiar, though I have tried to incorporate some new ideas (and some old ones worth reviving), and to highlight techniques which are particularly relevant to salad growing. The individual plants are covered in Part II.

First, however, I would like to mention record keeping. Whether one is an old hand or a newcomer to vegetable growing, keeping a gardening diary is an invaluable habit. Every garden and every household is unique, and in due course one's personal diary becomes a far more practical guide into how much of what to sow and when than any gardening book! Moreover, gardening is an inexact science and however small or humble one's plot, there is always scope for experimenting usefully with new varieties and slightly different methods in one's own conditions, and noting the results. I am always glad to hear from anyone who has made any 'discoveries' in connection with growing salad plants.

I

SOIL FERTILITY

If anyone were to ask me what are the most important factors in growing vegetables, especially salads, successfully, I would reply without hesitation: soil fertility and shelter. So soil fertility is a good starting point.

First, what exactly is soil? It looks solid, but in an average garden slightly less than half the volume of soil is solid matter; the rest is air and water, essential for both the animal and plant life in the soil. All organisms need water, and plants absorb much of their food, elements such as nitrogen, phosphorus, potassium, calcium, magnesium and sulphur, and half a dozen others known as trace elements, in water through their roots. Roots also take in oxygen from the soil as part of the plant's breathing process. Indeed, in waterlogged airless soils plants cannot survive.

The solid part of the soil is made up of mineral particles of sand, silt and clay, which have been formed over the centuries by the breakdown of rocks. Some of the nutrients required by plants are found in these particles, particularly in the clays. An important five per cent of the solid material in the soil is organic matter. This is a mixture of the remains of plants and animals, decomposing vegetation and humus, and the tiny microorganisms living in the soil. The organic matter can be looked upon as the main storehouse of the essential nutrients which plants need. But before the nutrients can be made available or released to plants, the organic matter has to be broken down into humus.

This is one of the most important processes taking place in the soil, and is performed by micro-organisms such as bacteria. Soil fertility largely depends on creating the optimum conditions for the micro-organisms to work, that is ensuring they have adequate moisture and oxygen, that the soil is not too acid or too alkaline for them, and that there is an adequate supply of organic matter for them to work on. A key factor here is soil structure, this and humus being closely related.

SOIL STRUCTURE AND SOIL TYPES: The mineral and organic particles in the soil join together to form small lumps or crumbs of varying sizes. In good soil these are stable. Around them a network of spaces or pores is built up, and with the crumbs make up the soil structure. The spaces between the crumbs form channels which are the aeration and drainage system of the soil. When it rains, the surplus water drains off through the channels preventing the soil from becoming waterlogged; but the rest of the water remains in the smallest pores, forming a moisture reservoir for roots and soil organisms. The large spaces between the crumbs are filled with air.

One of the main differences between sand, silt and clay, explaining their different character, is their ability to form crumbs. Sandy soils have large particles which are very reluctant to stick together: the spaces between the particles are large, so water drains away easily and the soil contains plenty of air. Sandy soils therefore warm up quickly in spring, but dry out rapidly in summer. They are usually poor in nutrients, which are washed out in the drainage water.

A clay soil is the other extreme; because of the unique chemistry of clay, the minute particles have a tendency to stick together. Pure clay is sticky, there are few spaces for air, and water cannot drain through it easily. When it does dry out it is apt to form hard, impenetrable clumps. It is, however, rich in nutrients.

The ideal soil is a 'good loam' – a balanced mixture of sand, silt and clay. The sandy elements make for good drainage and aeration, the clay for richness, retention of water in summer, and the cohesion essential for the formation of crumbs.

THE IMPORTANCE OF HUMUS: The crumbs of a well-structured soil are formed by contrasting actions: by particles of sand and silt being bound together and by clods of clay being broken apart. In both cases the main agent is humus. Humus not only has the ability to coat particles of sand and silt so that they cohere, but it plays a vital intermediary role in the breakdown of large clay clods into small clods, then into crumbs.

Humus also has great water-holding capacity, which is particularly important in sandy soil, helping to prevent nutrients being washed out so rapidly. Humus is also a source of nutrients in itself, so clearly in the long term the structure and fertility of virtually any soil can be improved by the addition of organic matter which will be converted into humus. (Organic matter is any material of animal or vegetable origin, such as manure or compost.)

OTHER INFLUENCES ON SOIL FERTILITY:

Earthworms: in tunnelling they break up clods and improve aeration and drainage, pull organic matter down into their burrows, and help to incorporate humus with the mineral elements of the soil. They may even secrete a substance which helps in the formation of soil crumbs. Worms also help to control plant diseases by removing the plant debris in which some fungus diseases over-winter. They flourish in soil rich in humus; and are noticeably active where the soil surface is kept mulched.

Plant roots: the ramification of plant roots through the soil helps to build up crumbs in sandy or silty soils, and to break down clods in clay soil. This is one reason why soil seems to improve simply by use. It also explains why the best soil structure is found in fields which have been down to grass for many years – a classical method of improving soil structure is to turn it over to grass for a time.

Soil acidity: another factor with a bearing on soil fertility, acidity is measured on the pH scale, on a range 0–14, the neutral point being 7, the pH of pure water. A soil with a pH below 7 is acid; with a pH above 7 is alkaline. (The change from one pH level to the next indicates a tenfold increase or decrease in acidity or alkalinity.) Acidity can be measured fairly simply with amateur soil-testing kits, which, if used carefully, are accurate enough. Broadly speaking, the acidity of a soil reflects the amount of calcium (lime or chalk) in it; the higher the calcium level the more alkaline the soil and the higher the pH. In our humid climate rain is continually washing calcium out of the soil, so it has a tendency to become more acid all the time. This is most apparent in parts of the country with very high rainfall, in cities and industrialized areas where acid in the atmosphere effectively washes out calcium even faster, and on light sandy soils. Heavy soils such as clays are less likely to become very acid.

Most vegetables, with the exception of brassicas, do best on soils with a pH of 6–6.5, that is, slightly acid. In fact, most soils in Britain are slightly acid. The result of too acid or alkaline a soil is that nutrients either become unavailable, or are so concentrated that they become toxic; in addition the micro-organisms which break down humus cease to function, and earthworms move out of the soil.

In Britain the most common pH problem is over-acidity. This is corrected by liming, but as over-liming is harmful, it should only be carried out if it seems to be really necessary. If plants are doing well, and if there is a large worm population, assume everything is all right. If plenty of humus is being worked into the soil regularly, an acidity problem is less likely to develop.

Indications that a soil is too acid and needs liming are a sour look – moss growing on the surface, weeds such as sorrel and docks, and vegetation on the surface which is not rotting. Liming should rarely be carried out more than once every three or four years, unless acidity is a notable problem. Liming needs time to take effect; several dressings over the course of two or three years may be needed to bring a very acid soil to a neutral point. For an average dressing, apply ground limestone or chalk at the rate of 500 g per sq m (1 lb per sq yd). Lime is best applied in the autumn and worked well into the soil: but never apply it at the same time as fertilizers or manure and, ideally, allow six months between liming and sowing or planting. It can also be added indirectly to the soil by using spent mushroom compost (which has chalk in it) or by working lime into a compost heap.

Drainage: one of the commonest causes of infertility is poor drainage. In a waterlogged soil animal and plant life is starved of oxygen with dire consequences, soil structure deteriorates, and the soil is cold. Improved drainage often produces almost miraculous results in a 'difficult' garden. Signs of poor drainage include: water lying on the surface several days after heavy rain; water encountered when digging a foot or less deep; poor vegetation (plants with a mass of small shallow roots rather than deep roots); lack of worms; and soil that is greyish, bluish, blackish or mottled rather than brown.

Some causes of poor drainage include: very heavy topsoil (usually clay) with little humus in it; hard pan in the soil; topsoil lying over impervious rock, or a layer of impervious subsoil; and low-lying land.

Where there is heavy topsoil, work in plenty of bulky organic matter. If this fails to have an appreciable effect within a year or so, artificial drains will be needed to remove water lying near the surface: the same applies where there is an impermeable layer or low-lying land. Often, simple trench drains are sufficient, laid either at the lower end of the slope, or down the sides of a level area. Dig about 30 cm (1 ft) wide, and 60–90 cm (2–3 ft) deep; fill the bottom third with clinker, stone and broken brick before replacing the soil in the top layer. Another method of improving drainage is to grow plants on raised beds, but the snag is that the soil dries out faster in hot weather.

A hard pan is a very hard layer which is occasionally found at varying depths in the subsoil. It may have been caused by the deposit of a layer of mineral salts, or by compaction of the soil; in either case the answer is to break it up with a spade or pick-axe.

IMPROVING AND MAINTAINING FERTILITY: If one is unlucky enough to be faced with gardening on poor, infertile soil the main steps for improvement can be summarized as follows: improve drainage if necessary; work in plenty of bulky organic matter; check acidity, especially in city gardens, and if necessary, correct by liming.

In poor soils it is worth concentrating initially on creating pockets of fertility, by working any available compost into a small concentrated area. Salad crops are ideal for the first sowings in these pockets as they are mostly shallow rooting, have a short life cycle, and give quick returns. At the other end of the scale potatoes and Jerusalem artichokes are useful crops to plant first in a below-par garden. This is especially true where the problem is heavy soil, since they break it up remarkably well.

Soil structure is a fragile commodity and should be treated with care. It can be destroyed by cultivating soil when it is very wet or very dry, by heavy rain beating on the bare surface, or by walking on the surface frequently. During the summer months (and possibly all the year round on light soils) it is good practice to keep the soil surface permanently covered in order to avoid unnecessary damage. This can be done by growing crops, by covering the soil with a mulch or, failing all else, by allowing weeds to grow – provided they are dug in before they go to seed!

THE BED SYSTEM

To avoid excessive tramping on the soil, divide the growing area into narrow beds which are easily worked from the paths between them. I am a firm believer in this old system and find a width of about 90 cm (1 yd) convenient, separated by paths of about 38 cm (15 in) wide. Beds of this width are also handy for covering with low polythene tunnels.

MANURES AND FERTILIZERS

Manures and fertilizers have two functions: to improve soil structure and to supply plants with the nutrients they require. The first can only be accomplished with bulky organic manures; the second can be achieved with bulky manures and artificial fertilizers. As seen from the previous chapter, adding organic matter to the soil is of prime importance and should be borne in mind when deciding on the type of fertilizer or manure to be used.

BULKY MANURES: Horse, cow, pig, poultry and other animal manures can all be used, preferably well rotted and mixed with plenty of straw and litter. Fresh manure should never come into direct contact with roots; it is also difficult to work into the soil. Poultry manure can be very strong, so should be applied more sparingly than other animal manures.

Treated sewage sludge (if guaranteed free of toxic metals), municipal waste, spent hops and spent mushroom compost are useful alternative forms of bulky manure. Mushroom compost usually contains a high proportion of chalk; it is inadvisable to apply it every year.

Seaweed is excellent, as it contains about the same amount of organic matter and nitrogen as farmyard manure, as well as numerous trace elements. It can be used fresh, dried or composted. If spread on the ground in summer it may attract flies; if so, cover it with a thin sprinkling of soil.

Peat is a useful conditioner in sandy, clay and chalky soils, though it is low in nutrients. A layer at least an inch thick should be worked into the surface.

Straw is also useful either incorporated in layers in a compost heap, or composted on its own. Do this by building up a heap in layers about 15 cm (6 in) thick, up to a height of 2 m (6 ft), watering each layer thoroughly and sprinkling layers alternately with lime and a source of nitrogen (such as ammonium sulphate, poultry manure or a compost activator). It should be ready within a few months.

COMPOST: 20th-century man's answer to the disappearance of bulky animal manures from our daily lives! It is made from vegetable and animal waste, and every gardener should consider making a compost heap his top priority. The heat generated in a really well-made heap destroys weed seed and disease organisms, though in this wet climate it is not always easy to maintain the ideal temperature. Good compost should look like soil – blackish brown, crumbly, uniform in texture and with no half-decayed vegetable stalks in it. A fair amount of raw material is needed to build up a heap quickly, which can be a problem in a small household. Beg or borrow from friends, neighbours or greengrocers who throw out rotten produce. Cut down nettles and other weeds, gather fallen weeds, appropriate unwanted grass cuttings from parks and churchyards – a great deal of priceless organic material is wasted in our society. Almost anything of animal or vegetable origin is suitable for composting, such as any kitchen waste; garden waste – lawn mowings, weeds, vegetable remains (bruise or chop very solid material such as old sprout stalks), bonfire ash, autumn leaves (even pine needles) and green bracken; and animal manures. Material to avoid includes: diseased plant material (burn this); roots of perennial weeds such as couch grass, bindweed and ground elder (unless they have been killed by drying in the sun); woody material (unless shredded or cut very small); and non-rotting material such as plastics and man-made fibres.

The decomposition of waste in a compost heap is brought about by bacteria. To operate effectively, they need air, moisture, and a source of nitrogen. The nitrogen source can be fresh green leafy material, animal manure (poultry is very good), nitrogenous fertilizers such as ammonium sulphate, concentrated organic fertilizers such as seaweed extracts, or a commercial compost activator.

When building a heap, strong corner posts or a rigid frame are advisable as a full heap or bin is bulky and weighty. For good ventilation at least three sides should be made of material which is not completely solid – wire, synthetic netting, slats, or poles laid horizontally with gaps between them. The larger the heap the higher the temperature which can be built up, but to get good compost the heap should be made reasonably fast. It is worth having two (even three) heaps side by side; while one is being built up the others are maturing or being used.

A compost heap should be built on soil. Start by forking over the ground, then make a drainage layer about 8 to 10 cm (3–4 in) thick, of clinkers, stones, rubble, tile drains or brushwood. Never make a heap on concrete; drainage will be impeded, and one wants worms to move into the heap when the temperature has cooled down. Pits are sometimes used; these conserve heat well, but run the risk of becoming waterlogged unless the underlying soil is properly drained.

Ideally, a heap should be built up in layers about 15–23 cm (6–9 in) thick, each separated with a layer of soil about 1 cm ($\frac{1}{2}$ in) thick. It is important that the material in each layer should be as mixed as possible. A layer of any one material (such as grass cuttings) becomes a solid mass, preventing aeration, drainage and bacterial activity. If the heap is short of fresh green nitrogenous material – likely in the winter months – sprinkle alternate layers with one of the other sources of nitrogen mentioned above. In acid soil, intermediate layers can be sprinkled with lime, but never add lime and a nitrogen source to the same layer. Add water if necessary to keep moist.

When the heap is about 1·3 m (4 ft) high, cover it with a layer of soil about 8 cm (3 in) thick, or with turves placed grass side down. Finally, cover the whole heap with black polythene or sacking to keep in the heat and prevent it drying out or becoming waterlogged. In summer a heap can be ready to use in 3–4 months; in winter it may take 6–8 months. It is best not to use compost until well decomposed, and so less likely to contain weed seeds and disease spores. With enough space a slow-rotting, long-term heap can be made with chopped-up woody material, evergreens and turves. This may take over a year to rot.

Bulky manures can be used in various ways: they can be dug into the ground at the rate of 3 or 4 buckets per sq m (2 to 3 buckets per sq yd); spread on the surface in a layer about 5 to 8 cm (2 to 3 in) thick, preferably in the autumn, and dug into the ground the following spring; worked into compost heaps; and used as a mulch around growing crops (if well rotted). Most soils benefit from an annual dressing of bulky manure.

The traditional method of working bulky manures and compost into the soil is by digging. On heavy soils this is best done in the autumn, ideally before Christmas, leaving the roughly-dug soil exposed to winter frosts which help to break down clods. On light soils where the soil structure may be destroyed by excessive winter weathering, it is probably best to delay digging until early spring, between January and March: the manure can be spread on the surface in autumn.

One should aim to dig over the garden once a year, incorporating manure or compost. Between crops a light forking is sufficient to prepare the soil for sowing or planting. As a general rule the deeper you dig the better the soil will become. Do not, however, bring clay subsoil to the surface; better to work in compost so that the subsoil gradually improves.

ARTIFICIAL FERTILIZERS: Where the soil is fertile, adequate crops can be grown without artificial fertilizers. They are useful, however, for supplying extra nutrients in poor soil and for helping to increase yields. Nitrogen is the element most likely to be in short supply, as it is rapidly washed out of the soil, and is needed in large quantities by fast-growing, leafy crops. Too much nitrogen, however, leads to lush, disease-prone growth, and inhibits germination in a seedbed.

Fertilizers may be applied as base dressings shortly before sowing or planting, or as top dressings or foliar feeds during growth. Nutrients should always be applied in a balanced form – nitrogen, for example, balanced by a little potash – so it is advisable to use commercially-prepared, balanced compounds. Fertilizers are available as powder, granules or pellets, or as liquids – the fertilizer value is the same. Solid fertilizers are spread on the soil and must be watered in; liquid fertilizers are normally watered on to the soil.

FOLIAR FEEDS: Some fertilizers, notably various proprietary organic fertilizers made from seaweed, can be sprayed directly on to the foliage. They are rapidly absorbed but plants can only take limited amounts of nutrients via the leaves. The ability to do so also varies during the day, so foliar feeding should be done in the evening or early morning. Foliar feeds are useful for supplementary feeding, for correcting trace element deficiencies (special products are sold for this), and for dry weather when fertilizers would need copious watering in.

My own manuring policy is to work some bulky manure into the whole garden every year, rotating home-made compost, farmyard manure and spent mushroom compost. During the growing season I boost growth with foliar feeds of seaweed extract, approximately once a month.

3

SHELTER, WATER AND WEEDS

Shelter, water and weeds all affect the quality of salad crops.

SHELTER: Research has shown that shelter from even light winds can increase plant yields by as much as 20–30 per cent. All ordinary vegetables seem to benefit from increased shelter, and for those on the climatic borderline in Britain, such as tomatoes, shelter can make the difference between success and failure. The combination of low temperatures and strong winds takes the greatest toll of plants, so by taking the edge off a keen wind, shelter tips the balance in the plant's favour. The value of cloches, plastic tunnels, greenhouses and the new slitted polythene mulches lies as much in providing shelter as in the higher temperatures they generate.

The ideal windbreak is not, as might be as imagined, a solid wall. It should be about 50 per cent permeable to the wind – a hedge or a closely-woven nylon fence. Wind simply jumps over a solid barrier, creating a far more damaging area of turbulence at some point on the far side. The effect of a windbreak lessens the further away it is: it is effective up to a distance of six to ten times its height, so 2-m (6-ft) high barriers would need to be about 12 m (40 ft) apart. Theoretically, windbreaks should be sited in the path of the prevailing wind; but as the direction of the prevailing wind is so variable, that is easier said than done!

Windbreaks are either living or artificial. The disadvantage of living windbreaks (trees or hedges) is that they compete with plants for nutrients, water and light, may create too much shade, and require some maintenance. Poplar, willow, and conifers such as *Cupressocyparis leylandii*, *Chamaecyparis lawsoniana* and *Thuja plicata* are often used. In the vegetable garden itself, sturdy annuals such as Jerusalem artichoke, sweet corn, cardoon and sunflower can be used as windbreaks, planted in rows at least three deep. Salads, and wind-susceptible crops such as dwarf beans, can be grown in their lee.

Artificial windbreaks such as lath or wattle fences, or modern net materials such as Rokolene or Netlon do not, of course, compete for nutrients and water, though they are less durable. Netting is easily attached to firmly anchored posts with battens; the force of wind blowing into netting can be very strong so corner posts may need to be reinforced to take the strain. Strips of nylon netting or hessian sacks 30 cm (1 ft) high can be strung between beds of vegetables, and even ordinary wire netting has some effect in breaking the force of a wind.

In built-up areas devastating wind tunnels can be created between buildings. It is worth planting trees or shrubs in such gaps (they may need artificial protection to start them off), or erecting fencing that extends well to either side of the gap – wind creeps cunningly around the edge of a windbreak!

Having stressed the importance of shelter, one should mention the reverse side of the coin. Vegetables should never be grown in claustrophobic conditions, which encourage the build-up of pests and diseases. Most do best in what is called an 'open site', free of deep shade created by buildings or large overhanging trees. Drips from trees can be very damaging. However, in summer some salad crops such as lettuce, cress and sorrel are apt to run to seed in positions exposed to full sun, and do better in light shade, provided the ground is reasonably moist.

WATER: Although a plant only grows really well if it has sufficient water, watering more than necessary is unwise as it can wash nutrients, especially nitrogen, out of reach of roots, it can discourage root growth, making plants more susceptible to drought, and it can weaken flavour. As water is an increasingly scarce resource and watering a laborious chore, one should use water as effectively and economically as possible.

It is helpful to know that much of the water lost from the surface layers of the soil, other than by drainage and transpiration through leaves, is by evaporation. Keeping soil mulched keeps down this loss. Soils which are rich in humus retain far more water than poor soils. Working organic matter thoroughly into the soil is one of the best ways of increasing the amount of water there. Loams and clay soils retain more moisture than sandy soils. Wherever possible roots compensate for lack of water near the surface by growing deeper into the soil. Deep cultivation makes this easier. On shallow soil overlying impermeable rock roots cannot grow deeper, so measures for conserving water in the soil are especially important. Plants compete with each other for soil moisture. The closer they are planted the stiffer the competition, and the more water required. Where water shortage is likely, grow plants further apart than otherwise to compensate. Weeds compete seriously for water, so remove them as soon as possible. Evaporation occurs rapidly from the top centimetre or so of soil. Once the surface is dry it slows down, the dry soil layer effectively becoming a mulch. So in dry weather disturb the surface as little as possible; deep hoeing will only increase water loss.

Plants' water requirements vary according to the type of plant and at different stages in its life cycle. Time and water can be saved by confining watering to these 'critical periods', explained below.

Germination: seed will not germinate in dry conditions; seed-beds or drills must always be watered.

Transplanting: plants should always be transplanted into moist soil, and/or watered gently daily after transplanting until they are well established.

When applying fertilizers: solid fertilizers applied as a top dress-ing should always be watered in, particularly if the soil is dry.

Leafy crops: the principal effect of watering is to increase leaf growth, so leafy crops such as lettuce, spinach, celery, brassicas and many salads would benefit from heavy waterings, 10–15 litres per sq m (2–3 gal per sq yd) per week, during the summer months. Where this is impossible, they should be given up to 20 litres per sq m (4 gal per sq yd) about two weeks before maturing.

'Fruiting' vegetables: vegetables grown for their fruits – toma-toes, cucumbers, peas, for example – need water most when flowering and fruiting. Once they are well established extra watering is unnecessary until they come into flower (unless grown indoors), when they would benefit from about 5 litres per sq m (1 gal per sq yd) every two or three days.

Root crops: these need a steady water supply while growing, but excess water leads to the development of foliage at the ex-pense of the roots. Water regularly to prevent the soil drying out.

An important general rule when watering is never just to

sprinkle the soil surface, as this simply brings roots to the surface. One thorough watering is far more beneficial than several light ones. Young seedlings and small plants should always be watered gently and thoroughly, using a can with a fine rose, a hose with a nozzle which can be adjusted to a fine spray, a house plant can with a narrow spout, or a sprinkler.

Where water is likely to be in short supply over a long period, I would suggest the following to make the best use of water. First, water seedbeds or seed drills very thoroughly. In hot weather water the bottom of the seed drill only, covering the seeds with dry soil; water well when transplanting, confining water to the area immediately around the plant and then mulching; restrict heavy watering to a period shortly before plants mature; sink clay pots into the soil near large plants and confine watering to the pot; water in the evenings to minimize evaporation; but allow time for plants to dry off before nightfall.

To water while you are away: make wicks 1–2 cm ($\frac{1}{2}$–$\frac{3}{4}$ in) thick from glass-fibre lagging, wool or soft string. Dangle one end in a bucket of water, the other near the plant's root or in its pot; water will seep along the wick to the plant. Also, cover the soil near plants and the surface of pots with stones to minimize evaporation.

WEEDS: Weeds are *persona non grata* in the vegetable garden, because they compete for water, nutrients, space and light. Many also harbour pests and diseases. Aphids over-winter in groundsel and chickweed, which, along with shepherd's purse and fat hen, also harbour lettuce mosaic virus in winter. This poses a dilemma for salad eaters – chickweed, shepherd's purse and fat hen being worthy additions to a salad!

Annual weeds are the most numerous – annual meadow grass, chickweed and groundsel being some of the commonest. They go to seed – some prolifically – at least once, sometimes several times, in one year, The top layer of soil is riddled with weed seed, much of which, fortunately, is lost when the soil is cultivated. In fact it really does take the proverbial seven years for one year's seed to disappear from the topsoil. Seed deeper in the soil can remain dormant for many years, so when ground is cultivated for the first time, there is a huge flush of weed growth initially.

The practical implications are: prevent all weeds going to seed; cultivate the ground, so gradually reducing weed seed; during the growing season cultivate as shallowly as possible to prevent more weed being brought to the surface, particularly with soil only recently cultivated.

Annual weeds are easily controlled with hoeing and mulching. For hoeing amongst salad crops my favourite tool is an onion hoe – small, light to use, easily controlled, shallow in action. Hoe when the soil is dry so that weeds can be left on the surface to dry before being composted. In wet conditions they may contrive to re-root.

Mulching is an invaluable means of weed control; though some weeds push their way through, they are easily pulled out. For vegetables sown outside, weed competition starts to be really serious about three weeks after the vegetable seedlings have germinated. Tackle them before this.

One of the most efficient ways of suppressing weeds in salad crops is to grow plants spaced equidistantly in 'blocks' rather than in traditional rows. Broad-leaved, low-growing plants such as lettuce can suppress weeds effectively. It has been proved that the most competitive weeds are those between rather than within rows; so by eliminating rows, one has an effective measure against weeds. Spacing has to be such that the mature plants will eventually blanket the ground. When the plants are small, hoeing between them, or mulching, will probably still be necessary.

Perennial weeds stay in the soil from one year to the next, often propagating themselves with creeping roots or stems. Dock, dandelion, bindweed, ground elder, couch grass, creeping thistle, and horsetail are some of the worst. As using weedkillers is impractical amongst salad crops, they have to be dug out, taking care to remove even small pieces of root which can still sprout.

Weeds are rich in mineral nutrients and organic matter, and should normally be put on the compost heap. Exceptions are weeds which are going to seed (unless it is a very efficient heap), and the fresh roots of perennials.

WEEDKILLERS: When taking over a neglected garden weedkillers may be necessary to clear the ground initially and rid it of perennials. A non-selective contact weedkiller such as a paraquat/

diquat mixture (Weedol) is useful for clearing surface weeds; Dalapon is effective against couch and other grasses, and 2, 4–D against broad-leaved perennials such as nettle, dock and thistle. Note: Use all weedkillers with great care and strictly in accordance with the manufacturer's instructions.

4

PESTS AND DISEASES

Fortunately there are not many serious pests and diseases of salad crops. This chapter takes a quick look at the remedies for those most commonly met.

Birds: salad plants are particularly conspicuous and vulnerable in winter and spring. Protect seedlings from small birds with a single strand of strong black cotton along the rows a few inches above ground level; or use netting slung over low wire hoops; or make bird scarers from anything which flaps, glints or makes a noise. Where birds are a serious problem, permanent wire or netting cages may be the only solution.

ANIMAL PESTS

Rabbits: often a serious pest in rural gardens. Erect low wire-netting fencing of approximately 4·5-cm (1¾-in) mesh, buried at least 10 cm (4 in) underground with the wire turned out to deter excavation.

Moles may do tremendous damage. Set traps in the main runs, preferably on firm ground; or put spiky material such as rose cuttings down the runs; or use gas or poison. Planting caper spurge is, in my experience, quite useless!

Mice and voles nibble off young plants and seedlings, especially in winter. Set mouse traps regularly.

Rats also nibble plants when hard-pressed in winter – even gnawing through heavy gauge polythene to reach them. Use rat poison – or call in the rat man!

Cats: very difficult! Wire netting or brushwood over seedbeds protects seedlings at their most vulnerable.

FIG. 1 – SOIL PESTS

Chemical control: Various proprietary chemicals are sold for control of soil pests, worked into the soil 5 cm (2 in) deep before sowing or planting. As they also kill beneficial soil life, and some (e.g. Gamma BHC) cause tainting in root crops, I hesitate to recommend their use in small gardens.

SOIL PESTS

PEST	Appearance	Adult Form	Time and Nature of Damage	Simple Control Measures
TURNIP MOTH / CUTWORM	Fat caterpillar, Distinct head, Sucker feet, Soil coloured, Up to 5 cm (2 in) long	Noctuid moth e.g. Turnip, heart and dart moth and others	May to Sept. Eats away plant stems at ground level	Destroy caterpillars, Search soil near damaged plant (by torchlight at night)
CRANEFLY / LEATHERJACKET	Legless, No distinct head, Fat and soft, Earthy colour, Up to 4 cm (1½ in) long	Cranefly or Daddy-long-legs	March to July, Stems bitten through at surface level, Ragged feeding on lower leaves	Ensure soil well drained, Clear and dig land before and September, especially if previously grass
WIREWORM / CLICK BEETLE	3 prs good legs, Tough, wire-like, golden yellow, shiny body, About 2.5 cm (1 in) long	Click beetle	March to Sept. Stems bitten below soil level; tomato stems tunnelled above ground	Numbers decrease once ground is cultivated
COCKCHAFER / CHAFER BUGS	3 prs strong legs, Large brown head, Tail end body swollen, Lies with body bent, Whitish; inactive, Up to 4 cm (1½ in) long	May-bug (Cockchafer), June-bug (Garden chafer)	July to Oct. Roots gnawed 5 cm (2 in) or more below soil surface	Keep garden clean and weed free
MILLIPEDES	2 prs legs on most segments, Slow moving. *Flat group:* Flat, light brown, 1.5 to 2 cm (½ in) long. *Snake group:* Smooth round bodies up to 2 cm (¾ in) long; usually black and shiny; curl up when disturbed	Do not confuse with centipedes which are: fast moving; have one pair legs per segment; are beneficial, eating small slugs etc.	April to July, Eat seed and stems of young plants, roots, tubers	Search near damaged plants and remove

SOIL PESTS (see fig. 1): Most of these are the caterpillar or grub stages of insects such as moths, beetles and craneflies. (See fig. 1 for details of identification, damage and control.) They tend to attack seedlings and young plants at and below ground level, particularly in relatively freshly cultivated ground and neglected gardens. Lettuce are often attacked. Watch out for wilting young plants, dig them up, search carefully through the soil around the roots and the culprit may be found – a shiny yellow wireworm, a fat leatherjacket, or even a slug.

Plant potatoes initially in new ground as a catch crop. Although the crop will be badly damaged many of the pests will be removed when the potatoes are lifted. At some stage in their life cycle many of these pests use weeds as hosts or hide under debris, so it is important to keep the garden weedfree and to burn or compost all debris. Chemical control should be a last resort. The chemicals which control soil pests also harm beneficial soil insects, may taint crops, and there is always a risk of harmful residues remaining in the soil.

Slugs: a terrible nuisance on salad crops, being active all the year, especially in damp weather, and attacking leaves and stems at ground level and roots in the soil. In some areas snails are a similar problem, especially in chalky soils and where there is debris for shelter. Slugs are night feeders, and one of the best methods of control is to search for them at night by torchlight. Damp nights are best for 'slugging'! Slugs can also be killed with methiocarb and metaldehyde pellets, placed in heaps around vulnerable plants. Cover baits with a tile or leaf, as they can be poisonous to birds and domestic animals. If methiocarb is used, allow a week before eating nearby crops. Metaldehyde is less toxic; it is best applied on bare ground in dry weather. The organic slug killer Fertosan is safer to use but not easy to get. Renew slug baits frequently and place them near, but not touching salad plants, as decaying pellets can encourage botrytis infections on lettuce.

Eelworms are minute soil creatures which cause various devastating plant 'sicknesses'. Of the salad crops, onion, tomato and radish can be affected. Some make cysts which enable them to hibernate in the soil for many years. There are no known remedies; the best prevention lies in crop rotation, if possible at least on a three-year cycle. (See p. 54.)

BENEFICIAL INSECTS: There are many beneficial insects in the soil. If an unidentified creature is fast-moving the odds are that it feeds on the animal kingdom and is likely to be beneficial. The slow movers tend to be vegetable eaters and are therefore pests. Don't automatically squash everything!

INSECT PESTS: Probably the most harmful group of insects on salad plants are *aphids* or greenfly, which can completely cover the stems, leaves or roots. They build up rapidly, especially in hot weather. There are many species of aphid, each usually attacking specific plants or groups of plants. They pierce the tissue, feed on the sap and weaken the plant, often transmitting virus diseases in the process.

Aphids have many natural predators such as ladybirds, hover-fly larvae and ground beetles, which may be killed when chemical insecticides are used. Inspect plants regularly to catch attacks in their early stages. Aphids can be controlled with the relatively safe insecticides derris and pyrethrum (used separately or mixed together for most effectiveness), or long-term protection can be given with systemic insecticides such as dimethoate, which are absorbed into the sap and, over a certain period, kill aphids landing on the foliage. Pieces of aluminium foil placed on the soil bright side up are now believed to deter aphids.

GREENHOUSE PESTS: Whitefly and red spider can be serious on greenhouse salad crops, especially in hot dry conditions. As a preventive measure avoid overcrowding, ventilate well, damp down frequently to create a moist atmosphere. Liquid derris gives some control against red spider; whitefly is difficult to control when established. In both cases biological control, that is the introduction of a natural predator, is possible. (See p. 194 for suppliers of predators.)

FUNGUS DISEASES (see fig. 2): Serious salad diseases caused by fungi are grey mould (botrytis) and downy mildew on lettuce, tomato and cucumber; powdery mildew on cucumber; blight and stem rot on tomato; various onion rots; celery leaf spot and what are collectively called 'damping off' diseases, which account for seed failing to germinate or seedlings keeling over and dying

FIG. 2 – LETTUCE DISEASES

a Downy mildew: blotchy areas appear on the outer leaves, and white spores on the underside of the leaves   *b* Botrytis or grey mould: leaves decay and may be covered in grey spores. The plant often rots off just above ground level

shortly after germination. Fungus spores are spread from infected plants by wind, rain and in debris. Some, such as onion neck rot, are carried in the seed. Attack is always most likely on weak plants, particularly where the skin has been damaged or bruised.

It is difficult to control fungus diseases once established. Fungicides have to be applied in anticipation or when an attack is in its early stages. They are less likely to leave harmful residues than insecticides, but must be used carefully. Plants should be sprayed gently but thoroughly. Avoid spraying in full sun or when plants are wilted. Fungicides are of two types: 'protectants' which remain on the leaf surface and kill spores on the leaf (they are liable to be washed off by rain so need to be applied frequently); and 'systemics' which are absorbed into the plant's sap, so are effective over a longer period.

Seed is sometimes treated chemically to kill seed-borne disease, or to give protection against, for example, damping off disease. Buy treated seed where possible.

A great deal of disease on salad crops can be prevented by following a few simple rules of good husbandry: grow plants well, in fertile, well-drained soil (weak plants are most vulnerable); sow thinly (seedling diseases are more likely where seedlings are overcrowded); sow on warm soil, warmed beforehand with cloches if necessary (seedlings never 'get away' under cold conditions, and it is the lingering seedlings which succumb to damping off disease); do not plant too close; handle plants carefully, especially onions at harvest, winter lettuce at planting and hoeing; remove diseased leaves from plants and burn any diseased material; keep pots and seed boxes clean (never sow in dirty boxes); keep water tanks and tubs covered; in greenhouses err on the side of over-ventilation; when watering in the evening make sure leaves can dry before night; rotate crops as much as possible.

RESISTANT VARIETIES: Plant breeders are continually developing varieties which are resistant or tolerant to certain diseases. Unfortunately, the fungi then develop new strains which overcome the resistance – which keeps the plant breeders in business! However, use resistant varieties where available. So far, resistance breeding has been more successful against diseases than pests. The lettuces Avoncrisp and Avondefiance, however, have a very high degree of resistance to lettuce root aphis.

VIRUS DISEASES: These serious, incurable diseases are caused by minute sub-microscopic particles. Commonest symptoms are badly stunted growth, and mottled, twisted, often yellow leaves. Viruses are spread by human contact, by knives being used on one plant and then on the next, by a number of insects, notably aphids, even by fungi and soil eelworm, and can be carried in the seed.

Of salad crops, cucumber is susceptible to cucumber mosaic virus, lettuce to lettuce mosaic virus and beet western yellows virus, and tomato to tomato mosaic virus. Uproot and burn any suspiciously stunted plants as soon as they are noticed, try to keep aphids under control, and make use of virus-resistant varieties of lettuce, cucumber and tomato where possible.

THE USE OF CHEMICALS: I, personally, feel that chemicals should be used as little as possible on salad crops because they kill pollinating and beneficial insects and fungi; may leave harmful residues on plants and are potentially dangerous to children and domestic animals. Insects and fungi build up resistance to specific chemicals, so the less they are used the longer any one will be effective when really urgent measures are required.

If using chemicals, take great care, always follow the manufacturer's instructions meticulously, and always spray in the evening or in dull weather, when pollinating insects are not flying. Some pesticides can be mixed with others or with liquid fertilizers and/or foliar feeds, and applied together. Consult the manufacturer's instructions.

5

SEED AND SOWING 'INDOORS'

Most salad plants are raised from seed, so knowing and understanding seed is a vital part of the grower's armoury.

SEED STORAGE: Seed naturally deteriorates with age, losing its viability (its ability to germinate) and vigour. This is accelerated when it is stored in moist and warm conditions; and minimized when it is stored in cool dry conditions. Many gardening failures probably stem from the habit of keeping seed packets in damp garden sheds or hot kitchens! Seed should therefore be stored in as dry and as cool a place as possible, ideally in a tin or jar in which there is a bag or dish of silica gel to absorb any moisture in the air. If cobalt-chloride-treated silica gel is used it will turn pink when moist, and should then be dried in an oven for 2–3 hours until it turns blue again. If ordinary silica gel is used, dry it periodically as a safeguard.

Open packets of seed are particularly liable to deteriorate. Wherever possible, buy seed in air-sealed foil packs. These are the best insurance against deterioration until they are opened – but once opened, seed starts to deteriorate normally. In reasonable conditions most salad seed can be kept for at least three years. If the viability is in doubt, try germinating a few on moist blotting paper before sowing on a larger scale.

F_1 *hybrid seed* is seed obtained by crossing two inbred parent lines. Resulting plants are usually of exceptional vigour and high quality. It is more expensive than ordinary seed, but in most cases is well worth the price.

Pelleted seeds are individually coated with a protective substance which breaks down in the soil. They look like tiny balls, and were originally developed for commercial growers to sow mechanically. Individual pelleted seeds are easy to handle and can be accurately spaced. This virtually eliminates the need for thinning. Germination problems are sometimes encountered with pelleted seed, and the soil must be kept moist until the seed has germinated.

Seed tapes and 'sheets': various systems of incorporating seeds into tapes, or within two fine tissue-like paper sheets are being developed. Until recently they were of dubious value, but some of the seed sheets now being developed on the Continent look promising. Seeds are spaced out in the paper sheets an inch or so apart. The sheets are 'sown' by placing them on the soil or in a seed tray, and covering them with soil or compost in the normal way. When used indoors they eliminate the need to prick out; outdoors they minimize the need for thinning.

Chitted seed is newly germinated seed, with the seedling root showing. It is now being sold by mail order firms, sent in blotting paper in plastic sachets, and should be pricked out as soon as possible. Chitted seeds save amateurs the necessity of germinating seed with heat. I have used chitted cucumber and geranium seeds, and in both cases had excellent results, notwithstanding the fragile appearance of the seeds on arrival.

Fluid sowing is a recently developed sowing technique whereby seeds are germinated on paper tissues indoors, mixed with a gel (wallpaper paste which does not contain a fungicide can be used) and sown into seed trays or in the soil outdoors. It enables difficult seeds to be started earlier and flourish even when sowing conditions are unfavourable. It is particularly promising for sowing lettuce under hot conditions, for celery and for outdoor tomatoes, enabling a crop to be direct sown outdoors – normally impractical in Britain. However, for most salads sowing in individual blocks (see p. 35) is probably equally effective and at the same time simpler.

Saving your own seed is a practice which has largely died out, and the trend today is to advise against it – for sound reasons. First, the risk of cross pollination between varieties and between species is high, so one can rarely be 100 per cent sure of getting pure seed. Then seed crops require long periods of dry sunny weather when ripening to ensure good quality seed, and the English summer, when most seed is ripening, is notoriously humid and unreliable. Lastly, modern seedsmen take stringent measures to procure excellent quality, disease-free seed of high purity and cleanliness, with good germinating properties – hard to equal in normal amateur conditions.

However, having said this, it is sometimes necessary for salad growers to be able to save some of their own seed. This applies particularly to the useful, but uncommon salad crops. Once a source has been found, it may well be prudent to save your own seed in case the supply runs out! It is also useful to save seed of those salads which lend themselves to being broadcast in patches – an extravagant practice. However, by saving seed from just a few plants, one can afford to be extravagant!

It is easiest to save seed from the winter hardy salads, which naturally run to seed early in the year. They stand a far higher chance of the seed maturing and ripening than those plants which naturally seed in late summer or autumn. The following are some of the best prospects for seed saving: chicories, endives, hardy lettuce, winter radish, celeriac, rocket, land cress, corn salad, chervil, Japanese Mizuna greens, claytonia, cress and borage. To maintain the quality of your stock it is advisable to start again with commercial seed every two or three years.

A few guides to saving seed: never save F_1 hybrid seed – it will not breed true; never try to save seed of more than one variety of any crop – unless they are a considerable distance apart; only save seed from the very best plants – strong and disease-free; never save seed from plants which have bolted or gone to seed prematurely. Seeding plants can grow very lanky and unwieldy so ensure they will not be in the way and interfere with other crops. Support and tie them upright if they are liable to fall over, which can result in mouldy, diseased seed pods (a promising plant can often be transplanted, before it starts to go to seed, into an out-of-the-way corner, or even better, into a greenhouse or plastic tunnel); make sure plants are well watered at ground level when flowering and when the seed is forming, to get plump seeds; as far as possible allow the seed pods to ripen and dry on the plant (in continuously wet weather it may be advisable to pick them when nearly ripe and hang them in a dry place to finish ripening-off: otherwise cut them down just before the seed pods burst naturally, and hang or lie them flat in a cool dry place until the pods can be cracked open easily); when completely dry, spread them on sheets of paper, crack the pods, and collect the seed in the paper, blowing off as much dust and debris as possible; keep in dry envelopes, stored in a tin. (See p. 27.)

Many of the crops mentioned above will seed themselves naturally if the seed pods are not collected. In due course a thick crop of seedlings will emerge which can be transplanted, thinned out or, in some cases, allowed to grow thickly and close cropped with scissors.

SOWING 'INDOORS': This means sowing in protected conditions, normally in seed boxes or pots – for example in a cold or heated greenhouse, on a window-sill indoors, in a cold frame or under cloches, which enables sowing several weeks earlier than would be possible outdoors. This method is good for: tender half-hardy crops, such as tomato and pepper which in our climate would not have time to mature if sown directly outside; crops needing a long growing season such as celeriac, celery and some onions; exceptionally early crops (spring lettuce); specific germination problems (lettuce may not germinate outdoors in high summer temperatures, but can be sown in cooler conditions indoors); economy of garden space by having seedlings ready to plant as soon as the previous crop is harvested; better quality plants.

Traditionally, the main stages in raising salad plants indoors are:

Stage I: Sowing seed in special compost in small containers, often in a propagator or with artificial heat.

Stage II: Pricking out – transplanting very small seedlings into a tray to space them out and give more growing room.

Stage III: Potting on – transplanting the small plants into individual pots when the tray is outgrown. (Mainly done for plants to be grown indoors, such as tomato and cucumber.)

Stage IV: Hardening off – gradually accustoming plants to lower temperatures.

Stage V: Planting outside or in greenhouses.

The pricking out stage is the most fiddly and liable to be neglected. It can be eliminated by: sowing individual seeds in soil or peat compost blocks; sowing seeds direct into very small pots, or expandable 'pots' such as Jiffy 7s; sowing seeds well spaced out initially – say 2·5–4 cm (1–1½ in) apart in most cases. To sow indoors containers, compost, and a means of creating a warm, damp atmosphere to encourage germination are needed.

Containers: seed trays or boxes 5 cm (2 in) deep are ideal. Some are sold with fitting plastic domes to encourage germination. Clay and plastic pots can also be used, as can the small plastic pots used for yoghurt and margarine, but make drainage holes in the bottom.

Composts for sowing and potting are light-textured soil or peat-based mixtures. (There is no connection with the compost from a compost heap.)

Peat composts are easy and light to use; sterile, so free from weed seed, and of a porous texture to encourage rapid root growth. Disadvantages are that they dry out rapidly and are sometimes difficult to re-wet. Three types are now sold: sowing, potting and blocking. Sowing compost is finest in texture, and necessary for sowing very small seed. Potting and blocking composts are coarser, with more nutrients, so can feed and support seedlings longer. Blocking composts have an additive which makes them more easily compressed.

Theoretically one sows in sowing compost, and pricks out into potting compost. Salads, however, can all be sown direct into potting (or blocking) compost, but well spaced out, so that pricking out will be unnecessary.

Soil-based composts for amateur use are gradually being superseded by modern peat-based composts. Soil-based composts are made from sieved loam, peat and sand, mixed to a formula devised by the John Innes Institute. They are heavier to handle than peat-based composts but less liable to dry out, which is an asset in later stages of growth or with plants grown to maturity in pots.

Seed can be sown into John Innes Seed Compost or, alternatively, direct into John Innes Potting Compost No. 1 (JIP. 1), potting on into JIP. 2 later.

Home-made compost suitable for sowing can be made by mixing two parts of good quality peat with one part of coarse builder's or silver sand. The peat can be soaked first in a weak solution of liquid seaweed to encourage healthy seedling growth. Sowing compost can also be made by sieving the topsoil from a hardwood forest through a ·25 cm ($\frac{1}{8}$ in) sieve.

For potting on, mix peat and sand with at least an equal weight of good sieved loam, to which some well-crumbled compost-heap compost, or a basic fertilizer can be added.

The underlying principle of sowing, both indoors and out, is to sow into soil or compost of a sufficiently light texture to encourage germination. No nutrients are required yet, indeed, if the compost is too rich seedlings will be lush and weak. Never, for example, sow into compost-heap compost, which would be much too rich. Once seedlings are growing they need nutrients to support their rapid development. If started in poor soil, sand, or compost, they must then be moved into something richer and stronger.

Atmosphere: it is not necessary to have a heated greenhouse for sowing indoors, but most seeds germinate better in warm soil, and benefit from what is called 'bottom heat'. This can be provided in several ways, such as: starting seeds in a warm cupboard, or above a radiator (but not directly on it), or installing a heated propagator on a greenhouse bench, using electric cables covered with sand. The Jiffy Soil Heating Unit is recommended for this (see Appendix II). Free-standing propagators can also be made and heated with paraffin, gas or electric heaters designed for use in greenhouses.

With the exception of tomatoes (where plants are easily bought) no salad plants have to be started with artificial heat. It does, however, lead to faster germination, which usually means better plants and earlier crops.

Now for a word of warning about the 'post germination' problem! As soon as there is a sniff of spring around the corner, gardeners get itchy fingers and start sowing indoors. Unfortunately, many of those fingers get burnt! While it is relatively easy to germinate seeds early in the year, especially with a propagator, it is much more difficult to provide growing conditions in the weeks after germination before it is safe to plant outdoors. One cannot plant outside until all frost risk is past, and in much of Britain ground frosts endure until the end of May or even early June.

FIG. 3 – SOWING INDOORS
a Seed tray or pot being filled with compost   *b* Surface being firmed
c Water being soaked up into the compost   *d* Sowing seed   *e* Sifting compost over the seed

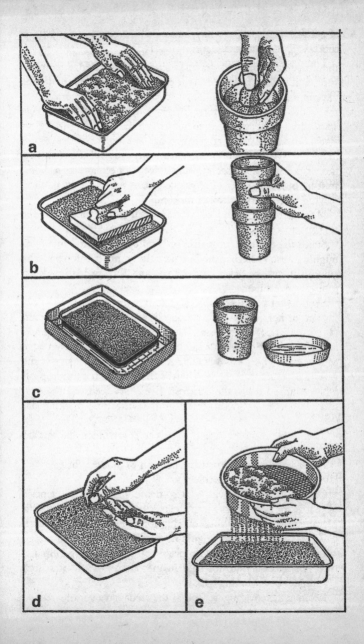

Seedlings soon grow out of the limited space of a propagator, and to continue growing steadily they must have good light (or they become lanky and drawn), reasonably warm day temperatures and at least frost-free night temperatures. These conditions are often hard to meet in domestic conditions. The moral is not to start raising too many seedlings too early – unless you have somewhere light and warm to house them.

PROCEDURE FOR RAISING PLANTS INDOORS (see fig. 3):

Stage 1 – Sowing. Using peat-based composts: fill the seed tray, box or pot with compost. If using a deep pot economize on compost by putting a layer of moistened foam rubber in the bottom, leaving 5 cm (2 in) headroom for compost.

Make sure edges and corners are well filled, then press the surface smooth.

Stand the container in a dish or bowl of water until it is thoroughly moist. (Alternatively, prepare the compost beforehand by tipping it into a bucket, watering it and leaving it to soak up moisture overnight.)

Sow the seed thinly on the surface. Whether you will be pricking out or not, sow seed thinly, ideally spacing it about 1–2.5 cm ($\frac{1}{2}$–1 in) apart. Some seeds are large enough to be picked up and sown by hand. Small seeds can be picked up on the broken edge of a piece of glass. Put them in a saucer, moisten the edge of the glass and touch a seed, which will then stick. It will drop off when touched on to the compost. Even tiny seed can be sown this way, making spacing easier and saving time pricking out (see fig. 4).

Sieve some compost over the seeds to cover them; the smaller the seed the less covering needed.

If moisture does not rise from beneath to moisten the covering layer, water gently with a fine rose.

Cover the seed tray with a fitted dome, pane of glass or piece of plastic, or pop the tray into a plastic bag to keep it moist until germination. (Remove this covering for about half an hour each day. This helps to prevent damping off diseases.)

Put the seed tray in a warm place or propagator to germinate. It is not necessary to put seed in the dark; indeed some seed germinates better in the light.

Remove the covering as soon as the seeds have germinated.

Using soil-based composts: if these are used it is advisable to put broken crocks, dry leaves, or a couple of layers of newspaper in the bottom of the seed tray to improve drainage. Start by watering the compost with a rose to make it just moist, then follow the same procedure as for peat-based composts.

Sowing in blocks (see fig. 4): for many years, commercial growers have been using small 'blocks' of sowing compost, measuring about 4 cubic cm (1½ in) with pelleted seeds sown in a small central depression. Using ordinary seed I have found blocks an ideal way of raising all salads.

They have several outstanding advantages: individual seedlings have an excellent start; no need to prick out, as blocks are planted out direct; they can be planted in dry, wet or adverse conditions in which normal, bare rooted plants would be liable to fail, as the block cushions the plant from the shock of transplant-

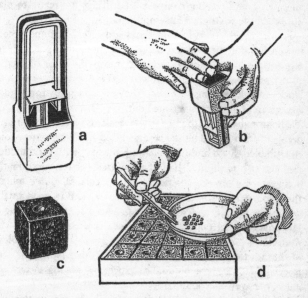

Fig. 4 – BLOCKING
a Hand-blocking tool *b* Packing compost into the blocker *c* Block with hole in the centre for the seed *d* Picking up individual seeds with a piece of glass to sow singly in a block

ing; a range of salad plants can be grown in a minimum of space: a standard seed tray holds about forty-five blocks, and each could be sown with a different type of plant if required.

Blocking is easiest if carried out with special blocking compost and a hand-blocking machine. Commercial hand-blockers, which make a minimum of ten to twelve blocks, are expensive; but fortunately single-block tools for amateurs have recently come on to the market. A rough and ready alternative is to put compost in a seed tray, wet it, then cut it into blocks with a kitchen knife. Ordinary potting compost can be used, although some experience is needed to get it to the right moisture content for blocks.

If a block has no hole in the top, make one with a small dibber, the end of a pencil or a nail. Sow the seed either by hand or by the broken glass method (see p. 34). Once blocks are sown make sure they do not dry out, as re-wetting is difficult. (This applies to all sowing and potting composts.) Seedlings are ready to plant out when the roots are visible on the outside of the block.

Plants raised in blocks sometimes grow very fast and become overcrowded in the seed tray before conditions are right for planting outside. As a holding operation, move a number of them to empty seed trays, spacing them out and filling gaps between the blocks with loose moist compost; they continue growing without a check until they can be planted out.

The drawback to growing single seeds in blocks is the risk of non-germination and blocks being wasted – although these could be crumbled down and used again. However, with good modern seed the risk is slight. I had one hundred per cent germination this year with several varieties of lettuce, corn salad and tomato, and good germination with most other seed. Buy good quality seed, store it well, and select plump, sound seeds for sowing. If germination is in doubt, sow 2–3 seeds in each block; but steel yourself for pulling out the extra seedlings to leave one per block, or the advantage of this method will be lost. Now that seed, especially F_1 seed, has become so expensive, sowing in blocks is in fact one way of economizing.

Sowing in individual pots: large seeds, such as cucumber, can be sown directly into small pots of about 5 cm (2 in) diameter, made of clay, rigid plastic, plastic film or peat, or in compressed Jiffy 7 discs which expand on watering. Plant roots grow through peat pots and Jiffy 7s, so the complete pot is planted out. Their tendency to dry out can be prevented by standing them in a container with moist peat or soil packed around them.

Once seeds have germinated they need to be watched carefully as they are very delicate. Keep tiny seedlings away from bright sunlight; shade them if they are on exposed south-facing window-sills, and turn them 90 degrees every day so that they do not become drawn towards the light. Keep them moist but not overwatered, watering either with a rose, or the soaking-up method, and keep away from draughts.

Stage II – Pricking out (see fig. 5): seedlings should never be crowded; the earlier they are pricked out the better, preferably as soon as the first two seed leaves appear. Only prick out healthy seedlings – the 'duds' never recover.

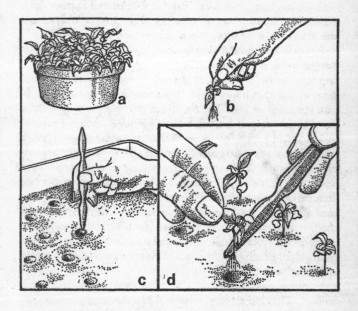

Fig. 5 – Pricking out
a Seedlings in the pot in which they were sown *b* Handling individual seedlings by the leaf *c* Making a hole for the seedling *d* Planting the seedlings

Prepare a tray or pot with moist compost, making it firm and smooth as for sowing. Better plants will be produced by pricking out into individual pots, but more compost and space will be required.

Water seedlings first, then lever them out gently with a plastic label or a knife blade, disturbing the roots as little as possible. Handle them by the leaves.

With a miniature dibber or large nail make a hole in the compost just large enough for the roots.

Hold the seedling in the hole and press compost gently around it, so that the seed leaves are finally just above soil level. Make sure the seedling's roots are in contact with the soil, and not hanging in an air pocket. Level the soil.

If necessary water, using a fine rose, or the soak up method.

Shade seedlings from direct sun for the first two or three days.

Stage III – Potting on: most salad plants can be planted out direct from trays or pots as soon as they have developed a sturdy root system and soil and weather conditions outside are suitable. Potting on is mainly necessary for plants which will be grown permanently in large pots. It is never advisable to move a plant from a small pot into a much larger one at one go; move to an intermediate size first. The technique is as for planting. Where a soil-based compost is used, put a good layer of crocks covered by old leaves in the bottom of the pot to ensure good drainage (unnecessary with peat-based compost). Always water a plant before knocking it out of a pot for potting on or planting.

Stage IV – Hardening off: plants grown indoors need to be acclimatized gradually to colder, more exposed conditions before they are planted outside; they may succumb or be set back by the first taste of inclement weather. Hardening off is especially important for plants raised in peat-based composts, which encourage rather lush 'soft' growth. Growth in soil-based compost is 'harder' and more resilient.

The first step in hardening off is to increase the ventilation indoors. Then move plants outside into a sheltered position during the day (or remove cloches and frame lights) but take them indoors, or protect them, at night. Gradually leave them outside for longer and longer periods, protecting them only on exceptionally cold nights. If this is done over a ten- to fourteen-day period, they may be deemed tough enough to plant out permanently.

6

SOWING OUTDOORS AND PLANTING

SOWING OUTDOORS: There are three methods of sowing outdoors: broadcast, in drills and singly. The key to successful sowing outdoors is in preparing the soil; indeed preparing a seedbed is probably one of the most skilled techniques in gardening.

In the ideal seedbed the ground should be firm but not solidly compacted – ideally, there should be a least a six-week gap between digging the soil and making the seedbed, to allow the soil to settle. The surface should be free of large stones and lumps of soil and should be raked to a fine tilth, that is with the soil crumbs about the size of large breadcrumbs. The soil should be moist and warm; not wet, cold or dry.

Preparing a seedbed: during the winter months most soils become wet, and work on the seedbed cannot begin until the surface has started to dry out. The art of seedbed making is in seizing the right moment. If soil sticks to your shoes when you walk on the surface, it is still too wet to work and is best left for a few more days. But do not wait until it has become completely dry and dusty – or you may have to water to break down the surface for a tilth. Clay and chalky soils have a nasty habit of being too wet one moment and drying into intractable solid lumps the next.

Assuming the soil has been dug over in winter and exposed to frost, or dug over early in spring, fork the top 5–8 cm (2–3 in) of soil lightly, or hoe it, to help dry out the surface. (This may be unnecessary on some soils.)

When the surface seems dry enough to work, possibly the same day, maybe a few days later, shuffle over the surface lightly to smooth and consolidate the soil; alternatively, use the back of the rake to break down lumps. Some persistent soil lumps can be broken up by hand. Rake off stones and remaining lumps of soil.

Rake the soil gently backwards and forwards until a fine tilth is obtained – the smaller the seed being sown the finer the tilth required. This procedure may have to be repeated several times to get the soil 'just right' – gradually getting a finer and finer surface. Sometimes a light shower of rain provides just the right conditions for raking the surface to a tilth; watering may be necessary if the soil becomes too dry.

If a good seedbed has been prepared but there is no time to sow immediately, cover the surface with a thin mulch of straw, hay, compost, even newspaper, to preserve the tilth and prevent it drying out until you are ready. The strong winds which are so common in spring dry out a surface in no time, and one can be back to square one again!

Broadcasting (see fig. 6) is a useful method of sowing various crops, for example: salads which will be cut and allowed to regrow such as cress, rocket, some types of chicory and lettuce, and packets of mixed salad seed; salads which require little space and no thinning such as radish, pickling onions and spring carrot; hardy overwintering salads such as parella lettuce and grumolo chicory. It is also a quick way of sowing when time is precious, though it is, of course, extravagant with seed.

Make sure the seedbed is weedfree, as it is difficult to weed in broadcast crops. In very weedy soil it is worth preparing the ground, allowing a flush of weeds to come up, and hoeing them off before sowing.

Prepare the seed-bed with a fine tilth as above, then scatter the seed by hand evenly over the surface. The quantity of seed required will vary – cress, for example, would be sown much thicker than radish or lettuce.

Rake over the plot in one direction, say north to south; then rake in the opposite direction.

If the soil is likely to dry out before the seed has germinated cover it with a light, easily moved mulch such as sheets of newspaper, sacks or straw. Keep inspecting the seedbed and remove the mulch as soon as any seedlings appear, or they will become white and drawn.

Sowing in drills is the commonest method of sowing outdoors. It is used for plants raised in a seedbed and later transplanted into their permanent positions, and plants which are normally difficult to transplant so are sown in their permanent positions

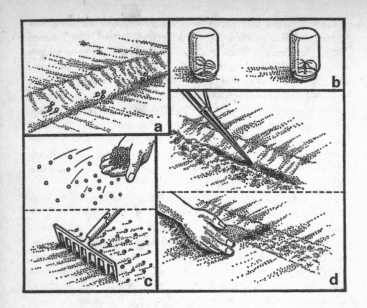

Fig. 6 – Sowing outdoors

a Station sowing *b* Sowing large seeds individually under jars *c*
Broadcasting *Above:* scattering seed evenly over the surface *Below:*
covering it up by raking in each direction *d* Sowing under dry conditions *Above:* watering the bottom of the drill *Below:* after the
seeds have been sown, covering with dry soil to prevent evaporation

and thinned out. This is often the case with summer lettuces,
chives and parsley, and root crops such as beetroot and radish.

Choose a day when the ground is moist and there is little
wind, and prepare a seedbed with a fine tilth as already described.

Mark out the position of the rows and, using the trowel blade
or a wooden label, make a miniature trench or drill in the soil
along the length of the line. The drill can be anything from
1–5 cm ($\frac{1}{2}$–2 in) deep, depending on the seed. As a general rule
seed needs to be covered by about twice its own depth of soil. So
tiny seed is barely covered; lettuce is sown about 1 cm ($\frac{1}{2}$ in)
deep, and so on.

Sow the seeds along the drill. Whatever you are sowing, sow THINLY. This is probably the most important and most ignored rule of gardening! New gardeners are always tempted to sow thickly just in case! In practice, germination is either so good that the vast majority of the seeds germinate (and have to be thinned out), or some other factor such as cold soil, bad weather, or the age of the seed prevents virtually all the seed germinating, so resowing is necessary anyway. Avoid shaking the seed packet along the rows; this is wasteful and hard to control. It is better to put a few seeds in the palm of the hand, and to take a pinch of seed at a time. The seed can be evenly spaced, station sown (groups of three or four seeds) or intersown (two different crops, which generally mature at different rates, sown in alternate rows). After sowing press the seed lightly into the bottom of the drill, and cover it with well-crumbled soil.

If sowing in adverse conditions, such as in very hot weather, before sowing dribble a little water into the bottom of the drill only, let it soak in, and sow directly on this base. Cover the seed with dry soil to act as a mulch (see fig. 6). In prolonged dry weather cover with newspaper or a similar mulch until the seeds have germinated (see p. 41). In very wet conditions spread a little peat along the bottom of the drill to improve sowing conditions.

Drills can also be drawn and the ground covered with cloches for a few days before sowing, to warm up the soil.

Sowing seeds singly (see fig. 6): very large seeds such as beans and cucumbers can be sown singly by making a hole with a small dibber and dropping them in. Make sure, however, that the seeds lie flat in the soil and are not suspended in a pocket of air at the bottom of the hole. Large seeds can be given an early start by sowing them outside under jam jars.

THINNING: Seedlings tend to grow very fast and rapidly become overcrowded, spindly or drawn, a state from which they never recover. Removing surplus seedlings or thinning – so that each plant has enough space to develop – is a vital operation.

Start thinning as soon as the seedlings are large enough to handle. Thin so that each seedling is just standing clear of its neighbours, and thin progressively to offset losses from pests and diseases. Choose a time when the soil is moist to minimize the shock to the roots of remaining plants – water an hour or so beforehand if necessary. Afterwards, firm the loose soil around any seedlings which have been disturbed, and then remove thinnings, as their smell may attract the plant's pests. Spare thinnings can often be transplanted; those of onion or lettuce can be mixed into salads.

TRANSPLANTING : Seedlings raised in seedbeds or under cover indoors eventually have to be planted in their permanent positions. Seedlings of most vegetables can be transplanted, but it is, of course, a shock to the plant to be uprooted. Young plants make new roots more easily than old, so usually the sooner a plant is moved the better.

Many nurserymen and garden centres now sell plants for transplanting. However, where possible, it is worth raising one's own. The advantages include: less risk of introducing disease into the garden; more choice (nurserymen have to limit themselves to the most popular); plants are at hand to transplant in their prime, and when soil conditions are most favourable.

When transplanting: choose a dull, overcast day, or transplant in the evening; if the soil is heavy, work in a little well-rotted compost or peat beforehand; if the soil is dry, water both the seedbed and the ground being planted beforehand – preferably overnight or several hours before – do not plant in waterlogged soil; lift seedlings carefully with a trowel, and always hold them by the leaves to avoid damaging the delicate root hairs; with a trowel (miniature trowel or small dibber for very small seedlings) make a hole large enough for the roots without cramping – hold the plant in the hole as you replace the soil; firm the soil round the stem with your fingers (firm planting is essential); tug a leaf when you have finished, and if the plant wobbles, replant it! Unless the soil is already wet, water around the plant with a rose on the can. It is a useful practice to mulch after planting; this cuts out much watering and weeding later. Very small seedlings may be swamped by mulching so wait until they are bigger; in very hot weather, shade plants until they are well established. Effective shades can be made with netting, or conical 'hats' of newspaper or cardboard. Gentle daily watering may be necessary for several days after planting until the plants look perky and well established. This will not be necessary if the plants are mulched. Some plants, such as outdoor tomatoes, require stakes: this prevents root disturbance later.

Spacing: As already mentioned, it makes sense to plant salad crops in blocks with equidistant spacing between plants, rather than in the traditional rows. Research has confirmed that this ensures the optimum use of space, water and nutrient resources, besides being an effective means of keeping down weeds.

7

MISCELLANEOUS SALAD TECHNIQUES

MULCHING: This is the term for covering the soil surface with a layer of material to prevent moisture loss. It is probably one of the most ancient gardening techniques in the world, developed centuries ago by highly skilled gardeners such as the Arabs and Chinese. It was also used long ago in Britain; a 13th-century accounts book for Norwich Cathedral records labourers being paid threepence a day for 'thatching' fields with straw!

As the majority of salads are leafy, thirsty crops, mulching is particularly relevant to salad growing, especially in dry parts of the country or in dry conditions. One of the most interesting techniques we encountered on our travels through Europe was the extensive use of mulching with sand, stone and gravel on very hot dry parts of the Spanish coast. Tomato and cucumber were amongst salad crops being mulched in this way – some being grown in the open, some under low plastic tunnels, some in greenhouses.

Apart from its prime function of conserving moisture, mulching has numerous other beneficial effects: it keeps down weeds; it improves the soil structure (partly by encouraging the activity of worms); it has an insulating effect, keeping the soil cooler in summer and warmer in winter (stone and sand mulches also throw out some heat at night); it keeps the top soil layers moist and enables roots to extract more nutrients; it prevents the soil becoming too compacted when walked on; when used under trailing or sprawling crops like cucumber or tomato it keeps the fruits clean and dry, so lessening the risk of fungus infection; organic mulches increase the organic matter and nutrients in the soil (they can either be dug in at the end of the season, or left on the surface for the worms to work in).

Ideal mulching materials should be slightly loose in texture, to allow water to penetrate to the soil. Straw, for example, is much looser in texture than lawn mowings, which become compacted if used fresh, and peat tends to absorb most of the rainfall before it reaches the soil. Some suitable organic mulches are compost, dried bracken, shredded or pulverized bark, spent mushroom compost, spent hops, seaweed, dried leaves, leaf-mould, wood shavings, spent cotton waste; and sawdust, peat and lawn mowings if not used too thickly. (Lawn mowings should be allowed to dry out for several days first, or nitrogen is lost from the soil as they are broken down by bacterial action.) Suitable inorganic mulches are sand, gravel, stones, clinkers and black plastic film.

Depth: as a rough guide at least an inch of mulch is needed to preserve moisture. The bulkier the material, the thicker the layer of mulch can be. Straw and mushroom compost, for example, can be at least 8 cm (3 in) deep. The Spanish sand mulches are often 10 cm (4 in) deep.

After planting is generally the best time to mulch. With spring planting, wait until the soil has had a chance to warm up. In summer, water thoroughly when planting and then mulch; this will cut down remarkably on the need to water during the summer. Similarly, much watering in greenhouses can be saved by mulching. Once seedlings are up, the ground between rows can be mulched, watering first if necessary.

Crops which will be overwintered in the soil such as winter radish or celeriac can be mulched in the autumn. This helps to conserve soil warmth and to preserve the soil structure; it also makes it easier to dig them up when the ground is frozen. Light soils can be mulched in winter with organic mulches to help preserve the soil structure. Heavy soils are best left until they have dried out in spring. The important point about mulching is that it preserves the *status quo*. So never mulch very cold, very wet, or very dry soil.

Plastic mulches: various types of plastic film for mulching are now available to amateur gardeners.

a) Black film is already widely used for mulching strawberries and growing early potatoes – holes being cut in the film for the plants to grow through. Black film is a very effective means of controlling weeds. However, it tends to chill the soil, and if used over a long period has a detrimental effect on its biological life. For this reason the newer perforated black plastic film is preferable, as it allows some air and water to penetrate.

b) Brown film also prevents weed growth, but allows the soil to warm up more than black film.

c) White film is less useful for weed control but reflects light and heat up on to plants, encouraging ripening and earlier crops.

d) Perforated transparent film (see fig. 13): several types of mulching film are now being made, perforated with slits or small holes to enable the film to 'expand' as the plants grow. It conserves moisture (improving germination) and shelters plants (encouraging growth, bringing heavier yields), but does not necessarily protect plants from frost. The film is laid on seedbeds after sowing, or placed over young plants, and can either be dug into the soil at the unperforated edges or anchored with stones, clods of soil or wire pins. In most cases it must be removed a few weeks before the plants are mature. The time of removal is important and varies with the crop.

The use of perforated film (or 'floating cloches') is still experimental in this country. It looks promising for salad crops, especially those sown in autumn and early spring such as radish, lettuce, cress, carrot, onion, celery, parsley and annual herbs and for bush outdoor tomatoes. Cordon tomatoes can be grown in upright 'bags' of film, which are moved up the stake as the plant grows. So far I have only experimented with autumn-sown corn salad under perforated 'Xirofilm' – but it was most successful.

'CUT-AND-COME-AGAIN' TECHNIQUES (see fig. 7): A surprising number of leafy salad plants can be cut down to within 2·5–5 cm (1–2 in) above ground level, and will throw up further crops of leaves. Some – rocket, chicories, cress, Welsh onion for example – can be cut four or five times. Others, including claytonia, Japanese greens, some lettuce, chop suey greens, Abyssinian mustard, not quite so often.

To make the most of this technique the soil must be fertile, and the crop well watered. Occasional liquid feeds encourage growth. Cut the plants off clean with a sharp knife or scissors and remove any rotting leaves or debris.

It is sometimes hard to judge when to make the first cut. When it looks worth doing is probably the best advice one can

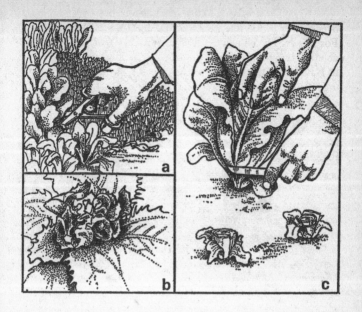

FIG. 7 – CUT-AND-COME-AGAIN TECHNIQUES
a Cutting a patch of seedlings *b* Batavian endive re-growing after the
first cut *c* Taking the first cut from a 'cutting' type of lettuce. The
cut stumps in the foreground will re-sprout

give. Surprisingly quite small stems and stumps will in fact
throw out new growth! The cut-and-come-again technique gives
quick returns (it is often used when plants are still seedlings) and
brings high yields from small patches of ground.

BLANCHING AND FORCING: Many of the salad plants used in
autumn, winter and early spring – endives, chicories and dandelions, for example – are naturally bitter. To make them sweeter
and more palatable they need to be blanched, literally 'whitened',
by being kept in the dark.

Blanching normally takes about fifteen days, and as there is a
high risk of the plants rotting during the process in cold, damp,
winter conditions, it is best to blanch just a few at a time – enough
to keep up a regular supply. Whole plants are more liable to rot
than trimmed plants; and curled-leaved types more than broad-

49

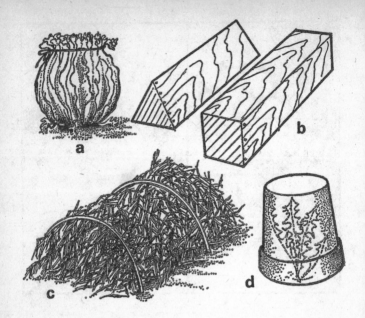

Fig. 8 – Blanching methods
a Tying up leaves *b* Covering with a wooden structure *c* Covering with bracken held in place with wire hoops *d* Using an upturned flower pot. The drainage hole must be blocked to exclude light

leaved. To minimize the risk of rotting remove any dead, decayed or diseased leaves in the vicinity of the plant, and only cover or tie foliage when it is dry. There are numerous methods of blanching, and many variations on the themes suggested below.

In situ methods (see fig. 8): 1. Tie up leaves near the top with raffia. This simple method only blanches the central leaves, but is quick and easy. 2. Cover plants with large upturned flowerpots. If the leaves are sprawly tie them loosely first. Block drainage holes to exclude light. 3. Cover plants with planks made into an inverted V or box. 4. Cover plants with a loose layer of straw, kept in place if necessary with wire hoops. (Good for red chicory.) Straw the plants in autumn before cold weather sets in. 5. Cover trimmed chicories and dandelion with about 20 cm (8 in) of sand, light soil, cinders, or black plastic over a wire frame. Done in the autumn, this will give blanched shoots for the spring.

Transplanted methods (see fig. 9): these have an element of forcing in them, as they usually bring on the plants a little earlier.

1. Lift plants in autumn and replant them closely in frames, darkened by covering with straw mats or black polythene. (Useful for blanching endive heads.) 2. Alternatively lift roots in autumn or during the winter months and replant a few at a time in damp soil in pots or boxes, or direct into the soil under greenhouse staging or benches. Pots or boxes can be put in a dark cellar or shed, cold room or under the greenhouse bench. Where they are not put into a naturally dark environment, darken them artificially by covering with an inverted pot or box of the same size, with all drainage holes or cracks blocked. An area under a greenhouse bench can be darkened with black polythene.

This second method is useful for a winter supply of chicory before the outdoor crop is ready. Witloof chicory roots are trimmed to about 2.5 cm (1 in) above neck level before planting. With red chicories the leaves are simply tied, encouraging the formation of tight hearts. Plants can be brought on a little earlier with slight heat (such as a moderately warm airing cupboard); but it is generally held that the flavour is better if they are allowed to develop naturally. To avoid digging up roots in midwinter, they can be lifted in autumn and stored flat in boxes of moist earth, peat or sand until required.

3. Cellars are still used on the Continent for storing and forcing winter vegetables. The following method of forcing dandelion, wild chicory, and small Witloof chicory roots (or large ones which have already been forced once) is used in Belgium (see fig. 9f). A heap of soil about 10 cm (4 in) deep is built up against a cellar wall, and trimmed roots are laid on this layer, with necks protruding over the edge. They are covered with another 10-cm (4-in) of soil, another layer of roots and so on, then watered with a rose on the can. (If the final layer of soil is made about 20 cm (8 in) deep, the final layer of roots can be planted upright.) The blanched leaves are cut as they are ready, just above the neck. Many will resprout several times.

STORING VEGETABLES: The quality and flavour of all vegetables deteriorate with storage, so vegetables should only be stored when necessary (for winter reserves or when they risk being destroyed

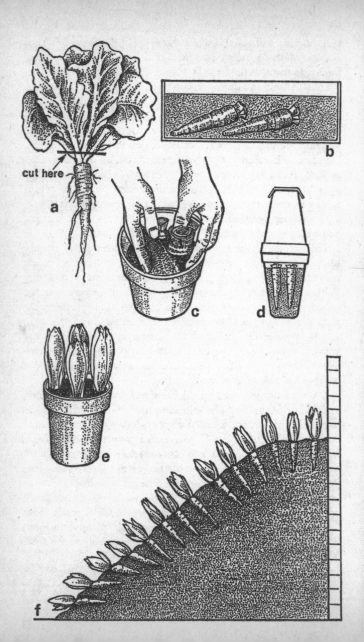

cut here

a

b

c

d

e

f

by bad weather). Only store vegetables in prime condition; reject any which are diseased, pest damaged, or showing signs of bruising or rotting. Handle vegetables for storage very gently.

Vegetables can be stored: in soil – roots such as beet and carrot can be left in well-drained soil, covered with several inches of straw or bracken; in boxes in sheds – most roots can be stored in layers of slightly damp sand, peat, or weathered ashes in dry, frost-proof sheds (cut or twist off stems before storing); in clamps – roots can be stored outdoors, or in cellars, in simple clamps. Start with an 8-cm (3-in) layer of straw on the ground; pile the roots on the straw, cover with 15 cm (6 in) of soil, and a final layer of 15 cm (6 in) of straw. Some means of ventilation, such as a wedge of straw, or a piece of pipe, running through the heap and protruding above it, is advisable. Storage-type cabbage can be clamped, putting straw between each head. Witloof and Sugar Loaf types of chicory are sometimes stored in clamps, heads turned inwards, the whole heap covered with straw; hanging – winter cabbage can be stored for several weeks suspended by the stem in dry sheds or cellars and onions suspended in nets; short-term storage – leafy crops such as lettuce, endive, summer cabbage and chicories keep best for short periods in plastic bags in a fridge.

FIG. 9 – FORCING TECHNIQUES
a–d Stages in forcing Witloof chicory a Roots being cut off above the neck b Storage in moist sand until required for forcing c Planting several roots in a large pot for forcing in the dark d Covering with a pot of the same size with light excluded e The resulting chicons f Belgian method of forcing chicory and dandelions in a cellar. (For details see page 51.)

8

PLANNING AND SITING

Rotation, harvesting season and accessibility in winter are some of the factors to consider when planning a kitchen garden.

ROTATION: The main purpose of rotation is to discourage the build-up of certain soil pests and diseases. Most diseases only attack one crop, or a range of botanically closely related vegetables, and become far more serious when that crop or group is grown continuously on one site. The following salad crop diseases can be guarded against by rotation: onion neck rot (four-year rotation); onion white rot (at least four-year rotation); various carrot root rots (one- or two-year rotation); clubroot in brassicas and related crops such as radishes (three-year rotation).

Most soil pests are unaffected by rotation, being able to move in search of their hosts. One exception is lettuce root aphid. Where lettuces have been attacked by root aphids, avoid planting in that ground for at least a year. Rotation is also the only remedy against eelworm, the minimum cycle being three years. Those likely to attack salad crops are onion stem and bulb eelworm, brassica cyst eelworm on brassicas and radishes, and potato cyst eelworm in potatoes and tomatoes. (Tomatoes are unaffected by the disease but are a host.)

For rotation purposes vegetables should be divided into the following groups: potatoes and tomatoes; onion family (onion, leek, garlic); brassicas (cabbage, radish, turnip); legumes (peas, beans); roots (carrot, salsify); miscellaneous (celery, lettuce, spinach).

In the average-sized garden it is obviously very difficult to devise a full rotation scheme. It is usually a question of compromise, though it is easier to work out a flexible rotation system where the garden is divided into a number of narrow beds, rather than into large beds. The principles to observe are: wherever possible, and for as long as possible, follow each crop with a crop from a different group; watch for any signs of disease build-up in the soil.

HARVESTING SEASON: Within the broad outline of the rotation system, it is advisable to grow close together crops which will be sown or harvested at the same time. This enables a piece of ground to be cleared at one go to make room for something else. Examples include: spring-sown salads (spring onion, young carrot, lettuce); summer crops (outdoor tomatoes, pepper, cucumber); late autumn crops (Chinese cabbage, endives, Japanese greens); hardy overwintering crops (celeriac, chicories, corn salad, land cress, claytonia, winter radish).

SITING: Salad crops for the winter should, ideally, be as near a path as possible to avoid treading on cultivated ground. (This is another case where narrow beds are practical.) Dwarf-growing winter salads – lamb's lettuce, salad burnet and winter savory – can be used as edgings to paths or beds. It is always useful to have winter herbs near the house – and remember to mark the ends of winter salad rows with a tall stick, so that they can be found if covered with snow !

Every garden has its problem corners – too wet, too dry, or too shady for most vegetables; but some salad plants and herbs can do reasonably well in difficult areas as suggested below.

Moderately shaded areas: angelica, chickweed, chop suey greens, chervil, cress, Hamburg and ordinary parsley, lettuce and radish (in summer), sorrel. Red lettuce, incidentally, develop a deeper colour when grown in light shade.

Damp, heavy soil: chickweed, chicories, hairy bitter cress, land cress, and celery and celeriac if the soil is reasonably fertile.

Dry soil: nasturtiums, pickling onions, thyme and other herbs.

Many salad crops can be blended effectively or unobtrusively into flower beds – as edgings, in small groups or patches in the centre of a bed, or, where appropriate, as tall architectural plants at the back of a border. They do, however, generally need more fertile conditions and more moisture than flowers, so do cater for this !

Plants suitable for edgings include: golden and green purslane, which like light soil but must not be allowed to dry out; winter purslane (claytonia) – plant in autumn for winter and spring;

cress – keep it cropped; grumolo chicory – forms beautiful dwarf rosettes in winter, but should be dug up before it seeds in early summer; chop suey greens – keep cropped or allow to flower after use; lettuce – red and green salad bowl types and oak-leaved lettuce are the most suitable, as well as some of the red Italian lettuces, and those whose leaves can be picked off individually so the overall effect is not lost when they are used; sedums – various sedum species can be used in salads (see p. 93); curled parsley, chives, chervil and salad burnet – useful and decorative edgings if flowering shoots are kept trimmed; golden and ordinary marjoram, silver and gold thymes, hyssop and winter savory – useful, pretty, permanent herb edgings.

Medium-sized plants are: beetroot – the purplish foliage can be very decorative; carrot – seed can be broadcast together with annual flower seed to make an effective and useful display; red chicories – green in summer, turning red and variegated in winter, best sown early summer; dill – delicate, feathery foliage; sages – purple, golden and variegated sages are all ornamental and useful in small quantities in salads; peppers – some of the cayenne peppers are attractive plants with delicate foliage; tomatoes – dwarf varieties such as Pixie are not out of place in a flower border.

For the back of the border: fennel, borage, angelica, lovage and Sweet Cicely are tall, handsome plants, all of which can be used in salads.

Flowers such as borage, nasturtium, calendula (pot marigold), bergamot, pansies, violets, geraniums, chrysanthemums, roses, anchusa, and the flowers of rosemary, sage and lavender, can all be used in salads (see pp. 94 to 101).

CATCH CROPPING AND INTERCROPPING: Salad crops are amongst the fastest growing and smallest of vegetables, so are particularly suited to intensive, space-saving techniques such as intercropping and catch cropping.

Catch cropping: no ground in a garden need ever be idle; in the gap between one long-term crop (such as winter brassicas) being cleared and another (such as peas or sweet corn) there is often an opportunity for sowing a quick salad crop.

Here, patches come into their own, especially if used for those salads which are broadcast and cut for use as seedlings. They can either be left in the ground for their full term of several cuts, or cleared after one or two cuts if the ground is required. Cress, mustard, rocket, chop suey greens, mixed salad can be used in this way. So can lettuce and Sugar Loaf and red chicory, particularly when grown for use as seedlings rather than as mature plants. Block-raised plants are also very useful for establishing a catch crop quickly.

'Growing bags' can be used for a quick catch crop when their main summer crop – say tomato or pepper – is finished. There should be enough fertilizer residue in the bag to sustain a crop of cress, rocket, corn salad or claytonia or, with a little fertilizer, winter lettuce. These would be useful for salads during the winter and spring months. Put the bags in a sheltered position, preferably in a greenhouse or frame. Used bags are also handy for raising seedlings in spring.

Intercropping (see fig. 10): two or more crops can often be grown together in the same piece of ground if one is fast and the other slow maturing, or if one is tall and the other dwarf or spreading.

John Evelyn had a few suggestions for his gardener in the 17th century: 'One may sow Reddish & Carrots together on the same bed: so as the first may be drawn, whilst the other is ready: or sow Lettuce, purselan, parsneps, carrots, Reddish on the same beds, & gather each kind in their season, leaving the parsneps to Winter ...'

Here are a few 20th-century ideas: Between fairly close rows of slow-growing crops such as shallots, leeks, maincrop onions or maincrop carrots, sow radish, spring onions, cress, mustard; or plant small lettuces (such as Tom Thumb) or corn salad.

Between slow-growing widely-spaced crops such as brassicas, celeriac, marrow, pumpkin, or between blocks of peas, dwarf beans or broad beans, sow as above, plus slightly larger salad crops such as rocket, medium-sized lettuce, Japanese greens, Chinese mustard and chop suey greens.

Under sweet corn: all salads suggested above can be grown under sweet corn, preferably planted at the same time. Mature sweet corn usually only shades the ground lightly, so the salad plants may be left for their full term if kept well watered. Also, sprawling plants such as cucumber and marrow can be grown under sweet corn; so can dwarf beans.

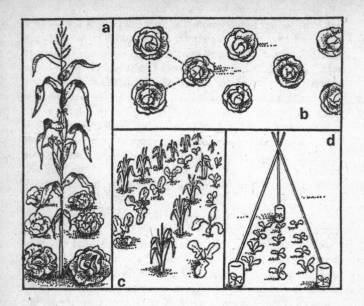

FIG. 10 – INTERSOWING AND SPACING
a Undercropping sweet corn with salad plants *b* Equidistant spacing which is ideal for many salad plants *c* Using space between a long-term crop such as leeks for a quick salad crop *d* Undercropping climbing plants. Cucumbers are sown under the jam jars, but the salad crop will have been cleared by the time the cucumbers have grown up the poles

Beneath climbing marrow, cucumber or beans when grown on tripods: radish or cress could be sown, or salads such as lettuce, corn salad and chop suey greens can be planted on the ground between them. They will have matured, or can be cleared, before the ground is shaded by the climbing plant.

Between station-sown, long-term crops: radish, small lettuce and spring onion are particularly suited for sowing between the 'stations' of slow-maturing crops such as parsnip, salsify, scor-zonera. If the long-term crop is sown at least 23 cm (9 in) apart the secondary crop can be sown between. It will be mature and cleared before the main crop has grown to occupy the space.

9

PROTECTIVE CROPPING

Cloches, frames, low plastic tunnels, walk-in polythene tunnels, glass- and plastic-clad greenhouses are all forms of protection which are of immense value to salad growers who want fresh, varied, good quality salads all year. Protective cropping is the key to salads both earlier and later in the year, and to being able to indulge in tender crops like tomato, cucumber and pepper – which are ill at ease outdoors in the average British summer. This book will only deal with unheated structures. For salad growing heat is unnecessary, expensive and, many people maintain, leads to an inferior, insipid flavour.

BENEFITS OF PROTECTION: '*Growing Days*' The majority of the plants we cultivate only grow when the mean daily temperature rises above 6°C (43°F), a temperature reached some time in spring; they cease growing when it falls below 6°C (43°F), some time in late autumn. The days between these two points are termed 'growing days', the number varying in different parts of the country from about 300 a year in Cornwall to 250 in the north of England, eastern Scotland and other cold areas – an appreciable difference.

All forms of protection warm up the soil and air around plants and, to a greater or lesser degree, slow down the rate at which heat is radiated from the soil at night. This effectively increases the number of growing days for any protected crop. Protection is therefore particularly valuable in cold, high and exposed areas where the growing season is shortest. A gain of as much as three weeks at the beginning and end of the season can be made by protecting crops. Another important point is that, provided plants have sufficient moisture, the higher the temperature rises the faster they grow; so protection increases the rate of growth.

Protection against frost: Salad crops vary in the amount of frost they can stand without being killed or damaged. Cloches and greenhouses give some protection against frost, though on cold clear nights, due to soil radiation, the air temperature under cloches and plastic tunnels can be as low, or even lower, than the temperature outside. (The only real guarantee against frost is a heated structure.)

The importance of unheated protection lies in minimizing the effect of frost by: keeping plants dry; protecting them from wind (the combination of low temperatures and strong wind is extremely damaging); improving soil tilth around plants (frost therefore penetrates less deeply and for less time). Further protection against frost damage can be given by: spraying cloches with water immediately before a heavy frost is expected (the ice layer formed gives extra insulation); spraying plants the morning after a frost before the sun is on them (this enables them to thaw out gently, and often prevents fatalities).

Protection from wind and birds: While a surprising number of salad plants survive remarkably low winter temperatures, when exposed to the full brunt of winter weather the leaves become battered, tough and coarse. Birds also do a lot of damage, especially in spring, both destroying plants entirely, and by making them unsightly. The quality of salads is improved beyond recognition when the plants are protected.

TYPES OF MATERIAL: Gardeners today have a choice of many materials, ranging from glass to plastics and polythene film, from which to make cloches, frames and greenhouses. These brief notes give only an indication of the main materials. Fortunately cheap and simple forms of protection give good results.

Glass has three important qualities. First, it transmits a great deal of light, which is particularly important in winter, when lack of light is a limiting factor on plant growth. Secondly, it traps heat exceptionally well. During the day the earth absorbs the sun's energy in the form of short waves; but at night heat is lost by radiation of long waves from the soil. Unlike most plastic materials, glass to some extent holds back the long waves, so retaining some heat. Thirdly, it does not deteriorate with age.

Its disadvantages are that it is expensive, heavy, breakable and awkward to erect. Most glass cloches were traditionally made in a tent shape (from two pieces) or a barn shape, from four pieces. There are also flat-topped types. For low-growing salads, tents and low barn cloches made from panes 45 × 30 cm (18 × 12 in) are quite adequate, though tomatoes require larger ones. Various devices are sold for joining panes of glass together to make cloches, the best known being the Rumsey clip (see fig. 12a). Broken glass can be mended with an appropriate glue.

Rigid plastics and synthetic materials, both transparent and opaque, such as fibreglass, glass resin, polyvinyl chloride sheets and acrylic sheeting (Perspex), do not usually look as nice as glass, but tend to be cheaper and easier to handle. Some are available both as corrugated and flat sheets.

A number of the transparent plastics are almost as good as glass for light transmission, although as moisture condenses on plastics, some light is cut out. The opaque plastics look as if they would be unsuitable for plant growth, but in fact it has been shown that plant leaves make very efficient use of such even, diffuse light. A few rigid plastics such as polyvinyl chloride are like glass in being impermeable to long wave transmission, so retaining some heat at night. Corrugated materials lose more heat than flat sheets, but have more rigidity and are usually easier to erect.

Many plastics become brittle with age, the greatest risk being degradation due to ultra-violet radiation. For this reason plastics should always be stored out of sunlight. Where possible buy 'ultra-violet (u-v) treated' plastics, which last longer. Plastics are lighter than glass, so require more anchorage, but they are more flexible, and can more easily be made into protective structures of any shape or size.

Semi-rigid plastics, for instance the double layer propylene/ethylene 'board', sold in this country as Correx, is one of the most useful new materials for amateur gardeners. The fluted channels between the two layers give it a corrugated appearance, and because of the double layers, heat loss is minimized and insulation properties are good. Plants grow well in the diffuse light created by this material. Its average life expectancy is three to five years if it has been 'u-v treated'. It can be attached to metal or wooden frames. At ground level it is generally best to use it with the flutes running horizontally, otherwise moisture and dirt may be sucked up by the flutes, causing discoloration.

Wire-reinforced plastics are cheap materials with a relatively short life span, but are nonetheless useful for making cloches

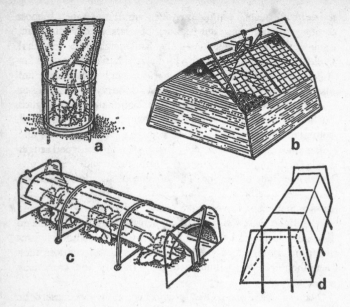

FIG. 11 – TYPES OF CLOCHE

a The Devon cloche: polythene stretched over a wire frame *b* The Westray cloche: glass and polypropylene combined with bird-proof netting *c* The Essex cloche: sliding panels to assist ventilation *d* Cloche made with double-layered polypropylene

and other protective structures. They can easily be bent into any required shape.

CLOCHES (see fig. 11): As it is impossible to describe the many makes of cloche on the market, the following are some of the practical factors – other than cost and appearance – to consider when choosing or making cloches.

Choose materials with good *light transmission*, bearing in mind that an evenly diffused light is acceptable. The light factor is most important: in the short days of autumn and winter; when cloches are being used to grow, rather than merely protect plants; in industrial areas where atmospheric pollution reduces the light.

Stability and anchorage are the worst problems with cloches – and of course they are most useful in exposed areas and in autumn, winter and spring when cold winds and gales are most frequent. Avoid flimsy cloches; one is constantly retrieving them, whole or in pieces, from one's own and neighbours' gardens! Avoid sharp angles which catch the wind. Good features include: stout anchoring pins or legs which can be dug firmly into the ground; holes or hooks in the roofs through which string or wire is threaded for extra anchorage; flanges at the base which can be weighted down. In exposed areas, putting pea sticks on each side of cloches gives extra protection from the wind and makes them more stable. A useful tip with glass is to rub all edges with a carborundum stone when putting them up.

Handling and storage are important, for one of the great advantages of cloches is their versatility; so make sure they are easily moved. Many women find the larger sized glass cloches awkward and heavy to handle. Modern cloches such as the Westray, which combine glass and Correx in one unit, are much lighter to lift and move. Cloches which are awkward to erect and dismantle tend to spend much of their life idle. Those which stack or fold on top of each other when not in use are an asset.

Draught prevention and ventilation must be considered. The ends of cloches must always be closed or wind tunnels are created, so completely offsetting the benefits. Ends can be closed with: closely fitting pieces which hook on to the main body; anchoring rods inserted down the vertical flutes of double-layered polypropylene; panels of glass or plastic, held in place with canes or sticks. Put the canes into the ground at an angle rather than upright, or they work themselves loose (see fig. 12a).

There must be some ventilation, such as gaps between plastic cloches, or between the panes in glass cloches. In hot weather additional ventilation is necessary, or they must be removed. Methods of ventilation include: removable sides or panels, or means of raising them; sides which can be rolled back; ventilator holes in the material; netting over the framework which allows glass or plastic panels to be removed, while maintaining protection against birds.

Size must be such that crops are covered with some room to spare, to keep air circulating and help prevent disease. In summer, foliage should not be too near glass or it will scorch; in winter, plants touching glass may be affected by frost. Cloche height

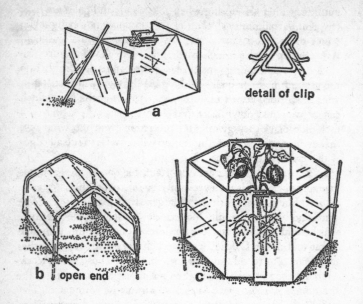

detail of clip

a

b open end

c

Fig. 12 – Cloche techniques

a The Rumsey clip being used to join panes of glass; note the end panels are held in place with a stick in the soil at a 45° angle, not upright   *b* Cloche made by inserting straightened coat-hanger or wires into a plastic bag   *c* Cloches used on their sides to wrap around plants which have outgrown them

can be increased by: using the side or roof extensions available on some models; standing them on bricks or boards; siting them over a trench – only advisable on very light, well-drained soil.

With some of the flexible materials the width/height ratio can be adjusted to cover a wider or narrower area of ground. Some cloches can also be used on their sides 'wrapped' around plants which have outgrown them, anchored with a cane through the handle, or one on each side.

Primitive cloches can be made from large plastic bags, slipping bent pieces of wire (such as coat-hangers) down each side of the bag, and piercing the plastic with the wire for anchorage (see fig. 12b). Another way is to nail polythene film between two frames made of battens. Four of these frameworks will make a single tent-shaped cloche. A row of these can make a small tunnel with one closing panel at each end.

A few more points should be made about cloches. To take advantage of cloches, they should always be put on good soil, into which plenty of organic matter has been worked. This encourages growth and helps water to penetrate. In winter it is worth stirring the soil around cloched plants to keep the roots aerated.

There is generally no need to remove small cloches for watering. Rain-water runs down the sides of cloches, percolating to the roots. Equally, they can be watered from above with a can or hose. However, it may be necessary to remove them to water small seedlings, and large cloches may have to be removed to ensure that water is reaching the roots. They can, of course, be lifted off when it rains. In summer, the soil surface under cloches dries out rapidly. Poke a finger an inch or so into the soil to see if it is moist beneath the surface. Mulching cuts down on the need for watering.

The strength and weakness of cloches lies in their mobility. They have to be moved for many gardening operations, which is a drawback; but they can be moved from crop to crop, wherever protection would be most beneficial, which is their great advantage over more permanent structures such as frames and greenhouses. They can also be used all the year round.

In spring use them as outlined below.

To prepare the soil for sowing: put cloches on the soil to warm it up for sowing; and over wet soil to dry it out before preparation of a seedbed.

For early sowings: in boxes or pots or *in situ*. Virtually all salad crops can be started off ten or more days earlier in spring by sowing under cloches. To make maximum use of precious space under cloches, intercrop as much as possible. Radish, corn salad, spring onion, carrot, beetroot, seedling crops can all be carefully sown towards the outside of the cloches, with lettuce, peas and dwarf beans down the middle.

For early plantings: all salad plants which have been sown indoors in boxes or blocks can be planted out earlier under cloches.

Tender seedlings and young plants raised in propagators indoors can be hardened off by putting pots or boxes under cloches. Move the cloches a little further apart each day, then leave them off during the day but cover the plants at night. Finally expose the plants continually before planting out in permanent positions.

Cloches can be used *inside* unheated greenhouses and tunnels early in the year. Soil and air temperatures under the cloches are a few degrees higher than in the rest of the greenhouse. This enables tender crops such as tomatoes to be planted out earlier, and other salad crops to be brought on faster. In the lean days of early spring, these extra days of growth are invaluable.

In late spring/early summer use cloches for sowing tender crops, e.g. cucumber, purslane, basil; planting tender crops, e.g. tomato, cucumber, pepper. In both these cases cloches can be removed when they are outgrown or needed elsewhere.

In summer (where cloches are large enough), tender crops can be grown to maturity – for example pepper, cucumber (trained horizontally), tomatoes grown as bushes or trained horizontally.

In autumn use to accelerate ripening of cut down or bush tomato plants; for ripening onions and seed crops. In both cases support the crops to keep off the ground; for covering late summer sowings and plantings of endive, lettuce and other salads for use either in autumn, winter or early spring, or for transplanting the following spring; for late sowings of radish.

In winter use for protecting overwintering salad crops for use during the winter, for example winter lettuce and other hardy salads; Sugar Loaf types of chicory and endive (which will survive some winters but not others); for protecting overwintering seedlings for planting out in spring; inside greenhouses and tunnels to give extra protection to winter salads, particularly those on the borderline of hardiness.

The most efficient way of using cloches is *strip cropping*, whereby vegetable sowing and planting is planned so that cloches can be moved to and fro between adjacent strips of ground. Strip cropping is a subject on its own, but one simple example based primarily on salad crops is given below.

	Strip 1	Strip 2
OCTOBER	*Winter hardy lettuce planted under cloches; intersown with radish for late autumn use*	
MARCH/ APRIL	Cloches removed for lettuce to mature unprotected	*Spring salads (lettuce, corn salad, Japanese greens, seedling patches) sown under cloches*
MAY/ JUNE	*Tomatoes (or cucumber or pepper) planted under cloches. If large enough, crops can mature under them*	Spring salads followed by short summer crops such as dwarf French beans grown in the open
EARLY OCTOBER		*Sugar Loaf chicory, endive or winter lettuce planted out under cloches*

Italic type shows crops covered by cloches in any one season.

Low POLYTHENE TUNNELS (see fig. 13c): Low tunnels made from polythene sheeting stretched over wire hoops are the cheapest form of protective cropping. The sheeting, cut to the required length, is kept in position with strings over the film, tied on each side of the hoops. Tie the strings on one side with a firm, long-term knot, and on the other with a loose knot, to make moving the tunnels a quicker and easier operation – especially in cold, finger-numbing weather! The strings can be left permanently attached to the hoops. (Fine wire is sometimes used instead of string.) The ends of the sheeting are bunched together and simply knotted around a stake, which is put into the soil at an angle of 45°, about 60 cm (2 ft) beyond the last hoop. It is something of an art to get a low tunnel nicely taut!

Sheeting sold for low tunnels is lightweight (150 gauge), so is apt to tear. The tunnel shape does, however, stand up to strong winds surprisingly well. Rips, if caught early, can be mended with plastic tape. Buy 'u-v' treated film wherever possible, and always store it out of sunlight when not in use. Film is sold in various widths, and it is best to err on the wide side so that hoops will be amply covered, with extra plastic at the edges to give additional anchorage in winter and windy weather; either bury the edges in the soil, or weight them with pieces of wood, piping or stones. The ends can also be weighted instead of being tied.

One of the advantages of low tunnels over cloches is that the sheeting is simply pushed to one side for watering, cultivation, picking and ventilation – although in windy weather it is apt to blow back unless securely fastened. Heavy snow should be brushed off or the tunnel sags on to the crops.

Low tunnels are used for the same purposes as cloches, although they are most useful in winter and spring. In summer they tend to create too humid and close an atmosphere, unless well ventiliated. In Spain and Italy low tunnels are widely used in spring (when temperatures approach our summer temperatures) for early plantings of melon and tomato; 'portholes' are cut at regular intervals along their length for ventilation. They are also useful inside greenhouses and large tunnels for bringing on salad crops, and for early plantings of indoor tomatoes.
FRAMES: The garden frame is virtually a bottomless box with a sloping lid or roof; a halfway house between a cloche and a greenhouse. More substantial than a cloche, it is more permanent and offers more protection, but is less mobile and flexible. In the past frames were built over hotbeds of fermenting manure and were extensively used for forcing early salads. Today they are sometimes heated with electric cables in the soil.

FIG. 13 – USING POLYTHENE FILM
a Large walk-in polythene tunnel 1.5 to 2 m (5 to 6 ft) high *b* Perforated film cloche over a tomato plant *c* Low polythene film tunnel, about 30 cm (12 in) high *d* Simple frame design using polythene film nailed or stapled to a wooden frame, and dug into the soil at ground level. A light top can be made by nailing polythene between battens. An extra batten nailed to the front makes a ridge against which the top can rest when in use *e* Lean-to frame. The front of the frame is made by nailing slats to a plank which is half buried in the ground. Polythene is nailed to the slats with battens. A movable piece can be made in one end to serve as a door and for ventilation *f* Perforated film laid flat over spring and autumn salad crops

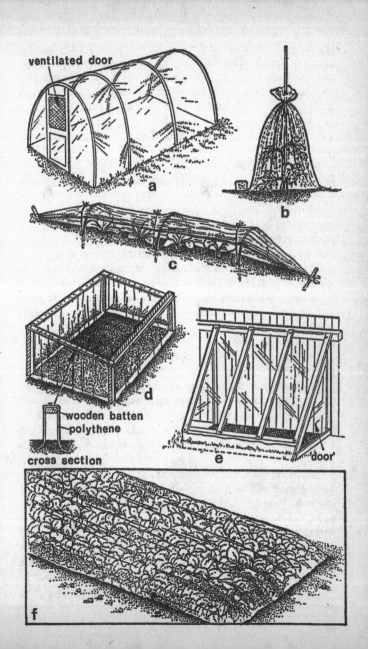

ventilated door

a

b

c

d

wooden batten
polythene
cross section

e

door

f

Frames can be portable or permanent, lean-to or free-standing, single or double span. The sides of permanent frames were traditionally made of brick, concrete or wood. Portable frames – commoner today – have frames of timber, galvanized steel or aluminium, the sides often being of transparent material such as glass, rigid plastic, or even film. For a cheaply constructed frame made from polythene film of 500 or 600 gauge, see fig. 13d.

Similarly, the roof, traditionally a glass 'light' in a wooden frame, can be of rigid plastic or film. Some are hinged to open upwards; others slide on or off sideways or forwards – factors to consider when erecting a frame in a confined area. Where lights are made of lightweight material there should be some means of anchorage in wintry or windy weather.

Frames are normally made lower at the front and higher at the back, to catch the maximum light, being sited, wherever possible, in a south-facing position. For low-growing salads a height of 18 cm (7 in) in front and 23 cm (9 in) at the back is adequate. Larger crops such as cucumbers, self-blanching celery and melons would require deeper frames, say 45 cm (18 in) at the back to 30 cm (12 in) in front.

A simple triangular lean-to structure built against a wall to protect summer tomatoes and peppers would need to be several feet high at the back, reaching down to ground level at the front (see fig. 13e). Glass- and plastic-sided frames let in maximum light, an important factor late and early in the year. A non-opaque-sided frame will have better insulation, but it should not be too deep, or seedlings and young plants will be drawn towards the light.

Frames should never be under trees or in the shade. It is worth having good soil in a frame, working in plenty of well-rotted compost. Ventilation is important, as frames are relatively airtight and a muggy atmosphere encourages disease. They can normally be ventilated by propping the roof lights open or sliding them back; in summer the lights can be removed completely. When watering, try to water the soil rather than the leaves, to minimize the risk of fungus diseases. Seed boxes in deep frames may have to be raised on upturned boxes or pots to prevent seedlings becoming too drawn.

Frames are used mainly for the same purposes as cloches, though they cannot be moved from one crop to another so readily. Being generally more substantial than cloches, they are more suitable for providing frost-free protection in winter. They can be used for: raising plants in early spring in boxes or *in situ*, for transplanting; growing early crops of spring salads; hardening off; growing tender crops in summer; overwintering mature lettuce and other hardy salads; overwintering seedlings for spring planting; forcing and blanching chicories and endives; storing winter vegetables; maintaining a winter supply of parsley, mint and other herbs, by lifting mature roots in the autumn, and planting them in the frame; forcing early roots of mint and seakale in spring.

GREENHOUSES: A greenhouse is a luxury for salad growers, although the classical permanent greenhouse – heated or unheated – has always been used for growing tomato and cucumber. The drawback is that where tomatoes are grown for several years consecutively in the same greenhouse soil, the soil becomes 'sick' through a build-up of pests and diseases.

The alternatives then are: to sterilize the soil (either with steam or chemically); to replace it with fresh soil; to grow tomatoes in pots, bags or in specialized sterile systems such as ring culture or hydroponics.

POLYTHENE TUNNELS: Small 'walk-in' polythene tunnels (see fig. 13a), on the pattern of those used by commercial growers, offer a viable and cheap alternative to a permanent greenhouse for amateurs. Essentially these consist of heavy (500 or 600 gauge) polythene film, stretched over a frame of galvanized tubular hoops, anchored by being dug into the soil in a trench, about 23–30 cm (9–12 in) deep, around the base. Such tunnels are easy to erect; the plastic, which should last three to five years, is cheaply and easily replaced when necessary, and if the soil does become stale, it is only a minor operation to move the tunnel to an adjacent site. In my experience, these polythene tunnels are excellent for growing salad crops all the year round, their one drawback being the problem of ventilation. High temperature and humidity, conducive to disease, can easily build up under the film. The answer is to have maximum ventilation, with ventilation panels in any doors, and if necessary cutting portholes the size of dinner plates in the film 45 cm (18 in) or so above ground level. Large pieces of polythene can be taped over the holes to close them in winter.

Apart from purpose-made polythene tunnels, handy amateurs can easily build themselves 'mini' tunnels, or simple greenhouse-shaped structures, using polythene sheeting and a timber or galvanized pipe framework.

To get the maximum life out of polythene film the following points are worth noting: always use heavy gauge, 'u-v' treated film; make sure there are no projections or rough edges on the framework which might cause friction and wear (pad them with rubber or felt); fit sheeting as tightly as possible, as flapping leads to wear and tear. Nail to battens where necessary. If possible, erect film on a warm day when it is slack and supple and can more easily be pulled taut.

There are a number of easily-assembled polythene structures on the market today, falling into a category somewhere between a giant frame and a small greenhouse: all are useful for extending the salad season, and improving salad quality all the year round.

Many greenhouses are idle in winter and could easily be used for growing winter salads. Endives and lettuce can be planted as late as November to give useful crops the following spring, and patches of rocket, cress, chop suey greens, seedling chicories and Abyssinian greens sown in early spring can be very productive. They can be sacrificed with little loss when it is time to plant tomatoes or other summer crops.

Apart from the risk of soil becoming stale, the only drawback to greenhouses (and tunnels) is that virtually all watering has to be done by hand. This can be minimized to some extent by working in plenty of organic matter and by keeping crops well mulched once watered.

Part II
Plants

Now to the actual plants which can be used in salads, starting with chapters on the less conventional: seed sprouting, weeds and wild plants, flowers and herbs. With vegetables it is hard to draw the line between those grown primarily for use raw in salads, and the many dual-purpose vegetables – beans, potatoes, asparagus for example – which are normally used as hot cooked vegetables but are also excellent cooked and used cold as salads. Some of these I have called 'secondary vegetables', and have covered very briefly at the end of the main vegetable section.

These chapters are written almost in note form, partly to save space, partly to make reference easier. When I started growing vegetables in earnest I always seemed to be rushing indoors to look things up, fingers dirty, guiltily treading carpets with muddy boots, and I remember being very irritated by the need to wade through long paragraphs to extract the vital information I needed. So this is an attempt to overcome the 'information retrieval' problem!

A word on seed availability is necessary. Many of the plants I have found most useful in salads, especially in winter salads, are not, at the time of writing, commonly sold in this country. Now that I know they can be grown here successfully I am trying to encourage British seed firms to add them to their lists, and I am hopeful that they will become more easily available in the future (see Appendix II for suppliers). In the meantime, people travelling to the Continent will find no difficulty in buying them abroad, and I have tried to give foreign names where applicable. It is, incidentally, quite legal to import packets of commercially available seed for private use.

With the commonly-grown salads the problem is often too much choice! In most cases I have listed a few tested varieties;

but new varieties are constantly appearing and old favourites may disappear.

In these chapters dates of sowing, planting and harvesting must be treated as 'average', as there is great variation between different parts of the country, and from one year to the next. My own experience is based on East Anglian conditions, with fairly cold winters and relatively dry summers.

I have concentrated on the techniques of growing outdoors or in cold greenhouses, as few of us can now afford the luxury of heated greenhouses for salads. Wherever cold greenhouses are mentioned, frames or cloches could also be used, but are, of course, less efficient. I have also assumed that salad plants are being grown at equidistant spacing. So unless stated to the contrary, where the advice is to thin or plant say 10 cm (4 in) apart, the rows would also be 10 cm (4 in) apart.

SEED SPROUTNG

Seed sprouting: The idea of taking seeds, sprouting them, and eating the nutritious tiny young seedlings or sprouts is not new; it is probably at least five thousand years old. The Chinese and other ancient races such as the Aztecs and Navajo Indians practised it centuries ago, but it has only become popular in Europe and North America in the last few years. For salad lovers, seed sprouting opens up a whole new range of 'crops' which can be available at any time of year.

It is a useful technique for a number of reasons. Above all, it requires little space; several days' supplies can be grown in a jam jar on a window-sill. Results are rapid as most seeds, under normal conditions, will grow to an edible stage within four to five days. It is simple, requiring only the most rudimentary and inexpensive equipment, and it is economical. Many seeds yield up to ten times their weight when sprouted.

Sprouts are a highly nutritious form of food, particularly rich in vitamins and minerals such as iron, calcium, potassium and iodine. They can be used both raw and cooked in a wide range of recipes. Indeed they can rightly claim to be the ideal packaged food: nutritious, lightweight and easily stored.

Toxicity: It should be pointed out that legumes (beans, peas, alfalfa) can be toxic to humans *when eaten raw*. Among the most toxic raw are haricot beans. Of legumes used for sprouting, adzuki beans, lentils, alfalfa, fenugreek and buckwheat are relatively toxic. They should therefore not be eaten raw regularly, in large quantities (more than 140 g (5 oz) dry weight or 595 g (21 oz) wet weight, daily). Small quantities of raw legume sprouts would be unlikely to have harmful effects. (Mung and soya beans are amongst the least toxic.) Toxicity is reduced by sprouting and by cooking – frying, boiling or steaming. A nutritionist advises me that quick frying sprouted beans for a few minutes in oil, followed by ten minutes' steaming as part of a mixed vegetable dish, would render them safe.

No doubt many seeds could be sprouted and eaten, but it is only those which are tastiest and easy to sprout which have become widely used for the purpose. They include many beans, ranging from the well-known mung bean of Chinese bean sprout fame, to the round red adzuki, now commonplace in health food shops, to the familiar large white Lima bean. Of the cereals, rye, wheat, barley, rice and maize can all be sprouted. So can numerous legumes, such as alfalfa (lucerne), some types of clover, fenugreek and lentil. Amongst common garden plants, radish, pumpkin and sunflower are useful for sprouting. Other seeds which can be sprouted include bamboo, buckwheat, burdock, chickpea, Mexican chia, maize and mint.

Seeds for sprouting can be bought in foreign food stores, health food shops, and increasingly from the retail seed firms, amongst whom Thompson and Morgan can claim credit for having pioneered the sale of sprouting seeds in this country. With radish, sunflower, alfalfa and pumpkin there is no problem in growing one's own seed, though with pumpkin and sunflower it is necessary to get a variety with hull-less seeds, which are the only ones suitable for sprouting. (See Appendix II for suppliers.)

It is most important always to buy seed which is intended for sprouting or human consumption. Before being packeted, much seed today is treated with chemical dressings, generally insecticides or fungicides, and it goes without saying that such seed would be dangerous to use for sprouting. Remember, also, that seed for sprouting is living; it should be stored in cool dry conditions, preferably in airtight jars, to retain its viability.

There are several different methods of sprouting seed and a wide range of seeds sold for the purpose. It is worth experimenting with various methods and seeds to see which suits one best. This is a subject on which no two people agree!

PRINCIPLES OF SPROUTING: Although seed sprouting is easy, it is by no means foolproof. Sprouting seeds must have warmth, moisture and ventilation, but the combination of warmth and moisture encourages the growth of moulds. Far and away the greatest problem with sprouting seeds is to prevent this (particularly with beans). Cracked, dead or diseased seeds are especially liable to rot during the sprouting process.

There are three 'Golden Rules' for sprouting. Before you start, remove any obviously cracked, unhealthy or off-colour seed. Similarly, remove any other poor seeds you notice once sprouting has started. Keep the seeds fresh by rinsing them night and morning. (In a few cases it is advisable to rinse three times a day.) Successful sprouting seems to depend on developing an unshakeable routine! Even neglecting one rinse can result in seeds going 'sour', and once this has happened, there is no remedy other than throwing them out and starting again. It is also good practice to wash out the inside of the jars when sprouting, as they can become slimy. Grow the seed as fast as possible without actually forcing them. 'Lingering' seeds never grow well. For each kind there is an optimum temperature range, and finding it is largely a matter of trial and error. For the majority, temperatures between 13° and 21°C (55° and 70°F) are suitable. A few require higher temperatures.

Seeds can be sprouted in the dark or light; it is a question of whether you prefer the flavour of the crisp-textured, whitened sprouts obtained by growing in the dark, or the usually softer-textured, yellow and greenish shoots which have been grown in the light. Chinese bean sprouts are traditionally grown in the dark. I usually grow mung and similar beans in the dark, and most other sprouting seeds in the light.

For growing in the dark a cupboard is usually quite suitable provided it is not too close an atmosphere. An airing cupboard is handy in winter when window-sills may be cold. Otherwise, jars can be darkened by wrapping with black polythene or aluminium foil or by covering with an empty cereal packet. Dishes can be darkened by making foil covers.

If grown in the light the best place is an ordinary window-sill, avoiding a south-facing or very sunny window. Sometimes, seeds can be started in a warm place (a warm cupboard or above a moderately warm radiator), then moved to a window-sill to 'green up' before use.

METHODS OF SPROUTING (see fig. 14): One simple and efficient way of sprouting seeds is with a jam jar, and some means of pouring water in and out to rinse the seeds. This can be: a piece of muslin held over the top with an elastic band; a lid punctured with holes; a domestic strainer into which the seeds are emptied for rinsing. The drawback of muslin is that it is apt to discolour, and sometimes the seeds stick to the cloth making it difficult to pour out the water. If this happens, a corner can be carefully lifted to let out the water. If a strainer is used, seeds are tipped out of the jar into the strainer which is held under a tap to rinse them. They can then be spooned back into the jar. When grown in a jar, the entire sprout and the original seed can be eaten, so there is no wastage.

The procedure is as follows: remove any poor seeds; put a tablespoon or so of seed into the jar. You will need enough to make a layer between ·25 and ·5 cm ($\frac{1}{8}$ and $\frac{1}{4}$ in) deep in the jar, bearing in mind that the seeds will usually grow to ten times their original bulk. Run cold or tepid water into the seeds, shake them around and drain off the surplus water. Remember the seeds must always be moist, without actually lying in water. Put the jar where the seeds are to sprout – on a window-sill, in an airing cupboard, or above a radiator. The jar can be upright or on its side so that the seeds sprout more evenly. Twice a day, preferably morning and evening, run some cold or tepid water into the jar, swirl it around, and pour it out. If the sprouts grow out of their jar after a day or two, half can be transferred into another jar. They sometimes 'creep' up a jar at an astonishing rate. With the strainer method, careful handling is needed not to damage the young growths.

Some people find the 'dish method' easier; but as it is harder to rinse the sprouts and keep them fresh, they are more liable to 'go off'. For some reason seeds generally take longer to sprout in dishes than in jars. The aluminium foil dishes used for freezers are ideal.

Seeds can be laid on a moisture-retentive base such as cotton wool or flannel or, alternatively, simply spread over the bottom of the dish. Sprouting is faster where no base is used, though the risk of the seeds drying out is higher. Until the sprouts root into the base, as mung and other beans will do, they can be rinsed by pouring into a strainer. Seeds grown on a dish with some base stand up firmly and look attractive, but they have to be cut off at the base for use, so there is some wastage.

Fig. 14 – Seed sprouting methods
a Rinsing through a strainer for the jar method *b* Sproutakit *c* Simple jar method *d* Essex Sprouter *e* Dish method

Bowls can be used for sprouting seed, again using a strainer to rinse them. Another method sometimes recommended is to put the seeds in an unglazed dish in a dish of water to keep them moist.

There are several purpose-made sprouters on the market, some with two or three layers or tiers so that several types of seed can be sprouted at once. I have found the Sproutakit and the Essex Sprouter are successful. The Sproutakit is simply a plastic beaker with a screw lid into which a piece of rigid mesh is fitted for draining. The Essex Sprouter is a larger, two-layer moulded plastic kit with large holes in the lid for pouring water in and out. (See Appendix II for suppliers.)

USAGE AND STORAGE: Sprouts should be used at their tastiest and most nutritious. For each type there is an optimum size, rarely more than 2–2·5 cm ($\frac{3}{4}$–1 in) in length: they should never be overgrown. Once sprouts have reached their optimum size they can be kept in a fridge for three to four days. They keep best in a bowl of fresh water or in a closed plastic bag. Occasional rinsing with water preserves their freshness. Sprouts can be deep frozen like any other vegetable: blanch in boiling water or steam for a few minutes, then cool rapidly before freezing. They can be frozen without blanching, but should then be used within four to six weeks.

Apart from being used fresh in salads, sprouts can be used in many other ways – in soups, in baking, for stuffing, as an accompaniment to meat dishes. Many wholefood recipes make use of ground dried sprouts. For this purpose they can be dried gently in an oven, stored in jars, and ground just before use.

SOME COMMON SPROUTING SEEDS:

Beans: most beans sprout faster if first soaked overnight. Drain and rinse with fresh water before putting them to sprout. Jar or dish methods can be used for most beans, the jar method being more reliable.

Mung beans (Chinese bean sprouts) are normally ready in three to four days and are best eaten when 2 cm (¾ in) long. Green seed coats sometimes adhere to the seed sprouts. They are edible, but can be removed by tipping the sprouts into a bowl of water. Most of the seed coats will rise to the surface and can be skimmed off.

Adzuki and *alphatoco* are easily sprouted red and khaki coloured beans. Very similar in texture and flavour to mung beans, and should be grown in the same way. Normally ready in four to five days and best eaten when 2 cm (¾ in) long.

Soya: round bean about pea size, harder to sprout than mung and adzuki as it is more likely to ferment. Take special care to remove damaged seed. Normally ready within three to seven days. Use raw when no more than 2 cm (¾ in) long or flavour becomes very strong. For cooking, sprouts can be grown up to 3·5 cm (1¼ in) long.

Lima: large white bean. Pre-soak for two to three hours only, or may ferment. Normally ready in about six days. Use when no more than ·5 cm (¼ in) long or flavour deteriorates.

Alfalfa (lucerne) are small cress-like seeds. Can grow in dark or light; or start in dark, move to light after two days. Normally ready in four to six days. Eat from about 1–4 cm ($\frac{1}{2}$–1$\frac{1}{2}$ in) long, when green seed leaves appear.

Cereals (barley, rye, wheat): sometimes hard to obtain untreated seed for sprouting, but all cereals are easily sprouted in jars. Normally ready in three to five days. Wispy roots appear first; eat when shoots are about 1 cm ($\frac{1}{2}$ in) long or they become bitter.

Rice: use long or round grain, brown, unpolished rice. Easily sprouted; mild flavour. Ready in three to five days.

Fenugreek: mild curry-flavoured sprout; ready in two to four days. Eat when ·5 to 1 cm ($\frac{1}{4}$–$\frac{1}{2}$ in) long. Fenugreek is apt to stain muslin badly.

Lentils: red, brown, grey green, yellowish *whole* lentils are all suitable for sprouting, and grow very tasty crisp sprouts. Ready in three to six days. Use when about 1 cm ($\frac{1}{2}$ in) long.

Pumpkin: use unhulled seeds. Give three rinses a day. Ready in two to five days. Eat when 1 cm ($\frac{1}{2}$ in) long.

Sunflower: use unhulled seed. Seeds sprout slowly, so rinse thoroughly. Generally ready in five to eight days. Use when no more than ·5 cm ($\frac{1}{4}$ in) long or they become bitter.

Mixtures: various sprouting seed mixtures are now being sold. Some are based on beans, some on alfalfa, some on a balance of different seeds. The only snag is that the seeds may germinate at different rates.

Mustard and cress (see fig. 17): for growing indoors, the traditional method of growing mustard and cress on a dish is certainly the best. If grown in a jar, cress goes into an evil-smelling, stagnant and gelatinous mass! Mustard and cress can be grown in any dish lined with blotting paper, tissues, flannel or a piece of old cloth – anything for anchorage and moisture retention. The more substantial the base, the longer the crop will stand once ready. Mustard grows faster than cress, so if both are required together, it should be sown three days later, either in the same or in a separate dish.

Sow seed evenly on the moist base; to help retain a humid atmosphere and encourage germination cover with paper until it germinates. Though mustard and cress are normally grown on a window-sill, they are sometimes started in the dark, to draw up the seedlings, and moved into the light when about 2·5 cm (1 in) high. Never allow them to dry out while growing. In winter, cress is generally ready ten days after sowing (mustard seven days) if a day temperature of 15–18°C (59–65°F) is maintained, with night temperatures no lower than 5°C (41°F).

The seedlings can be eaten when 4–5 cm (1½–. in) high. If the base is very clean they can be pulled up by the roots and the entire seedling eaten. Otherwise cut them off at base level with scissors – when sometimes a second crop will grow up, probably from seeds which did not germinate the first time. If kept moist, mature seedlings will stand up to two weeks in good condition.

In the punnets of mustard and cress sold commercially, rape is often used instead of mustard. It has a larger leaf and slightly milder taste, and is a useful substitute. (For growing mustard and cress outdoors and in greenhouses, see p. 128.)

II

WILD PLANTS AND WEEDS

In his immense Victorian encyclopedia on gardening J. C. Loudon has a short but compact section on 'Edible wild plants, neglected or not in cultivation'. His main reason for including them was 'to enable the gentleman's gardener to point out resources to the poor in his neighbourhood in seasons of scarcity'. He adds rather ominously that 'all vegetables not absolutely poisonous may be rendered edible by proper preparation'.

In many parts of the world, however, the approach to the amazing storehouse of food in wild plants – from which all our cultivated vegetables derive – is far more enthusiastic. This enthusiasm is most noticeable in mountain areas, where, starved of fresh greenery during the long winter months, the spring tradition of gathering the first 'mountain herbs' for use in salads stretches from Europe to Japan.

I would never advocate a salad made entirely from wild plants; but it is great fun and a source of satisfaction and variety to add a few leaves of this or that to a salad. By all accounts, weeds and wild plants are an excellent source of vitamins and minerals, and many, with their long history of medicinal use, have 'healthy' properties as well.

The main problem with wild plants is identification. To paraphrase what the old salad sage Evelyn said three hundred years ago : they say that any fool can gather salads – you can hardly go wrong if you choose herbs which are young, tender and green – but many fatal mistakes have been made by those who took hemlock and aconites for garden parsley or parsnip; fine-leaved water dropwort for wild celery, and so on. One must be absolutely certain, basing identification on several parts of the plant, and consulting a good flora or book on wild plants until one is familiar with the plants.

The following are only very brief notes on some of the weeds and wild plants which can be eaten raw. I cannot pretend that I have tried more than a fraction of them myself, but since 'combing the literature', past and present, to discover what was used, I have found myself eyeing the untidy corners of my own garden and neighbouring hedgerows with intense interest. As a result, hardly a week goes by without trying something new in a salad – sometimes with delight; sometimes not!

This list is merely a starting point for those who want to pursue the matter further. Besides the common names, Latin names have been given for accurate identification. (Common names are misleading; the same name is sometimes applied to both an edible and a poisonous species!) It is illegal to dig up wild plants in the countryside – so take only a few leaves as you need them, or cultivate the plants in your garden. (See Appendix II for sources of wild plant seed.)

ALEXANDER (*Smyrnium olusatrum*). Biennial plant, up to 1·50 m (5 ft) high, common around coast. One of earliest to appear in spring. Whole plant edible once cultivated. Buds and spicy young leaves used in salads; stems used to be blanched. Spicy seeds can be used as pepper substitute. Do not confuse with very poisonous Hemlock Water Dropwort (*Oenanthe crocata*) found in similar places at same time.

BEECH (*Fagus sylvatica*): Very young leaves, sweet-tasting.

BLADDER CAMPION (*Silene vulgaris* or *S. cucubalus*): Widespread white-flowered roadside weed. Young mild-flavoured leaves and shoots eaten raw and cooked.

BROOKLIME (*Veronica beccabunga*): Common in streams, marshes, wet places. Young tops used in salads. Opinions differ as to whether it is more or less bitter than watercress.

BURDOCK, GREATER and LESSER (*Arctium lappa* and *A. minus*): Common, large-leaved rampant plant growing up to 1·5 m (5 ft) high, seeds eventually protected by 'burs'. Used all over the world, cooked and raw. Pick young leaf stems in spring, strip off peel, cut into small pieces for salads. Flavour described as 'intriguing and elusive'. Seeds can also be sprouted; remove hooked fruit cases first.

BURNET (*Sanguisorba officinalis* or *Poterium sanguisorba*) (see fig. 15): Common, virtually evergreen weed of chalky grassland. Leaves cucumber-flavoured. (For cultivation see p. 104.)

84

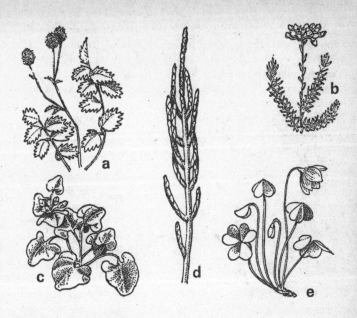

FIG. 15 – EDIBLE WILD PLANTS
a Salad burnet *b* Creeping jenny *c* Scurvy grass *d* Glasswort *e* Wood sorrel

CAT'S EAR (*Hypochoeris radicata*): Very common perennial weed in countryside and garden. Leaves green all year round; can be picked for salads.

CELERY, WILD or SMALLAGE (*Apium graveolens*): Found in damp places near sea; very strong-smelling. Leaves and young stems can be chopped into salads. (Do not confuse with hemlock or water dropwort.)

CHICKWEED (*Stellaria media*) (see fig. 16): Very common garden weed. I have used young growths and leaves in salads almost all the year round. Grows most lushly in slightly moist, shaded positions such as in the fruit cage. Worth 'nurturing' best patches. Chop with scissors; it regrows rapidly.

CHICORY, WILD (*Cichorium intybus*) (see fig. 23) (use of flowers see p. 95; cultivation see p. 116): Young leaves used whole in spring salads; chop older leaves to relieve tartness.

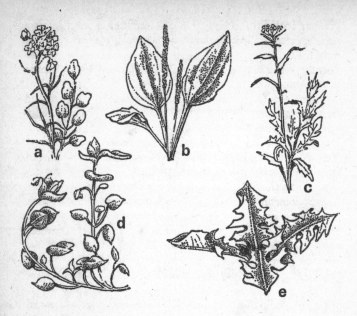

Fig. 16 – Edible weeds
a Lady's smock *b* Rat's tail plantain *c* Shepherd's purse *d* Chickweed *e* Dandelion

CORN SALAD OR LAMB'S LETTUCE (*Valerianella locusta*) (see fig. 18):
Native plant common on dry soils; very hardy, leaves remaining
green all winter. Young leaves, young flower stalks and flowers
all edible in salads. Easily grown in gardens. (For cultivation see
p. 126.)

CRESSES: Many wild cresses suitable for salads. Most have characteristic, pungent flavour. Many remain green all winter or appear very early in spring. Best to use young leaves. Easily cut with
scissors; regrow rapidly.

HAIRY BITTER CRESS (*Cardamine hirsuta*) (see fig. 17): Annual
weed common on waste land, bare ground in gardens. Small-
leaved, ground-hugging plant until flowering spikes shoot up
in spring. Seeds fired out of pods dramatically, resembling an
attack of midges if pods touched. Extremely hardy; very useful
in salads late into winter and early in spring. A patch will re-

generate itself in a garden; thin out seedlings to keep plants a reasonable size. Cloche a few plants in spring to make leaves more tender, larger.

WAVY or WOOD BITTER CRESS (*Cardamine flexuosa*): Very similar to above but fewer basal leaves.

GARDEN CRESS (*Lepidium sativum*) (see fig. 17): 'Mustard and cress' cress, often found wild as escape from gardens. Cultivated world-wide. (For cultivation see p. 128.)

PENNY CRESS, FIELD or COMMON (*Thlaspi arvense*) (see fig. 17): Very common annual weed in waste places, arable fields and gardens. Young leaves spicy addition to salads.

WATERCRESS (*Rorippa nasturtium-aquaticum*) (see fig. 18): Confusingly sometimes called brooklime. Common in running water. Cut older leaves off top of plants for salads, as more flavour than young leaves. Never pick from stagnant water or where water contaminated by pastures, because of risk of liver fluke infection. For this reason probably advisable to cultivate, or grow land cress instead, which has similar flavour. (For cultivation see p. 170.)

WINTER CRESS or YELLOW ROCKET (*Barbarea vulgaris*): Biennial or perennial evergreen cress with broad, deeply indented leaves, common on damp roadsides and waste places. Extremely hardy; can be used in salad all winter. Use basal leaves and leaves on flowering stems.

AMERICAN or LAND CRESS (*Barbarea verna*) (see fig. 17): Biennial evergreen, very similar to above, common on waste ground. Formerly widely cultivated as salad plant and for oily seeds. (For cultivation see p. 141.)

DAISY (*Bellis perennis*): Ubiquitous daisy of garden lawns. Young leaves used in salads. (Use of flowers see p. 97.)

DANDELION (*Taraxacum officinale*) (see fig. 16): Another ubiquitous weed, all parts of which have been used for centuries for culinary purposes. Leaves remain green almost all year; pick youngest for salads. Plants can be potted up to force for winter, or blanched *in situ* to make leaves more tender. (For cultivation see p. 133.)

EVENING PRIMROSE, LARGE and COMMON (*Oenothera erythrosepala* and *O. biennis*): Tall yellow-flowered biennial now found wild; originally introduced from America for garden cultivation for

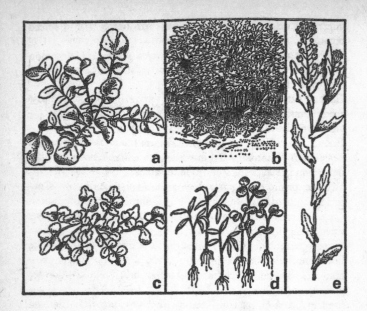

FIG. 17 – CRESSES
a Land cress *b* Cress patch grown in the ground *c* Hairy bitter
cress *d* Cress (left) and mustard (right) seedlings *e* Field penny
cress

edible root. (Cultivated like salsify, see p. 162.) Young leaves
eaten in salads.

FAT HEN or LAMB'S QUARTERS (*Chenopodium album*): Common
weed of waste and cultivated land. Young leaves eaten raw in
salads; also cooked like spinach. American Indian: made seeds
into cakes and gruel.

GLASSWORT or MARSH SAMPHIRE (*Salicornia europaea*) (see fig. 15):
Cactus-like plant found on salt marshes and shingle beaches; its
ashes once used in glass-making. For salads, young leaves and
shoots traditionally gathered June/July. Older growths, gathered
August/September, were cooked. Can apparently be grown in
gardens by sowing fresh-gathered seed in autumn in good, well-
drained soil. In the book *Food for Free* flavour described as crisp,

tangy and delectable. Young growths can be pickled in spiced vinegar.

GOATSBEARD or WILD SALSIFY (*Tragopogon pratensis*): Common weed in dry grassy places. Leaves and roots can be eaten raw. (For use of flowers see p. 100.)

GOLDEN SAXIFRAGE (*Chrysosplenium oppositifolium*): Plants of shady mountains, streams and wet ground. Leaves gathered for salads; the *cresson des roches* of the Vosges.

GOOD KING HENRY, ALL-GOOD or MERCURY (*Chenopodium bonus-henricus*): Wayside perennial, generally cooked like asparagus but young growths and asparagus-like shoots, which appear very early in spring, can be used raw in salads. (For cultivation see p. 173.)

Do not confuse with Dog's Mercury (*Mercurialis perennis*) – similar but very poisonous.

HAWTHORN (*Crataegus monogyna*): Very young leaves and flower buds chopped into salads. Said to have nutty taste.

MILK or HOLY THISTLE (*Silybum marianum*): Biennial thistle with beautiful white-veined foliage. Young leaves and stems (peeled and chopped) used in salads. Roots can also be eaten raw and cooked. Easily grown in garden. Sow in spring, thin or plant 60 cm (2 ft) apart.

HORSE RADISH (*Armoracia rusticana*, *A. lapathifolia*, or *Cochlearia armoracia*): Large dock-like plant, common in hedgerows, roadsides. Roots peeled and used raw in salads or to make sauce. (For cultivation see p. 139.)

JACK BY THE HEDGE or GARLIC MUSTARD (*Alliaria petiolata*): Common hedgerow weed appearing very early in the year. Bruised leaves have faint garlic smell. Use finely chopped in salads, or cook.

LADY'S SMOCK or CUCKOO FLOWER (*Cardamine pratensis*) (see fig. 16): Pretty pale purple flower found in damp meadows and streamsides. Leaves remain green late in winter; watercress spiciness. In spring, pick young leaves from lower rosette.

LETTUCE, GREATER PRICKLY or ACRID (*Lactuca virosa*): Common in south-east on chalky soil near coast. Leaves used in sala but said to be bitter.

LETTUCE, WALL (*Mycelis muralis*): Perennial growing up to 1 m (3 ft) high on walls. Leaves eaten in salads.

LIME (*Tilia europaea*): Use young leaves, before they roughen, with sprinkling of lemon juice.

LUNGWORT (*Pulmonaria officinalis*): Perennial grown as garden plant and sometimes found wild as escape. Young leaves chopped into spring salads.

MARSH THISTLE (*Cirsium palustre* or *Carduus palustris*): In salads use raw young shoots and stalks, after removing prickles and peeling.

MUSTARD (*Sinapis alba*): 'Mustard and cress' mustard; cultivated as green manure and for seeds from which mustard is extracted; often found wild. Young seedlings eaten in salads, but difficult to identify at this stage in field, so probably more practical to grow at home. (For cultivation see p. 81.)

NIPPLEWORT (*Lapsana communis*): Common weed and wayside plant. Leaves edible raw.

OX-EYE DAISY (*Chrysanthemum leucanthemum*) (see p. 97): Young leaves used in salads in Italy.

PARSLEY PIERT (*Aphanes arvensis*): Small plant with pretty foliage found mainly on dry soils. Old salad plant; pickled and eaten raw in Hebrides.

PLANTAIN, BUCKSHORN (*Plantago coronopus*): Common plant in coastal regions. French used to cultivate, sowing in spring and thinning to 13 cm (5 in) apart. Cut flowers off as they appear to maintain steady supply of tender leaves for salads.

PLANTAIN, RAT'S TAIL (*Plantago major*) (see fig. 16): Very common countryside and garden weed famous for its ability to survive trampling. Eat central young leaves; pleasant slightly mustardy taste.

POPPY, FIELD (*Papaver rhoeas*): Common red-flowered poppy. Young leaves eaten raw in Mediterranean; seeds used to decorate buns. Do not confuse with Red Horned Poppy, *Glaucium corniculatum*.

PURSLANE (*Portulaca oleracea*): Succulent plant found on sandy soils. Used raw and pickled in salads; Evelyn recommended 'leaves of middling size'. (For cultivation see p. 158.)

PURSLANE, SEA (*Halimione portulacoides*): Succulent, grey- and silver-leaved plant of salt marshes. Leaves used in salads, but need careful washing.

RAMPION (*Campanula rapunculus*): Now uncommon plant,

found on gravelly soils. Once widely cultivated both for sweet, turnip-like roots, which were eaten cooked and raw in salads, and for young leaves, which were used raw. Evelyn also suggested earthing up stems to blanch, and eating seed leaves and young tops.

RAMSONS or WOOD GARLIC (*Allium ursinum*): Common in damp woods. Leaves can be chopped into salads for garlic flavour.

RED SHANK or RED LEG (*Polygonum persicaria*): Very common weed of arable land. Use leaves raw or cooked.

Do not confuse with extremely acrid Water Pepper, *Polygonum hydropiper*, found in damp places.

ROCK SAMPHIRE (*Crithmum maritimum*): Fleshy-leaved plant found on cliffs and shingle. Leaves and stems cooked, or pickled for salads.

SALSIFY, WILD or GOATSBEARD (*Tragopogon pratensis*): Narrow-leaved weed with dandelion-like flowers. Flowers, buds, young leaves, shoots and roots used in salads. (For flowers see p. 100; cultivation see p. 162.)

SCURVY GRASS (*Cochlearia officinalis*) (see fig. 15): Little, shiny-leaved plant found on coastal cliffs. Used to be cultivated, sowing in shady position in spring. (Thicker Danish scurvy grass, *C. danica*, considered better for cultivation.) Leaves rich in Vitamin C, eaten raw in salads.

SEAKALE (*Crambe maritima*) (see fig. 26): Native perennial plant found on sand and shingle beaches, now becoming scarce: pick sparingly. Traditional practice was to cover plant on seashore with 45 m (18 in) shingle, either in autumn when died down, or in early spring, and scrape away shingle to cut young shoots. (For cultivation see p. 163.)

SHEPHERD'S PURSE (*Capsella bursa-pastoris*) (see fig. 16): Very common weed, green much of year. Basal rosettes and stem leaves excellent raw in salads; distinctive flavour due to sulphur. Cultivated and sold in China for use raw or cooked like spinach. Said to be richer in Vitamin C than oranges. One snag – it harbours clubroot.

SORREL, COMMON (*Rumex acetosa*) and FRENCH or BUCKLER-LEAVED (*R. scutatus*) (see fig. 18): Found wild in grassland, woods, roadsides; appears very early in year. Sharp lemon taste of leaves wonderful in salads. (For cultivation see p. 165.)

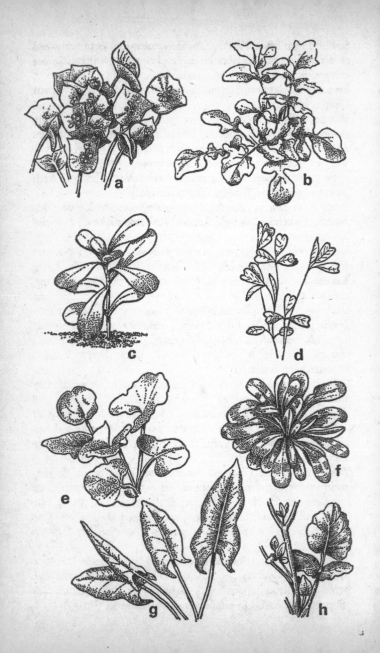

Sow or FIELD MILK THISTLE (*Sonchus arvensis*): Common weed of damp places and arable land. Trim bristles off leaves before using raw.

STONECROP, CREEPING JENNY, STONE ORPINE or TRIP MADAM (*Sedum reflexum*) (see fig. 15): Succulent-leaved perennial found wild on walls and rocks. Extensively used in salads in past. Easily grown in rock gardens and dry borders, sowing seed outdoors April, or dividing roots in spring.

Other edible sedums: *Sedum acre* – used in small quantities as pepper substitute; *Sedum album* – used in salads or cooked; *Sedum rosea* – used in salads in Greenland.

STRAWBERRY (*Fragaria vesca*): Young leaves of wild and culti-vated strawberries can be eaten raw. (Not personally impressed by the flavour!)

VALERIAN, RED (*Centranthus* or *Kentranthus ruber*): Red- and white-flowered forms found on dry banks and walls. Very young leaves eaten in salads. Cultivated in gardens by sowing in spring and planting out about 60 cm (2 ft) apart; or by dividing old plants in spring or autumn.

WALL ROCKET or WALL MUSTARD (*Diplotaxis muralis*): Found on rocks, walls, waste ground. Leaves eaten raw in Mediter-ranean.

WINTERGREEN, COMMON (*Pyrola minor*): Berried evergreen plant found woods, moors, rocks, dunes. Young tender leaves used in salads in North America.

WOOD SORREL – old English name ALLELUIA (*Oxalis acetosella*) (see fig. 15): Delicate folded clover-like leaves among first to appear in woods in spring. Leaves have sharp sorrel flavour; long usage in salads.

YARROW or MILFOIL (*Achillea millefolium*): Very common weed, green most of the year. Use feathery leaves in small quantities in salads; can also strip leaves from stems and cook.

FIG. 18 – MISCELLANEOUS SALAD PLANTS
a Claytonia *b* Rocket *c* Purslane *d* Alfalfa *e* Buckler-leaved sorrel
f Corn salad or lamb's lettuce *g* Common sorrel *h* Watercress

12

FLOWERS IN SALADS

It is strange that the use of flowers in cookery and salads has become so alien to us. Our ancestors made copious use of flowers, and all over the world flowers of such plants as chrysanthemums, marrows and numerous mustards are still grown and sold for cooking.

In the past violets, primroses, cowslips and many other flowers used in salads were collected from the wild. Today, the need to preserve wild species is paramount, so wild flowers should only be collected where they are in abundance. It is now illegal to dig them up – unless they are scheduled weeds or on your private land: so for wild flowers in salads they must be cultivated in corners of the garden. (See Appendix II for sources of wild flower seed.)

Flowers should be gathered at their freshest, early in the day when the dew has just dried on them. Always handle them gently, preferably cutting with a knife or scissors, and carry them in a flat basket so they are squashed as little as possible. They can be gently washed if necessary and patted dry with paper towelling. If not required immediately keep them in a closed plastic bag in a fridge. Just before use the flowers or petals can be freshened by dipping in ice-cold water.

The stems must be cut off before use, and with large flowers, the green receptacle at the base of the flower. With many flowers in the daisy family, such as marigolds, the individual petals have to be pulled off gently.

Flowers are mainly added to salads for their lovely colours and textures, but, of course, their delicate scents and flavours also contribute to the overall taste. They can either be used whole, or chopped into a confetti-like mixture to sprinkle over the top. It is always best to add the flowers at the last minute, just before serving. Flowers can also be dried or pickled for use in salads.

The following are brief notes on some of the flowers, both

edible and ornamental, which can be used in salads. Latin names are also given, as an aid to accurate identification.

ANCHUSA (*Anchusa italica*): Perennial garden flower, 1·3 m (4 ft) high. Lovely bright blue flowers at their best in June. Likes ordinary soil in sunny border. Plant in October or March, or treat as biennial, sowing seed May, overwintering small plants in cold frame and planting out in spring. Cut down main stem after flowering; smaller growths will prolong flowering season. Flowers blend beautifully in salads with rose petals and rosemary flowers.

BERGAMOT (*Monarda didyma*): Perennial, 30–60 cm (1–2 ft) high, spreading. Flowers scarlet, occasionally purple, lavender, white, pink; flowering July to September; traditionally dried for tea. Does best on moist, rich soil. Divide plants every two to three years, replanting youngest parts. Flowers beautiful on salads with borage. Leaves also edible but bitter.

BORAGE (*Borago officinalis*) (see fig. 19): Annual, 1 m (3 ft) high; bulky plants. Bright blue star-like petals contrast starkly with black anthers. Flowers June until frost. Likes reasonable, well-drained soil. Sow: February to March indoors; March to May outdoors *in situ* for main summer crop, thinning to 25–35 cm (10–14 in) apart; July to August for late crop outdoors or to transplant into greenhouse for winter leaves, late flowers, and possibly very early flowers following year if greenhouse frost-free. Once established, borage seeds itself; just thin out seedlings. Flowers sweet-flavoured, but remove hairy green sepals before eating. Young leaves edible finely chopped in salads or boiled.

BROOM, COMMON (*Cytisus scoparius*) (see fig. 20): Hardy shrub, grows wild and can be cultivated. Thrives on poor soil, dry conditions. Bright yellow flowers May/June; buds April/May. Best transplanted young. Prune back nearly into old growth after flowering. Broom buds and flowers extensively used in past in salads, fresh and pickled.

Do not eat too much, as excessive quantities are toxic.

CHICORY, WILD or SUCCORY (*Cichorium intybus*) (see fig. 23): Dandelion-like plant with flowering spikes 30 to 120 cm (1–4 ft) high. Beautiful flowers of varying shades of blue, flowering June–October. Either collect wild chicory flowers (commonly found on chalk) or let a few plants of cultivated chicory flower. Pick

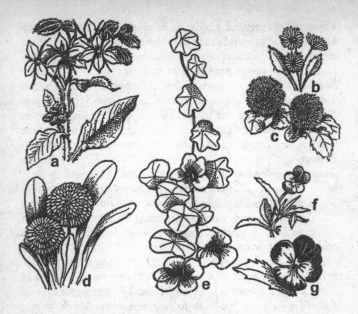

F IG. 19 – E DIBLE GARDEN FLOWERS
a Borage *b* Common daisy *c* Double daisy *d* Pot marigold *e* Nasturtium *f* Heartsease *g* Garden pansy

flowers just before using as they close up and fade very rapidly;
use petals or whole flower. Flavour slightly bitter; reminiscent
of chicory leaves, but milder. Flowers can be pickled. (For cultivation see p. 114.)

C HRYSANTHEMUM : Special varieties of chrysanthemum are used
for culinary purposes in Japan and China. Here, the many forms
of the ordinary, tender, florist's chrysanthemum (*C. morifolium*
or *C. Sinense*) can be substituted. Grows 60–120 cm (2–4 ft) high.
Ordinary garden soil. Feed regularly in growing season. Lift for
winter in cold areas, replanting or taking cuttings in spring. To
use, pull individual petals off flower heads. Before putting in
salads, blanch by dipping into boiling water for one second.

C OWSLIP (*Primula veris*) (see fig. 20): Familiar yellow wild flower
of spring, flowering April to May; found on chalky and alkaline
meadows, becoming rare due to overpicking. Grows best on

heavy clay soil; open site. Sow March/April or autumn in leafy compost in seed boxes or shaded frame; germination slow. Plant in permanent positions in autumn. Use leaves and flowers in salads; flowers can be pickled.

DAISY (*Bellis perennis*) (see fig. 19): Common little white-flowered perennial daisy of lawn and field, flowering May to October, so common it is no crime to pick it wild! Flowers open in bright sunshine, close in poor light. Far prettier open, so pick directly before use if possible; otherwise pick when open, keep in closed plastic bag at room temperature until needed. Use flowers whole in salads; leaves can also be used; and individual petals of larger forms. Cultivated double and large forms can be grown for salads. Sow in seed boxes in April for flowering the same year, or June/July for flowering the following season.

DAISY, OX-EYE or MARGUERITE (*Leucanthemum vulgare* or *Chrysanthemum leucanthemum*): Very common wild white daisy, flowering May to August. Pick off petals for salads.

ELDER (*Sambucus nigra*) (see fig. 20): Shrubby native tree of hedgerows, covered in June and July with bunches of sweet-smelling, creamy blossoms, each thousands of tiny flowers. Tolerates most soils. Easily grown in gardens. Can raise from 20–25-cm (8–10-in) hardwood cuttings taken in autumn; will be ready for planting within a year. When trees become too large cut back to stump, which will resprout. Never wash flowers or fragrance is lost. Shake heads over salad before serving, and tiny flowers will drop off easily. For salads, North American Indians used leaves and flowers, and in England buds and flowers were pickled.

EVERGREEN ALKANET (*Pentaglottis sempervirens*): Blue perennial flowers up to 80 cm (32 in) high, found in hedges and waste places, often as an escape; closely related to anchusa. Flowers April to June. Can be raised from seed or by division of plants in October. Like anchusa, flowers can be used in salads.

HARDHEADS or LESSER KNAPWEED (*Centaurea nigra*): Very common hedgerow plant up to 35 cm (14 in) high with thistle-like feathery purple flowers, June to September. Petals used in salads in the past.

HOLLYHOCK (*Althaea rosea*): Familiar tall perennial of cottage gardens, numerous colours. Old forms up to 2 m (6 ft) high;

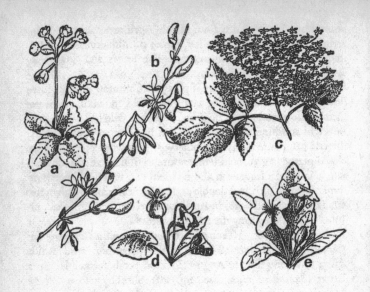

Fig. 20 – Edible wild flowers
a Cowslip *b* Broom *c* Elderflower *d* Violet *e* Primrose

newer forms such as Majorette are semi-dwarf. Likes rich moist soil. Tall ones need staking. Grow as biennial as old plants get rust disease. Sow May to July in seedbed, thin to 15 cm (6 in) apart, plant out September 1 m (3 ft) apart. Keep watered and mulched in summer. (In cold areas overwinter in frames, plant out spring.) Petals and cooked buds used in salads.

LAVENDER (*Lavandula spica; L. vera*): Bush with spikes of blue-purple flowers in summer. Likes well-drained soil; sheltered position. Propagate by cuttings in shaded frame in August, or rooted outdoors in September/October: trim back plants in March to prevent straggliness: best to replant every five years. Chopped flowers and leaves used sparingly in salads, desserts, jellies. Salads were once served on beds of lettuce and lavender sprigs.

MARIGOLD (*Calendula officinalis*) (see fig. 19): (This is English or Pot marigold, not African marigold, French marigold or *Tagetes sp.*) Annual, usually about 30 cm (1 ft) high, with flowers of lemon, orange and related shades, flowering early summer to

November. Prefers loamy soil, sunny position. Sow March onwards, *in situ* (very thinly), or in boxes or blocks indoors. Important to thin very early to 25 cm (10 in) apart, otherwise they become floppy. Can also be sown in open or cold greenhouse August/September for very early flowers following year. Remove dead flower heads to prolong flowering. Historically one of the most widely-used medicinal and culinary flowers; saffron substitute. Use young leaves and petals whole and chopped in salads; flowers can be dried and pickled.

NASTURTIUM (*Tropaeolum majus*) (see fig. 19): Climbing, trailing and dwarf annuals; red and yellow flowers, flowering early summer until frost. Likes sunny position; does well even on poor soils and dry banks. Sow spring, *in situ* or indoors. (In 17th century raised early on hotbeds.) Thin or plant so as to be 23 cm (9 in) apart. Leaves (whole or chopped), flowers and buds have long usage in salads for hot, peppery flavour. Plants with purplish foliage seem to have a better flavour. Seeds pickled as caper substitute. Pick when green soon after flowers wither. Where wanted primarily for leaves, grow in richer soil. (For nasturtium recipes see p. 188.)

PANSY, GARDEN (*Viola wittrockiana*), PANSY, WILD or HEARTS-EASE (*Viola tricolor*) (see fig. 19): Other wild and hybrid pansies can be used, but not the scentless 'florist's' pansy. Low-growing annuals and perennials, flowers single and mixed colours, ranging from black to purple to yellow, flowering all summer. Likes well-worked soil, open or partial shade. Best treated as biennials: sow spring to early summer in open ground or cold frame. Plant in permanent position in autumn 15 cm (6 in) apart. Remove dead flowers. Flowers and leaves used in salads.

PRIMROSE (*Primula vulgaris*) (see fig. 20): Familiar wild perennial, up to 20 cm (8 in) high, lovely yellow flowers March to May, easily cultivated. Prefers humus-rich soil, semi-shade. Sow in leafy compost in spring, in boxes indoors or in frame in cool position, planting autumn or early following spring 15 cm (6 in) apart. Mulch with well-rotted compost in spring. Remove lower leaves to protect from slugs and snails; keep weed-free. Every three years divide mature plants, or leaves produced rather than flowers. Flowers and young leaves used in salads.

ROSE (*Rosa sp.*): Any roses, wild or cultivated, can be used in salads. Select those with most fragrance. To avoid destroying flowers take only those with petals on the verge of falling. They add beautiful colour and fragrance to salads; sprinkle on top either alone or mixed with other flowers. Rose petals have long been used for culinary purposes.

ROSEMARY (*Rosmarinus officinalis*): Perennial evergreen Mediterranean shrub; violet flowers in bloom early summer. Likes well-drained soil, sheltered sunny position. May succumb in severe winters. Raise from seed sown May (but slow growing); or take cuttings September in sandy soil. Plant spring about 1 m (3 ft) apart. Prune old plants in spring to keep tidy and encourage new growths. Flowers delicate and attractive in salads.

SAGE, COMMON (*Salvia officinalis*): Perennial bush about 60 cm (2 ft) high. Flowering forms: common blue-flowered sage; white and pink forms of common sage; blue-flowered form of red sage. (Broad-leaved sages are usually flowerless.) Normally bloom end May to July. Prefer light soil. Easiest to raise from seed, sown spring; or take heel or tip cuttings in May in sandy soil; plant following spring at least 60 cm (2 ft) apart. Nip back young growths in spring to keep compact. Renew plants every four years. Flowers aromatic; add fragrance and colour to salads. Chopped leaves can also be used sparingly.

SAGE, CLARY (*Salvia sclarea*): Annual garden flower up to 30 cm (1 ft) high with colourful bracts; flowers July onwards. Sow in March to May in open ground, thinning to about 23 cm (9 in) apart. Flowers and bracts can be used in salads. Also useful plant for drying for winter decoration.

SALSIFY (*Tragopogon porrifolius*) (see fig. 27): Normally grown for root. Beautiful purple flowers, June to September, and cooked buds, hot or cold, can be used in salads. Flowers open for relatively brief period in morning; close and fade fast when picked so pick just before use, or as soon as open; keep in closed bag in fridge; use petals only. (For cultivation see p. 162.)

Wild salsify or Goatsbeard (*Tragopogon pratensis*) has yellow flowers, June to September, which can be similarly used.

SCORZONERA (*Scorzonera hispanica*): Normally grown for root. Yellow flowers and buds excellent raw or cooked and cold in salads. Flowers June to September. (For cultivation see p. 163.)

SWEET VIOLET (*Viola odorata*) (see fig. 20): Small violet, occasionally white, flowers February to April. Easily cultivated in ordinary soil with plenty of humus, shaded position. Plant crowns in spring or autumn 23 cm (9 in) apart; or sow September to November in cold frame. Will germinate following spring for planting out, though germination erratic. Violets widely grown in past for cooking and as salad herb. In 15th century flowers eaten raw with onions and lettuce.

13

HERBS

There was a time when all salad plants were considered herbs – yet today salads and herbs are divorced in our minds, and the use of herbs in salads is perfunctory. Yet what a difference the skilled and discreet use of herbs can make to a salad! This was brought home to me many years ago in Ireland, when by chance I spent a night in a house where the overgrown garden had, until recently, been tended by a herbalist. Our hostess went out in the dusk to collect a few herbs to enliven our tired supper lettuce. The result was superb – a medley of subtle freshness I have never forgotten. Most of the herbs were unknown to me then, but the lesson was never lost.

On how to use herbs in salads I can do no better than quote that versatile gardening writer Eleanor Sinclair Rohde: 'It is just the suspicion of flavouring all through the salad that is required, not a salad entirely dominated by herbs.' Her method was to mix into the salad a piled tablespoon of very finely chopped herbs; she listed about twenty.

Certainly an infinite number of herbs can be used in salads to give infinite variety. The only rule to follow is that the stronger the herb, the more sparingly it should be used. To my mind, fresh herbs are always preferable to preserved, which poses a challenge in the winter months, when only a handful naturally remain green. Quite a number, however, lend themselves to being cut down in late summer, potted up in good, light, well-drained soil or compost, and brought into a cool greenhouse or grown on window-sills to provide fresh herbs during the winter.

Many of the more succulent herbs, such as chives and parsley, can be frozen successfully, either in sprigs, or chopped into water in ice-cube trays. (Thaw the cube in a strainer when needed.)

Herbs can, of course, also be dried: pick them in their prime, usually just before flowering, dry them slowly in a very cool oven or hang indoors covered with muslin to keep dust free, then store in air-tight jars.

The following brief notes cover some of the herbs most suitable for salads.

ALECOST or COSTMARY: Large-leaved perennial growing up to 1 m (3 ft) high. Tolerates any soil; best in sunny position. Divide plants annually in spring or autumn. Very strong distinct flavour; use sparingly, finely chopped.

ANGELICA: Beautiful vigorous biennial growing up to 2 m (6 ft) high. Likes rich, fairly moist soil. Sow fresh seed September, planting following spring or autumn 1.5 m (5 ft) apart. Plants left to flower will seed themselves, and seedlings can be transplanted. Use young stems and leaves sparingly in salads.

ANISE: Annual with delicate foliage growing about 30 cm (1 ft) high. Likes warm position, well-drained soil. Sow *in situ* April, thinning to about 15 cm (6 in) apart. Traditionally grown for seeds, but aniseed-flavoured leaves pleasant chopped into salads.

BALM, LEMON or MELISSA (see fig. 22): Perennial plant growing about 1 m (3 ft) high. Tolerates any soil but best where rich and moist; excellent ground-cover plant. Raise by dividing plants in autumn, or sow in May, eventually planting 60 cm (2 ft) apart. Delicate lemon scent; chop leaves into salad.

BASIL (see fig. 22): Tender Mediterranean herb, variable height up to about 45 cm (18 in). Many types: commonest are large-leaved common or sweet basil, and smaller-leaved dwarf or bush basil. In England, best grown in frames or greenhouses or very sheltered, sunny position outdoors. Sow March/April indoors. Plant indoors May; outdoors after risk of frost, about 13 cm (5 in) apart. For winter use trim back few plants (ideally bush basil) early September, pot up, bring indoors. Normally provides leaf until November or December. Unique, strong, clove-like flavour. Chop leaves sparingly into salads; use with tomatoes, or in basil sauce.

BORAGE: Young leaves traditionally used in salads; texture rather hairy so best chopped. Most appreciated late autumn to spring, so July/August sowing, transplanted into greenhouse, very useful. (Plants will remain green unless severe frost encountered.) Where grown primarily for leaves, chop off flower stalks to encourage bushiness. (For cultivation see p. 95.)

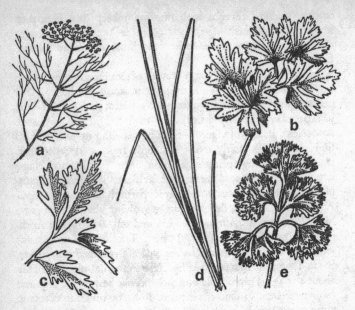

Fig. 21 – Herbs
a Dill *b* Broad-leaved parsley *c* Chervil *d* Chives *e* Curled parsley

Burnet, Salad (see fig. 15): Low-growing, exceptionally hardy perennial plant, sometimes found wild. Feathery leaves remain green all winter. Sow spring or summer *in situ*, thinning to about 15 cm (6 in) apart. Makes attractive bed edging. Leaves produced more abundantly if flower spikes cut off. Use young leaves raw; flavour reminiscent of cucumber. Japanese boil leaves lightly and dip in cold water for salads.

Chervil (see fig. 21): Hardy, rapidly-growing annual herb, parsley-like appearance, up to 60 cm (2 ft) high. Grow in slightly shady position, summer; sunny position, winter. Sow February to April *in situ* for summer use; August, outdoors, or in blocks in greenhouse, for winter/early spring use. Thin or plant to 10 cm (4 in) apart. Greenhouse crop may continue growing all winter. Plants left to flower will sow themselves; young seedlings can be transplanted in moist conditions. Useful herb all the year round; finely chopped, adds aniseed freshness to salads.

CHIVES (see fig. 21): Commonly-grown, tufted perennial up to 25 cm (10 in) high. Likes reasonable soil; makes excellent edge. Stands constant cutting. Sow spring, planting 23 cm (9 in) apart. Cut off flower stalks to encourage foliage. Divide plants annually in spring or autumn. Cloched plants in spring come on earlier. Chopped leaves add lovely mild onion flavour to salads.

CHINESE CHIVES. (For cultivation see p. 124.)

CORIANDER: Hardy annual up to 75 cm (2½ ft) high. Neglected here but wide culinary use all over world. Does best in light soil. Sow August/September to overwinter in open, or in frame for early summer use. Sow February to June for main summer crop; plant 23 cm (9 in) apart. Finely-chopped, fresh leaves excellent in salads. Leaves can be frozen but not dried; seeds used in curries.

DILL (see fig. 21): Feathery annual up to 60 cm (2 ft) high. Somewhat fragile plant; succumbs in adverse conditions, so grow in good soil, avoid exposed positions, keep moderately watered. Sow April to June *in situ*, thinning seedlings in stages eventually to 10 cm (4 in) apart or 24 cm (9 in) apart if growing for seed. Dill can also be sown indoors for transplanting; best to transplant groups of two or three seedlings together; or sow in compost blocks. Leaves, flowering heads and seeds all used in salads and cooking, and in dill pickles. Plant has unique delicate flavour of its own.

FENNEL: Fairly hardy, elegant perennial with feathery foliage up to 1.5 m (5 ft) tall. Tolerates most soils. Sow in spring *in situ*, thinning to 45 cm (18 in) apart. Can also propagate by dividing rootstocks in spring. To maintain constant supply of foliage keep plants cut to within 30 cm (1 ft) of ground and remove flower spikes. Chopped leaves and chopped and peeled young stalks used in salads and in cooking; aniseed flavour. Beautiful bronze variety can also be used. (For cultivation of swollen-stemmed Florence Fennel see p. 136.)

HYSSOP: Perennial, reasonably hardy, evergreen sub shrub, about 45 cm (18 in) tall, with attractive blue, pink, purple or white flowers. Likes light, well-drained soil; makes pretty low hedge if trimmed. Generally propagated by division in spring or autumn; can be sown in spring, thinning or planting 60 cm (2 ft) apart. Strong minty flavour; young leaves excellent chopped sparingly into salad.

LAVENDER: Leaves can be used very sparingly, finely chopped, in salads. (For cultivation see p. 98.)

LOVAGE (see fig. 22): Stately perennial growing up to 2·5 m (8 ft) tall. Prefers rich, moist soil. One of earliest plants to appear in spring. Easily raised in spring or autumn by sowing seed, eventually planting 60 cm (2 ft) apart, or by dividing roots; plants also seed themselves and seedlings can be transplanted. Strong celery flavour; chop leaves into salads or rub leaf around the salad bowl. Leaf stalks used to be blanched and eaten like celery.

MARJORAM (see fig. 22): Low-growing Mediterranean herb, 30–60 cm (1–2 ft) high with pleasant, characteristic flavour. Various forms: sweet or knotted – perhaps strongest and best flavoured, grown as annual here; pot – hardier, sprawling, perennial, dies back in winter; wild – can also be cultivated, good flavour. Prefer good soil, sunny position. Sow sweet marjoram indoors March, or outdoors May, planting about 18 cm (7 in) apart; can pot up late summer to bring indoors for winter use. Sow pot marjoram spring, or take cuttings early summer, or divide plants autumn. Plant 30 cm (1 ft) apart. Trim back foliage in autumn. All marjorams very useful cut finely in salads, and all dry well for winter use.

MINTS: Many types cultivated: garden or spearmint up to 45 cm (18 in) high; round-leaved apple and Bowles mints, up to 1·3 m (4 ft) high; pennyroyal, excellent ground-cover mint. Mostly rampant growers requiring rich, moist soil; should be moved every few years as they exhaust soil. Propagate by lifting and planting young shoots with roots in spring; or by dividing plants autumn or early spring and planting pieces of root horizontally 5 cm (2 in) deep, about 23 cm (9 in) apart. Can lift plants in October, plant in boxes, and bring indoors for fresh winter leaf. All mints strong-flavoured, good used sparingly in salads.

PARSLEY (see fig. 21): Fairly hardy, biennial herb, growing up to 60 cm (2 ft) high; both curled and plain- or broad-leaved forms cultivated. Likes good soil, plenty of moisture, light shade in summer. Sow: in spring for summer to autumn use; July/August for winter to early spring use, either overwintered outdoors, planted in greenhouses, or potted up to bring indoors. Germination slow; keep ground moist while germinating (good subject for sowing in blocks). Thin or plant to 23 cm (9 in) apart. Cut off flowering heads to prolong useful life. Foliage dies back to large extent in winter, but some generally remain green. Cover with cloches as safeguard, and to improve quality. Chopped foliage used in many types of salad; broad-leaved considered better flavoured.

PARSLEY, HAMBURG: Hardy form grown primarily for root, but parsley-flavoured foliage remains green all winter. Sow spring, moist situation, thinning to 23 cm (9 in) apart. Roots can be cooked or grated raw into salads.

ROSEMARY (for cultivation see p. 100): Chop leaves sparingly in salads.

SAGE: In past red sage, especially leaves from young shoots, much used in salads; remains usable all winter. (For cultivation, see p. 100.)

SAVORY: Summer savory, bushy annual up to 30 cm (12 in) high; winter savory, compact evergreen perennial. Both like sunny position; good soil for summer savory; well-drained for winter savory. Sow both in spring, thinning to 15 cm (6 in) apart. Winter savory also propagated by heel cuttings taken in spring, or by division of old plants. Both can be potted up for use indoors in winter. Both useful in various types of salad.

SWEET CICELY: Large-rooted, ornamental, slow-growing perennial up to 1·5 m (5 ft) tall. Grows best in rich, moist soil, partial shade. Sow fresh seed autumn, thinning to 8 cm (3 in) apart, planting in permanent position following autumn 60 cm (2 ft) apart; or divide roots carefully spring or autumn. Mature plants readily seed themselves; can transplant seedlings. Plants die down late and start growing early, so usable much of year. Leaves sweet aniseed taste; long used in salads and as sugar substitute. Roots boiled, cooled, and sliced in salads.

TANSY: Dark, curly-leaved, pretty plant, growing up to 60 cm (2 ft) high. Previously much used in salad; very strong flavour, use sparingly.

TARRAGON, FRENCH (see fig. 22): Narrow-leaved perennial growing up to 1 m (3 ft) high. Likes sunny position, well-drained, light soil. Divide roots spring or autumn; best planted spring, planting 60 cm (2 ft) apart. Cannot be raised from seed. Chop leaves into salads, or use to flavour vinegar. (Russian tarragon,

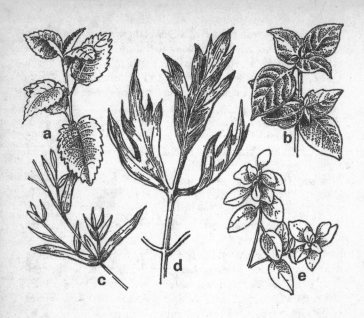

FIG. 22 – MORE HERBS
a Balm *b* Basil *c* Tarragon *d* Lovage *e* Marjoram

which can be raised from seed, is inferior in flavour and hardly
worth growing.)

THYME: Low-growing, sun-loving herbs. Many varieties grown;
common and lemon thyme most used in kitchen. Likes dry, well-
drained, sunny position; many thrive on chalky soils. Useful
edging plants. Propagated by dividing old plants; by taking cuttings in April/May; or by sowing seed in spring. Plant out about
30 cm (1 ft) apart. Keep plants trimmed; renew beds every few
years. Can pot up plants for winter use. Use sparingly in salads,
or to infuse salad dressings or vinegar.

14

SALAD PLANTS

ALFALFA, LUCERNE or PURPLE MEDICK (*Medicago sativa*) (see fig. 18): Rapidly-growing, evergreen, perennial member of clover family with decorative spikes of blue and violet flowers. Deep-rooted plants, growing over 1 m (3 ft) high. Mainly used for animal fodder, but edible and nutritious for humans.

Soil/situation: Grows in any soil; tolerates extremely dry conditions. Can be grown as hedge to divide different parts of garden.

Cultivation: Best sown spring and late autumn, either broadcast or in rows, thinning to 25 cm (10 in) apart. The seed sold for sprouting purposes is quite suitable to use. Unless seed required, cut back annually after flowering to encourage new growth.

Use in salads and cooking: Tips of young shoots used in salads almost all the year. (Older leaves tend to be bitter.) In China young shoots cooked lightly and mixed into meat dishes. Seeds can be sprouted (see p. 80).

AMERICAN CRESS (see Land Cress).

BEETROOT (*Beta vulgaris*): Roots can be flattish, round, or long and cylindrical. Red forms most common, but good-flavoured white and yellow forms also available. Sugar beet is also edible and sweet in salads, though rather colourless. Beet can be used fresh, stored, bottled or pickled in vinegar. Types: Early and maincrop, storage beet and pickling beet.

Soil/situation: Open site; deep, well-drained, moisture-retentive soil; neutral or slightly alkaline.

Cultivation:

Manuring: Roots liable to fork if grown on freshly-manured soil, so manure the previous autumn or for the preceding crop, or work in well-rotted compost before sowing or planting; lime if soil very acid.

Seed: Beetroot seed is botanically a fruit consisting of several seeds which may germinate in a cluster together. Early thinning is essential if reasonably-sized roots are to be obtained. Seedsmen sometimes offer 'monogerm' beet, that is, single, pelleted seeds. These are useful where obtainable. Beet seedlings can only be transplanted when very young or they are liable to bolt; risk is lessened by raising in blocks.

Bolting: Beetroot is naturally a biennial maritime plant. When grown in harsher inland conditions many varieties have a tendency to bolt, especially if sown early and growth checked by exposure to severe conditions such as frost or drought. Choose appropriate varieties for the season.

Watering: When grown slowly beet is woody and worthless. Best grown rapidly in soil which remains moist throughout its growing period. Water to prevent soil drying out; mulching is useful.

Size: Root size can be varied by choice of variety and spacing. Medium-sized beets are far more convenient to cook than prize-winning monsters. 'Baby' beet, up to about 4 cm (1½ in) diameter, useful for pickling and for salads. Pull in bunches with leaves attached. (Leaves can be boiled like spinach.)

Likely problems: Birds are very attracted to young seedlings – take preventive measures.

Harvesting and storage: Lift and handle beet carefully as cut and bruised roots 'bleed'. Twist off foliage to minimize bleeding. Store for winter either in clamps outside, or in boxes in a frost-proof shed in slightly damp sand or ashes.

Early crop under cloches: Use bolt-resistant variety (see below). Essential to encourage rapid germination by warming up soil with cloches about three weeks beforehand. Sow mid-February (mild districts only) to mid-March. Sow seed about 2 cm (¾ in) deep in rows about 15 cm (6 in) apart, or in broad bands about 10 cm (4 in) wide, scattering seed evenly across band. Pull bunches of young beet as required, or thin in stages to about 10 cm (4 in) apart. Should be ready in June.

Main summer crop for fresh use: Sow any variety, April to July. Thin when seedlings 8 cm (3 in) high, or earlier, to 10–15 cm (4–6 in) apart. Pull for use throughout summer. Make sure ground moist for July sowings.

Storage beet: Sow May, round or long varieties. Thin to 20

cm (8 in) apart if large roots wanted. Generally lifted late September/early November for storage.

Pickling beet: Either use thinnings or sow round variety fairly thickly, April onwards. Aim at approximately 200 plants per sq m (20 plants per sq ft).

Varieties: Bolt-resistant – Avonearly, Crimson Globe, Bolt-ardy. Maincrop – Detroit – Little Ball, Dwergina (good for July sowing and for pickles). Storage – Cheltenham Green Top, Housewives' Choice. Yellow – Burpee's Golden. White – Snowhite.

Use in salads and cooking: Cook beet whole until tender, in boiling water or by baking wrapped in foil. Use whole, diced or sliced in salads; small early beet are best flavoured. Yellow varieties very attractive in salads.

CELERIAC or TURNIP-ROOTED CELERY (*Apium graveolens* var. *rapaceum*) (see fig. 27): Relatively hardy, biennial member of celery family. Bushy plant with swollen bulbous stems. Bulb and leaves have pleasant, distinct celery flavour. Easier to grow than true celery; useful salad vegetable, particularly in colder months.

Soil/situation: Moisture-loving plant; natural habitat is marshy ground. Likes fertile, moisture-retentive soil, rich in organic matter. Prefers open position, but tolerates light shade.

Cultivation: Large plants only obtained with long growing season, abundant moisture throughout growth. Aim for steady, unchecked growth. Small plants, however, provide useful leaf almost all the year round. Sow in seed boxes or blocks February/March indoors in gentle heat; March/April in cold greenhouse or frame. Germination often erratic.

Prick out when seedlings large enough to handle. Harden off very carefully before planting outside in May, 30–38 cm (12–15 in) apart. Plant at soil level, do not bury stem. Weekly liquid feeding from June onwards beneficial. Keep well-watered and mulched throughout summer, or some plants may bolt. No earthing up is necessary.

Continental practice is to remove a ring of outer leaves every eight days, starting in September, until just a tuft of leaves remains. This probably encourages the development of nice clean bulbs. Celeriac can be left in the soil in winter, lifting as required. Cover roots and ground between plants with thick layer of bracken or straw to protect against frost. Roots can also be lifted in November, leaves trimmed, and stored under cover in boxes of sand. They probably keep best left in the soil.

Plants run to seed early summer in second season; any young seedlings can be transplanted or thinned and used as 'greenery' in salads or for flavouring. Leaves of small plants which fail to form bulbs (usually due to late planting) can be used until plants run to seed. Keep picking leaves to encourage fresh growth.

Varieties: Marble Ball, José.

Use in salads and cooking: Bulbs ready September/October onwards. Grate raw in salads, scrubbing first to remove soil from crevices. Grate just before use, squeezing lemon juice over gratings to prevent discoloration. Excellent cooked, eaten hot or cold.

Chop fresh leaves into salads. Leaves can be dried as celery substitute.

CELERY (*Apium graveolens*) (see fig. 26): Crop grown primarily for long leaf stalks, eaten raw or cooked. Foliage of some varieties used in salads.

Hardy winter celery: Traditionally grown in trenches with leaf stalks blanched artificially by earthing up to make them white and tender. There are white-, pink- and red-stemmed varieties.

Self-blanching: Newer, less hardy varieties, grown closer together on the flat, requiring less blanching. Probably less crispy and less flavoured than traditional winter celery, but good alternative for summer use.

American green: Green-stemmed, self-blanching celeries, good flavour; not hardy.

Green, branched or cutting celery: Hardy, bushy varieties grown on the Continent for use in soup, for garnishing and for salads. (French: *Céleri à couper, Céleri vert*; Italian: *Sedano da taglio*.)

Soil/situation: Open site; fertile, moisture-retentive soil, rich in organic matter, neutral or slightly alkaline. Peaty soils ideal.

Cultivation:

Seed: Susceptible to leaf spot, a serious seed-borne disease. Buy thiram-treated seed where possible. Germinates best in the light; sow shallowly, or on soil surface.

Bolting: Tendency to bolt if seedlings subjected to temperatures below 10°C (50°F) for more than twelve hours. If sown before about mid-March, be sure that temperatures of 10°C (50°F) can be maintained. Good hardening off over about two weeks and steady supply of moisture are important factors in preventing bolting.

Watering/feeding: All celery benefits from copious watering and regular liquid feeding during growing season.

Likely problems: Celery fly – Tiny maggots start attacking plants April/early May, causing blisters. Can have serious effect. Do not plant blistered seedlings; remove blisters on growing plants by hand, and burn diseased foliage. Avoid planting near infected parsnips, or where infected crop of parsnips grown in previous year. Can spray with pyrethrum, derris or dimethoate. Slugs are very partial to celery; take precautions.

Cultivation of different types:

Winter celery: Sow gentle heat late February/March. Prick out; harden off carefully. Plant out end May/early June, 30 cm (12 in) apart in double rows. On heavy soils plant on the flat, blanch by tying stems with brown paper. On medium and light soils plant in trench. Trench should ideally be prepared previous autumn, at least 38 cm (15 in) wide, by 30 cm (12 in) deep, working plenty of well-rotted manure or compost into bottom layer. Replace soil to within 8 cm (3 in) of soil level, leaving surplus on edge for earthing up.

Start earthing up about mid-August, drawing up about 8 cm (3 in) soil around stems; repeat at least twice more at two-week intervals until only tops exposed; tie plants loosely with raffia to keep upright. Where grown flat, blanch by tying brown paper or black polythene around stems in stages, about 8–10 cm (3–4 in) at a time. This type of celery is ready from November onwards.

Self-blanching celery: Sow, prick out, harden off, as for winter celery. Plant in compact blocks, plants 15–28 cm (6–11 in) apart end May/early June. (Closer spacing gives slender hearts; wider spacing gives higher yields, good blanching.) Growing in compact blocks encourages self blanching; tuck straw around outer plants for additional blanching. Ready for use July until September/October. (American green celery is grown similarly.)

Green cutting celery: Sow February to September in boxes

or seedbed. Plant 23–30 cm (9–12 in) apart. Can plant closer initially, removing alternate plants progressively. Use throughout summer, winter and early spring.

Varieties: Winter – Solid White, Giant Pink. Self blanching – Avonpearl (for early crop in July, sown mid-March), Lathom Self Blanching, Golden Self Blanching. American green – Greensnap, Tendercrisp.

Use in salads: May be necessary to discard outer stalks. Generally used as appetizer, dipping stalks into salt or olive oil. Chopped stalks and tender leaves mixed into salad.

CHICORY (*Cichorium intybus*) (see fig. 23): Large and variable family of perennial plants, cultivated since ancient times for roots, leaves, flowering shoots and flowers, for both culinary and medicinal use. Many are extremely useful salad plants, especially in autumn, winter and early spring. Characteristic flavour tends to be bitter, so for use in salads many are blanched, or shredded very finely.

Generally remarkably robust, disease-free and easy to grow. If few plants are allowed to run to seed, they will seed themselves. It is relatively easy to save seed as little cross pollination occurs naturally. All have beautiful flowers, which can be used raw in salads or pickled. Some forms almost unknown outside Italy; they deserve to be far better known. Wild chicory is native to this country (see p. 85).

In the following notes the chicories are divided somewhat arbitrarily into groups. In practice there is overlapping between groups, and within each group there are many varieties, with varying degrees of hardiness. Follow instructions on packets.

GRUMOLO CHICORY: One of my favourites. Survives abominable winter weather to produce beautiful, ground-hugging rosette of smooth, rounded, jade-like leaves in spring. Almost a green rosebud at ground level! In spring and summer plants looser in shape and grow taller; rosettes form in autumn and winter. Widely grown in Northern Italy.

FIG. 23 – TYPES OF CHICORY

a Sugar Loaf *b* Spadona cutting chicory *c* Grumolo chicory *d* Wild chicory *e* Hearting types of red chicory *Above*: var. Orchidea *Below*: var. Red Verona *f* Chicory flowers *g* Non-hearting red chicory, var. Treviso

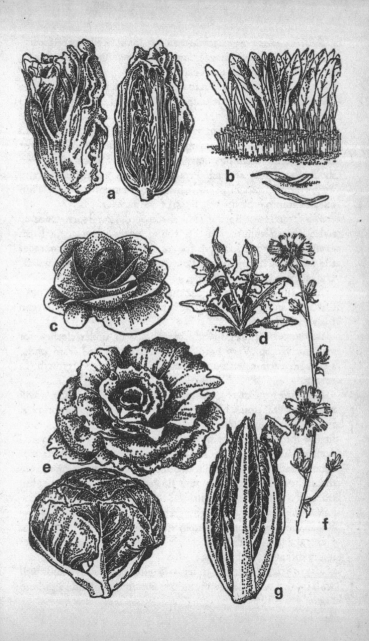

Soil/situation: Said to do best on light, well-worked, well-manured soils; but I have grown it successfully on very heavy, weed-infested, waterlogged clay!

Cultivation: A patch could be sown in a derelict corner of the garden and left to perpetuate itself. It can also be intercropped between sweet corn or brassicas. Generally sown broadcast as thinly as possible; alternatively, sow thinly in rows 15–20 cm (6–8 in) apart. Summer sowings should be covered with straw or sacking until seedlings have germinated. Mid-summer crop should be lightly shaded. Protect seedlings, young plants and winter crops from birds, which are very partial to them. Thin out in autumn if plants are on top of one another.

Main sowings: Spring (March onwards) outdoors. Once or twice during summer cut off young leaves when about 5 cm (2 in) high for use in salads (or for chickens!). This encourages the formation of the rosette. Leave plants from autumn onwards. Use late winter, early spring.

July/August in open, for use mainly in spring.

August in open, covering with plastic tunnels in late autumn for very early crop.

September/October in cold greenhouse or under cloches, for very early crop. Very hardy plants can be picked from under snow. Protection encourages earlier, more rapid growth in spring.

Harvesting: Cut rosettes just above ground level; plants will regrow several times, but never again quite as perfect as original rosette. Later leaves tend to be larger, but can still be used. Plants finally throw up flowering stalks over 2 m (6 ft) high covered with spikes of pale blue flowers. Either uproot at this stage if ground required, or leave a few for decorative value or to seed themselves. The leaves on the flowering stalks are bitter, but can be fed to hens and rabbits.

Varieties: Dark and light green forms are available. Some Italian names: Cicoria grumolo verde, ceriolo, sciroeu, cicorietta. General names for chicory, cicoria or radicchio. (Each variety has many different local names.)

Use in salads: Flavour bitter to English palate, but blends well with milder plants. Very useful late autumn, winter and early in the year, mainly February to May. Use small rosette leaves whole; larger leaves shredded. Flowers can be pickled.

GREEN CUTTING CHICORY: A number of fast-growing, green chicories are cultivated in Italy, primarily as cut-and-come-again crops. Mainly used when leaves are very small, only 5–8 cm (2-3 in) high, when they are at their sweetest and most tender. Leaves can also be used when plants are more mature, but sharper and more bitter in taste.

Cultivation: Broadcast thickly from March to September, in succession if a continuous supply of fresh young leaves is required. Cut seedlings and young leaves at ground level, generally at about 15-day intervals. Regrowth is very rapid.

During summer keep well watered, and unless sown on soil very rich in organic matter, give occasional liquid feeds. (Nitrogen requirements are very high.) When soil and weather conditions favourable, hardy varieties may be sown late in year (October/November, or January/February) in open, or under glass or plastic to provide crop of young leaves very early in spring. (These young plants withstand lower winter temperatures than mature plants.) Early protected spring crop can be excellent source of rapidly-growing, fresh salad when salad usually scarce.

Once beyond small leaf stage 'cutting' chicories can be: uprooted; left in ground and treated as perennial crop if space not required. If kept cropped some new leaves will be produced almost all the year round. Will prove very useful in winter (feed surplus to hens or rabbits); left in the ground until autumn, when Sugar Loaf types form small head. In Italy such plants uprooted and eaten with small portion of the root.

Varieties: Spadona (Sword, or Dog's Tongue) – fairly bitter but extremely hardy. Any Sugar Loaf type chicories (see separate section), for example Zuccherina or Bionda di Trieste – fairly sweet. Invernale di Milano (hardy) – fairly sweet. Italian – Cutting chicory is *Cicoria* or *Radicchio da taglio*.

Use in salads and cooking: If a perennial patch is established or successive sowings made, can be available all the year round. The younger the leaves are picked, the sweeter the taste. Small leaves traditionally blended with hard-boiled egg. Large leaves shredded into salads. Can also be cooked like spinach.

SUGAR LOAF CHICORY: Pale green chicories which form fairly tight, conical heads, so blanching themselves naturally to give crisp white salad. Sweeter than most chicories, but still more bitter than lettuce.

Soil/situation: Requires fertile, moisture-retentive soil.

Cultivation: Originally grown mainly for autumn/early winter crop, lifted and stored before severe weather. Improved modern varieties more likely to survive winter.

Sow *in situ* or transplant, thinning or planting 25 cm (10 in) apart. Sow: June/July so heads can form by autumn; August, in which case heads may form in autumn, but will otherwise form following spring. (Immature plants withstand lower winter temperatures better than mature, headed plants.)

Whether used in autumn, winter or spring, cut heads across neck and 4 cm ($1\frac{1}{2}$ in) above ground level and leave to resprout. Very useful crop of leaves may be produced over several subsequent months. Can also be grown as cutting chicory (see previous section).

Late autumn/winter crop benefits from cloche, low polythene tunnel, or straw protection. Biggest risk in winter is of rotting, especially when subjected to combination of prolonged cold and wet weather; remove rotting leaves but leave stump, as regeneration likely in spring.

Storage: Traditional method was to make circular heaps outdoors about 1 m (3 ft) high, with heads facing towards the centre. Heap was covered with straw. Also stored indoors in cellars or sheds.

Varieties: Bianco di Milano, Groenlof, Crystal Head, Elmo and Snowflake – all quite hardy.

Use in salads: Heads available, fresh or stored, between September and April; resprouted leaf until May or June. Very crisp, appealing salad. Hearts can be cut into small pieces or shredded. Use small leaves whole.

RED CHICORIES: Large group of relatively hardy plants grown widely in Italy, mainly for use during winter months. Many varieties, some with long narrow leaves, some with rounded leaves. Foliage generally green in summer and mild weather, but turning remarkable range of beautiful colours – pink, red, bronze, variegated – according to variety, with onset of cold weather.

In cold weather many varieties also form much-prized, tight, rounded hearts or 'heads' (possibly protective mechanism against cold weather). Heads sometimes form naturally; sometimes depend on artificial lifting and forcing. Head formation by no means a certainty: seems to depend on undefined factor.

Coloured chicories still relatively unknown and untried in this country. There is certainly room for experiment with different varieties (including many new varieties being introduced by plant breeders), and different techniques, to see what is most suitable for British conditions. Taste tends to be bitter; but is moderated by blanching with straw. Heads are more tender and crisper than outer leaves.

Soil/situation: Needs open position, fertile, preferably moisture-retentive soil, but tolerates both very wet and very dry conditions.

Cultivation: Less hardy varieties grown for autumn crop; hardier varieties for winter and spring use. Grown as both 'cutting' and 'heading' crops.

Cutting crop: Sow broadcast March to September. Cut young leaves when 5–10 cm (2–4 in) high. Can leave hardy varieties for cutting during winter, when leaves will become red. Can also thin out in autumn so that some plants will head up.

Heading crop: Sow *in situ* or transplant to 20–30 cm (8–12 in) apart depending on variety. Mainly sown May to July, though may get some bolting with May sowings. When transplanting, leaves are often trimmed back to within 8–10 cm (3–4 in) of base. May need to protect against slugs and birds.

Winter treatment: There are two main alternatives.

Leave plants *in situ*. Towards winter cover with 10 cm (4 in) of bracken, straw or dried leaves as protection against frost and to encourage heading (covering with low plastic tunnels seems to encourage rotting). Where soil is light, plants can be earthed up to assist blanching and heading.

Lift plants in succession for forcing. Trim ends of roots, cut back foliage to within 5 cm (2 in) of neck, pot up closely in boxes or pots of soil as for Witloof chicory (see below), and cover with straw or black polythene. Can be kept in cellar or stable, or brought on sooner in gentle heat (optimum temperature seems to be about 14°C (57°F). Sometimes leaves are tied together instead of being cut back. Less hardy varieties should be lifted before severe weather.

Harvesting: Cut heads, leaving 2·5 cm (1 in) or so above ground level. Stumps will resprout to give succession of small red leaves for use in salads until following June.

Varieties: Early – Treviso, Orchidea, Castelfranco. Hardy – Chioggia, Verona.

Use in salads and cooking: Headed types available October to May/June; seedling leaves all the year round. Leaves used whole or shredded in salad; in Italy, always with oil, vinegar and salt. Adds wonderful colour to winter salads. Red chicories also considered delicacy cooked: in soups, in rice dishes and grilled.

Sometimes small pieces of root eaten with heads.

WITLOOF or BRUSSELS CHICORY: Chicory originally grown for its parsnip-like root, which was added to coffee. Now forced, to develop the well-known, white, pointed 'chicons'. The technique was 'discovered' by a Begian farmer who threw his old chicory roots into a dark shed and found the resulting growths tender! Far more easily grown than people realize.

Soil/situation: Any reasonably fertile, but not freshly-manured soil; open site.

Cultivation: Sow thinly May/June *in situ*; germinates very easily. Thin to 15 cm (6 in) apart. Keep weeded and watered during summer so roots develop well.

Forcing methods: Before forcing summer foliage is cut off. Object of forcing is to stimulate the root into fresh growth in the dark, thus producing folded, blanched, near-white chicons. Forcing under warm conditions gives earlier supplies. Forcing at normal temperatures is said to produce better-flavoured chicons. Roots can be forced twice in succession, but second crop never so vigorous.

There are various methods of forcing (see fig. 9).

In situ: Best where soil reasonably light or sandy. In late October/November cut leaves off about 2·5 cm (1 in) above neck. Earth up roots so they are completely covered with soil. Can cover with cloches or straw to bring them on slightly earlier. Chicons will slowly force their way through between January and March, depending on the weather. Scrape back earth to harvest.

Lifting: Lift roots in late October/November. Reject very thin or fanged roots; ideal size is 2·5–5 cm (1–2 in) diameter across top of root. Trim off leaves 2·5 cm (1 in) above root. Trim roots so total length about 18 cm (7½ in). If roots are not required immediately for forcing, store horizontally in boxes of peat or moist sand in dry shed, or in shallow trenches in open. Use a few at a time to force in succession.

Forcing in pits or frames: Plant trimmed roots side by side in frame or shallow pit. Cover with 2·5 cm (1 in) sifted soil; water gently so soil works between roots. Two days later cover with 20 cm (8 in) of light soil or ashes. Cover this with layer of straw, and finally cover whole with black plastic or sheet of corrugated iron to ensure darkness and keep out rain.

Forcing indoors in pots: Prepare roots as above. Plant about three at a time closely together in any fairly moist soil in large 20–23-cm (8–9-in) flowerpot. Cover with inverted pot of same size, with drainage hole blocked to exclude light and bring indoors. Temperature need be no higher than 10°C (50°F) but slightly higher temperature accelerates growth. Water if soil liable to dry out. Chicons should form within about three weeks. Once chicons are ready, cut and keep in plastic bag in fridge; they will keep for three weeks.

Forcing under greenhouse staging: Roots can be planted in soil under greenhouse staging, if some method of excluding light is devised. Heavy black polythene is sometimes used.

Belgian method of forcing in cellars: See Dandelion, p. 133.

Soil-less methods of forcing: New varieties of chicory, for example Normato, have been developed for forcing commercially in plastic trays without the use of soil. Correct temperature and humidity probably far more critical for success than with traditional varieties, so probably not advisable under domestic conditions.

Use in salads and cooking: Chicons generally available between late November and March or April. Excellent crunchy, delicately flavoured, only slightly bitter salad. In Holland, sliced very finely and served with mayonnaise. Good eaten plain with cheese, or in mixed salad. Very versatile cooked vegetable, for example braised, or in casseroles; flavour quite different when cooked.

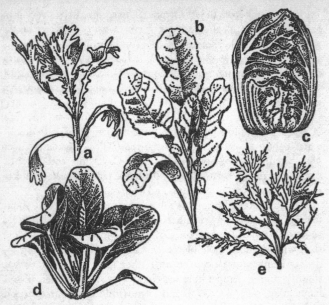

Fig. 24 – Oriental vegetables

a Chop suey greens *b* Abyssinian mustard Karate *c* Chinese cabbage *d* Pak Choi *e* Mizuna Japanese greens

CHINESE CABBAGE or PE-TSAI (*Brassica pekinensis*) (see fig. 24):
Vegetable resembling bloated cos lettuce or Sugar Loaf chicory rather than traditional European cabbage, up to 1·35 kg (3 lb) in weight. Some forms hearted, some loose-headed. Colour ranges from delicate light green to deep green. Leaves often have huge swollen white midribs, very prominent white veins giving a marbled look, and frilled and wavy leaf margins. Plant breeders have improved crop beyond recognition in recent years, producing excellent varieties for our climate. Extremely fast-maturing crop; ready six to twelve weeks from sowing.

Soil/situation: Likes fairly rich, moisture-retentive soil, limed if acid. Good 'follow on' crop for potatoes, early peas. Do not overcrowd autumn crop or rotting more likely in damp weather. Suitable crop for unheated greenhouses or frames in early summer and autumn.

Cultivation: By nature, a mild-weather, short-day crop, at its best in autumn. Has poor root system which dries out easily, therefore prone to bolting in dry conditions. Transplanting should be avoided if possible, unless using blocks. When sown in spring/early summer tendency to bolt if weather unduly cold. Now possible to sow earlier if: appropriate bolt-resistant varieties such as F_1 Tip Top are used; temperature kept above 10°C (50°F) during period between germination and planting out (two to four weeks according to season).

Sow *in situ* or in blocks, thinning or planting approximately 30 cm (12 in) apart; upright varieties can be planted closer.

Main sowings: For summer crop, try sowing F_1 Tip Top in blocks indoors for transplanting, or outdoors *in situ*, May/June. For main late summer/autumn/early winter sow outdoors July/August. For protected winter cut-and-come-again crop (see below) sow late August/early September.

Likely problems: Slugs – take precautions. Flea beetle – may attack seedlings – spray or dust with derris or pyrethrum. Clubroot – choose varieties that are resistant.

Harvesting: Harvest whole heads, cutting off at stump to encourage resprouting. Heads can be stored for about two months in cold cellars; several weeks in fridge. Plants generally do not withstand more than light f ost, but some varieties more frost-resistant than others. Can protect with cloches or low polythene tunnels in late autumn to prolong season and improve quality. May last well into New Year in mild winter.

Winter cut-and-come-again crop: Sow F_1 Tip Top late August/early September; plant in cold greenhouse about 13 cm (5 in) apart September/early October. Keep cutting leaves when no more than 8–10 cm (3–4 in) high for use in salads, keeping plants small. These cropped plants withstand far lower temperatures than mature plants. Very useful source of tender winter salading.

(F_1 Tip Top, grown this way 1978/79, survived – 10°C (14°F) producing fresh growth in mild spells throughout winter.)

Varieties: Wide and constantly expanding choice – F_1 Tip Top one of the most versatile; China King, Sampan, Santo, Nagaoka 50 Days, and many others also good. When in doubt select an F_1 variety.

Use in salads and cooking: Unique delicate fresh flavour and crisp texture; quite unlike British cabbage. Shred leaf and white leaf stalks into salads. Can also cook very lightly, using Chinese 'stir-fry' methods, or use to make soup. In China, Pe-Tsai is pickled.

CHINESE CHIVES (*Allium tuberosum* and *A. odoratum*) (see fig. 29): Delicate, perennial, flat-leaved chives with tuberous rhizomes, forming neat clumps 25–30 cm (10–12 in) high. Fragrant flowers, usually white. Various forms grown in China and Japan. Fresh leaves, blanched leaves, flowers, buds and flower stalks all edible, raw and cooked.

Soil/situation: Tolerates wide range of soil and climatic conditions.

Cultivation: Sow indoors or outdoors, in rows or broadcast, in spring. Transplant or thin to 15–20 cm (6–8 in) apart. Can also be grown successfully in pots. Once established, clumps are easily divided in spring or autumn. Best to remove flower buds in first year to encourage strong growth. Do not allow seeds to form or plants are weakened. Can cut foliage when leaves are about 15 cm (6 in) high; best not to strip entire plant. Lift and divide plants after fourth season. Plants can be left outdoors in winter, but die back during coldest weather. Pot up a clump in late summer for use indoors in winter. Plants can be blanched before flowering by covering with inverted pot. (Chinese use two curved roof tiles with clay placed over the gap.)

Varieties: Broad-leaved – used for blanching. Flowering Leek Tenderpole – used for flowers.

Use in salads and cooking: All parts of plant have very delicate flavour, blend of mild garlic and onions. Use as chives. Can be cooked, but very lightly or flavour lost. Leaves pickled in Japan. Flowers can be used fresh or dried; very mild flavour.

CHOP SUEY GREENS, GARLAND CHRYSANTHEMUM or SHUNGIKU (*Chrysanthemum carinatum*) (see fig. 24): Delicate yellow-flowered chrysanthemum of Mediterranean origin, with pretty, soft green, dissected foliage. About 18 cm (7 in) high when grown as vegetable; up to about 60 cm (2 ft) high when flowering. Seedlings and young growths used in Oriental cooking.

Soil/situation: Ordinary, fairly moist soil; does well on acid soils. Very pretty edging plant; a few plants left to flower will add colour to vegetable garden. Light shade preferable for summer sowings.

Cultivation: A crop which grows most lushly in spring and autumn.

Make earliest sowing February, indoors, or under cloches or frames outdoors. Sow successively about every ten weeks until mid-September. Sow broadcast, or in rows thinning to about 10 cm (4 in) apart. Can be intercropped between brassicas; or intersown between root crops, for example between station-sown parsnips 23 cm (9 in) apart. Ready for use six to eight weeks after sowing.

Cut broadcast seedlings when about 5 cm (2 in), young shoots when plants about 10 cm (4 in) high, cutting back to about 4 cm (1½ in) above ground level. Always use before flowering; flower buds bitter, and foliage becomes bitter once flowering starts. Pull up any plants which develop a woody stem and immediately run to flower. Plants will resprout several times; are eventually cut back by frost. Water frequently in summer and dry spells to delay flowering.

Use in salads and cooking: Available April to November with successive sowings. Aromatic, fairly strong flavour – not to everybody's taste! Use moderate quantities in salads. Gather just before using; flops fairly rapidly once picked.

Can also cook like spinach in minimum of water; use in Chinese recipes; or fry lightly in oil with garlic and bacon.

CLAYTONIA, WINTER PURSLANE or MINER'S LETTUCE (*Claytonia* or *Montia perfoliata*) (see fig. 18): Hardy annual with succulent leaves; early leaves narrow, later leaves curious rounded shape, wrapped around the stem. Introduced into Britain from American continent in 19th century; has become naturalized weed in some areas. Very pretty salad plant.

Soil/situation: Not fussy! Loudon's *Encyclopedia* (1860) says 'it has no pretensions to supersede spinach ... but in very poor soils, under trees, or in other peculiar circumstances it may be found an useful resource'.

Cultivation: Main sowing for winter use July/August (September sowings also possible). Sow April/May for summer crop. Sow: in blocks for transplanting; very thinly in rows, thinning to 13–15 cm (5–6 in) apart; broadcast thinly. Seeds are tiny and slippery so sowing thinly not easy, but necessary as seedlings become very entangled with each other and are difficult to thin. Claytonia very hardy, but advisable to cloche some plants in autumn, or protect with straw, or plant in frames or cold greenhouse as safeguard, and to get staggered winter-spring crop. Seedlings can be transplanted into cold greenhouse as late as December to give spring crop.

If plants well established by autumn, will give several cuts during winter. In very severe weather plants become 'blue' and may succumb; in this case protection advisable. From late February onwards plants vivid green; grow with extraordinary rapidity, quickly producing flowers on long stalks. Leaves, stalks and flowers all edible; cut carefully, leaving basal tuft intact for resprouting. Be careful not to uproot plants, which are very shallow rooting.

Plants run to seed and die June/July; leave few to seed themselves; seedlings easily transplanted autumn or following spring.

French: Claytone perfolie de Cuba.

Use in salads and cooking: Can be available all the year round if sown both spring and summer. Since 'discovering' claytonia in Belgium, it has become an indispensable ingredient in my early spring salads, supplying 'bulk'. Flavour is bland; texture cool and succulent; children love it.

Leaves can also be cooked like spinach.

CORN SALAD or LAMB'S LETTUCE (*Valerianella locusta*) (see fig. 18): Low-growing, hardy annual, rarely more than 10 cm (4 in) with small round or narrow leaves. Fragile-looking, but extraordinarily robust! Found wild all over Europe (see p. 86), but cultivated species more substantial. Widely grown on Continent; one of the most useful winter salad plants.

Soil/situation: Grows well on wide range of soils, tolerating fairly dry and fairly wet situations. Likes full sun, but can be used successfully for intersowing and intercropping in summer. On Continent, often broadcast on onion bed prior to onions being lifted. Shallow soil cultivation sufficient, but needs to be sown in firm soil.

Cultivation: Can be sown *in situ*, or transplanted, thinning or planting to about 10 cm (4 in) apart (use thinnings in salad).

Can also be broadcast and treated as cut-and-come-again crop; Italians use tiny young leaves in salad. However, I find corn salad more satisfactory when grown as single plants.

Germination can be slow in hot weather. Cover beds with wet sacking or newspaper until seedlings are through. Sowing possible early spring until winter, though plants tend to run to seed in mid-summer.

Main sowings: March/April outdoors for late May/early June crop. (This comes in at most useful time. Can sow or plant between early brassica plantings.) July outdoors for early autumn crop. August/September outdoors for main autumn, winter and spring crop. October and November in cold greenhouses, frames or under cloches for additional spring crop. This can be sown after summer crops cleared.

Quality and earliness of latter two sowings can be improved by use of low plastic tunnels or flat, perforated plastic mulches. Remove flat mulch ten days before harvesting.

Although very hardy, overwintered outdoor corn salad is always more tender and grows faster in spring if protected with cloches, straw or bracken in severe weather.

A few plants left in spring will seed themselves naturally.

Harvesting: Can start picking as soon as three to four leaves per plant. With more substantial plants, cut just above neck and leave to resprout. Leaves tend to become tougher once flowering starts; if flower spikes cut off plant may regenerate.

In early stages, flowers edible.

Varieties: Divided into two main types on Continent: *large seeded* – generally larger, floppier, narrow leaves, paler in colour; less hardy, more productive, used for early July sowings for early crop, for example Dutch Corn Salad, Large Leaved English, Valgros; *green* – more compact, crisper, rosette-shaped, with rounder, darker leaves; said to be hardier, better flavoured; generally sown end August/September for winter/spring use, for example Louviers, Verte D'Etampes, Verte de Cambrai. In practice I find little difference in hardiness and flavour between the two types!

Variegated forms: May be found occasionally in Continental catalogues, and mentioned in old gardening books. One with mottled, white-marbled leaves; one with bright yellow central leaves – colour intensified in cold weather giving 'rather pretty effect'.

Large Lettuce-leaved Italian (*Valerianella eriocarpa*): Long, large leaves; slightly less hardy, but said to remain in good condition longer in spring.

Use in salads and cooking: Can be available all the year round if sown spring, summer and autumn. Very mild flavour; some people adore, some find insipid. Soft, faintly greasy texture; blends well with other salad plants. At its best when freshly picked.

French: *Mache, Doucette, Boursette, Salade de blé*. Italian: *Valeriana, Lattughella di campagna, Songin*.

CRESS, GARDEN (*Lepidium sativum*): Hot-flavoured, delicate-leaved plant, of very ancient usage in salads. Early this century grown in huge quantities by London market gardeners in February and March under vines, and in hotbeds and temporary frames.

Although generally considered a seedling crop, grows rapidly to height of 30–60 cm (1–2 ft) when grown in soil, and extremely useful cut-and-come-again crop, especially very early in spring.

Soil/situation: As for white mustard (see p. 151). Cress is prettier than mustard, and could easily be grown in flower beds in spring, or in corners of ornamental garden.

Cultivation: For window-sill cultivation indoors see p. 81. For general cultivation outdoors see white mustard, p. 151.

In my experience, best 'value for money' with cress is late February/early March, sowing in cold greenhouse or under cloches, as a cut-and-come-again crop. Provided soil reasonably fertile and kept watered will resprout up to at least five times before losing vigour. Can be cut at almost any height from 4–15 cm (1½–6 in). (Patch sown in cold greenhouse 3 March 1979 was cut five times between 24 March and 12 June, with one seaweed foliar feed.)

Same technique can be applied to cress sown outdoors in spring; pays to lighten soil surface with peat or sand to encourage germination. In hot weather cress runs to seed and becomes tough far sooner, probably only allowing two or three cuts. Secret of tender cress is fast growth, light soil and adequate moisture. Besides using seedlings and very young cropped-off plants, leaves can be picked from stems of more mature plants.

Varieties: Common Cress, Fine-leaved Cress, Broad-leaved Cress (first two are most common in Britain). Australian Cress – not seen in modern catalogues, but gold-leaved variety sounds most distinctive and valuable if it could be found! Apparently rather like land cress in appearance, with more pointed leaves.

Use in salads and cooking: As for mustard; cress can be surprisingly hot, especially if grown in dry conditions and as it matures.

French: *Cresson alénois commun* (common cress), *à large feuille* (broad-leaved), *frisé* (curled), *doré* (Australian gold).

CUCUMBER and GHERKIN (*Cucumis sativus*): Greenhouse, indoor or frame cucumber – long smooth cucumber; very vigorous climbers. Ridge or outdoor – old ridge varieties short, stubby, prickly-skinned with tendency to sprawl rather than climb. (Gherkins are a type of ridge cucumber.) New Japanese varieties are much longer, smoother-skinned, climb readily, withstand poorer weather conditions.

Soil/situation: Sunny sheltered site; tolerate light shade in summer. Greenhouse may need to be shaded on south side in summer; diffuse light of materials like Correx (see p. 61) excellent for cucumbers. Roots need to ramble freely through highly organic, moisture-retentive, fairly fertile soil. Can be grown in large pots, boxes, or growing bags, indoors or outdoors, if root medium good. Will not tolerate frost.

Cultivation of greenhouse cucumbers requires: High soil and air temperatures (a heated greenhouse); constant pruning and training as growth is so vigorous; removal of male flowers to prevent fertilization (unless all-female-flowered varieties are grown); constant attention to ventilation and watering to prevent diseases which are encouraged by the warm, humid conditions which cucumbers require.

(For details of culture consult specialist book on subject.) Would recommend amateurs to grow, instead, new Japanese ridge varieties. These are suitable for cold greenhouses or outdoors.

Cultivation of ridge cucumbers: Prepare ground by digging holes (or trenches) about 30 cm (1 ft) deep, 45 cm (1½ ft) wide,

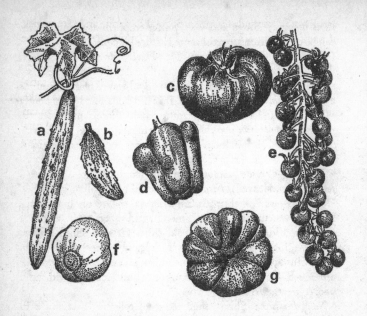

FIG. 25 – TYPES OF CUCUMBER, PEPPER AND TOMATO
a Ridge cucumber   *b* Gherkin   *c* Marmande-type tomato   *d* Green
pepper   *e* Small-fruited tomatoes   *f* Apple cucumber   *g* Tomato-
shaped pepper

filled with very well-rotted manure, compost or rotted straw.
Cover with about 15–20 cm (6–8 in) good soil, to make slight
mound. Sow five to six weeks before planting out; cucumbers
do better if transplanting is avoided.

Sowing alternatives: Indoors, mid-April, in gentle heat (propagator), in blocks or small pots. Sow two to three seeds per pot,
removing weakest seedlings; these plants can be transplanted
satisfactorily at 3–4 leaf stage; indoors, *in situ*, end April/early
May; outdoors, *in situ*, under cloches or jam jars late May. Harden
off thoroughly if planting outdoors.

Plant after all risk of frost is past – early to mid-May indoors;
late May/early June outdoors.

Plant 45 cm (1½ ft) apart if climbing; 90 cm (3 ft) apart if grown flat. Plant on mound; this ensures good drainage and lessens risk of plants rotting off at neck just about ground level. Cloche or frame protection or some shelter very useful in early stages. Mulch plants with thick layer of straw or well-rotted manure.

Support: Cucumbers can trail on ground; but far more satisfactory and cleaner crop if raised off ground. In greenhouse make simple framework by stretching wires across house about 30 cm (1 ft) apart, about 15 cm (6 in) from edge of house. (Follow contours of house from floor to roof ridge.) Train each plant up cane, string, or wire, attached at right angles to wire framework. Outdoors, erect any kind of strong frame or trellis.

Training: Old types of ridge cucumbers were stopped at 4/5 leaves; 4/5 laterals then developed from leaf axils; these in turn were stopped at about 45 cm (18 in) and most of fruit is borne on sub-laterals coming off these; sub-laterals then stopped two leaves beyond fruit; any non-fruiting laterals over 18 cm (7 in) long also nipped out.

New Japanese varieties bear fruit prolifically on main stem, so little stopping necessary.

Allow main stem to grow as high as space allows; stop when no room to train main shoot upwards or horizontally. Train laterals along wire framework; stop them when becoming entangled with neighbouring plants, or if showing no signs of fruiting.

Watering/feeding: Cucumbers need regular watering and feeding. Can feed with weak liquid feed every watering; foliar feeding particularly effective. Very beneficial to syringe or spray plants and greenhouse floor with water, once or twice daily in hot weather. (Creates a moist atmosphere which discourages red spider.)

Likely problems: The cucumber family is, unfortunately, prone to a fairly large number of pests and diseases. Avoid planting in cold soil and cold weather; keep well ventilated and syringed when hot; shut up greenhouses and frames early in evening when nights cold. Many varieties now being bred with resistance to one or more diseases; they are always worth growing.

Red spider: Worst under glass in hot weather; leaves become speckled white on back, then 'rusty'. Remove and burn leaves; spray with derris or systemic insecticides; syringe regularly with water. Can introduce predators (see p. 194).

Cucumber mosaic: Virus disease spread mainly by aphids; worst on outdoor crop. Leaves become mottled, yellow-green, growth stunted. Young plants probably die but established plants may outgrow it though yields are lower. Only remedy is to uproot and burn plants.

Powdery mildew: Powdery spots appear on leaves; keep plants well ventilated; spray with fungicide when first noticed.

Removing flowers: On old greenhouse varieties fruits formed without fertilization, and often became bitter and misshapen when fertilized. Therefore male flowers had to be removed (see fig. 30). There is no need to remove flowers on ridge cucumbers.

Production is liable to fall off in August after initial spurt. Remove dead leaves and surplus shoots with no signs of fruit; give foliar feed; top dress roots by covering with 5–8 cm (2–3 in) of soil mixed with well-rotted compost or basic fertilizer. This treatment often effective in stimulating further production, until onset of frost or low temperatures.

Harvesting: Unheated indoor crop ready late June onwards; outdoor crop mid-July to mid-September. Ends pointed in immature cucumber; rounded in mature cucumber. Keep picking to encourage formation of further fruit; do not allow fruits to yellow on plant. If a whole cucumber is too much to use, slice in half on plant; end will callous over and keep well (or grow new half-sized Mini-Cucumber).

Varieties: Japanese – F_1 Burpless (very digestible!), F_1 Burpee, Chinese Long Green, Kyoto Three Foot, Tokyo Slicer (and many others).

Gherkin – Venlo, Condor.

Apple Cucumber – Crystal Apple (very tasty, crisp, round cucumber).

Mini-Cucumber – F_1 Pepita (all-female greenhouse cucumber; can be grown in cool greenhouse).

Use in salads and cooking: Used sliced peeled or unpeeled. Also used in soups. For pickling use gherkins or ordinary cucumbers, either when small or sliced. Flowers can be used raw, fried in batter, or in soups.

DANDELION (*Taraxacum officinale*): Selected and greatly improved forms of common dandelion are widely cultivated on the Continent, especially in France, for use in autumn to early spring salads. Leaves either eaten green (more nutritious) or blanched (sweeter but less nutritious); roots also eaten. (For wild plant see p. 87.)

Soil/situation: Thrives on almost any soil and in any situation, other than waterlogged conditions.

Cultivation: Sow March to June *in situ* or in seedbed. Thin or plant 35 cm (14 in) apart; dandelions best not overcrowded. Alternatively, can thin to 5 cm (2 in) between seedlings, so that a group of small plants can be blanched under one pot. Keep weed-free; though there is a theory that dandelions left among weeds are naturally blanched. Generally used autumn onwards. Gather inner leaves as outer leaves are tough.

Blanching (see fig. 8): If preferred blanched, use one of the following methods, ideally blanching a few plants in succession for a continuous supply. Blanching takes 7–15 days.

In situ methods – Earth up plants in November with spade. (Leave ample space between rows where this method used.) Cut plants across neck when ready, earth up again for second picking in spring. This method is believed by many to produce the best flavour. Gather leaves together, tying gently if necessary. Cover with inverted pot with drainage hole blocked to exclude light. Make sure the pot is large enough to stand clear of foliage. Make wooden triangular or rectangular box to cover plants in winter. If not required until spring, cover plants by any of these methods when shoots appear in spring.

With all these methods growth can be accelerated by covering plants or pots with straw or dead leaves. Once plants are cut, expose them and allow to grow naturally for use the following autumn.

Lifting method – In cold climates dandelion plants are lifted October onwards, and forced like Witloof chicory, trimming leaves to 2·5 cm (1 in) above neck and potting up in dark (see p. 121 and fig. 9).

Belgian cellar method (see fig. 9) – Heap started with layer of soil 10 cm (4 in) thick on floor of dark cellar or shed. Dandelion roots laid side by side on soil, necks protruding over edge. Cover with a second layer of soil, second layer of roots, and so on. Water with rose on can and leave for three to four weeks.

If cut carefully when ready, about 1 cm ($\frac{1}{2}$ in) above root, it will resprout to give a second crop.

Varieties: Named varieties are rare in English catalogues. French varieties – Amélioré Géant – large-leaved, succulent, productive, upright form, good for forcing. Vert de Montmagny Amélioré – withstands damp well; good for use all winter. A Coeur Plein Amélioré – neat compact variety for winter use; almost self-blanching. French: *Pissenlit*.

Use in salads and cooking: Most valuable November–May. Raw leaves, especially lower parts, make very tasty, succulent salad. Roots also trimmed, scrubbed and used raw. Leaves also cooked like spinach and used in many recipes. All parts have culinary use, from flowers to roots.

ENDIVE (*Cichorium endivia*)(see fig. 26): Fairly hardy salad plants in chicory family; naturally rather bitter and normally blanched to sweeten. Tolerant of hot and cold conditions; therefore often grown as summer lettuce substitute (hot climates), winter lettuce substitute (cold climates).

Broad-leaved or Batavian – Many varieties grown on Continent, with much variation in leaf colour from bronzy-brown to green, some with fairly crisp, yellow-white hearts. New variety Golda relatively sweet and can be used without blanching. Broad-leaved types hardiest.

Curled – Very pretty plant with finely-divided crisp leaf, distinctive flavour. Generally less hardy and more liable to deteriorate in prolonged cold, damp weather.

Soil/situation: Open situation; fertile soil, moisture-retentive for summer crop.

Cultivation: Can be available all the year round with successive sowings. Sow *in situ* or transplant, planting 30 cm (12 in) apart to 35 cm (14 in) for larger, broad-leaved types. Thinnings can be transplanted to give succession. Summer sowings require rapid germination or they may bolt; cover until germinated.

Main sowings – both types: March (in frames), April (open) for May to August crop; June to July for autumn use. Broad-leaved only: August for winter use, grown indoors or outdoors

Fig. 26 – More miscellaneous salad plants
a Broad-leaved endive *b* self-blanching celery *c* Seakale *d* Curled endive *e* Iceplant

cloched; September/October, sown indoors or in frames, planted indoors for March to May protected crop. Golda only: November/January/February, sown indoors, spring-planted outdoors, for May onwards. Useful early outdoor crop.

Winter broad-leaved crop: In Britain undoubtedly most valuable as winter crop. To guarantee survival in cold districts should be grown with protection.

Alternative treatments: Grow to maturity and blanch; treat as cut-and-come-again crop (see fig. 7). In my experience the variety Cornet de Bordeaux will give constant leaf throughout winter and spring if treated this way; grown in cold plastic tunnel it remained in perfect condition all winter, when majority of winter lettuces grown under similar conditions became diseased and rotten. (Variety Golda would probably perform similarly.)

When grown outdoors, cut plants will withstand lower temperatures than mature plants, but likely to succumb eventually if subjected to prolonged severe, wet weather. Cloche or similar protection advisable.

Blanching: Necessary to blanch most varieties if one prefers sweeter taste. Plants normally ready for blanching two to three months after sowing; blanch ten to fifteen days before required. Blanch a few at a time; liable to rot fairly rapidly once blanched. Particularly important to ensure plants are dry before blanching; cover with cloches beforehand to dry if necessary. Can be blanched *in situ* or lifted and blanched under cover.

Methods of blanching (see fig. 8) – Draw up leaves above heart; tie towards top. (This method gives partial blanching.) Draw up leaves and tie; cover with large upturned flower pot with drainage hole blocked to exclude light; or with tiles or wooden box; or any structure which could be covered with mats or black plastic to exclude light. Or lift and plant in pots or boxes in dark cellar, or under darkened staging in greenhouse or in frame. Pots used for blanching can always be covered with straw or litter to hasten blanching process.

Varieties: Fine-leaved – Grosse Pancalière (good for summer), Ruffec and Wallonne (hardiest). Intermediate – Colmar, Cornette (good flavour). Broad-leaved – Cornet d'Anjou, Grande Maraichère Samy, Golda, Cornet de Bordeaux (hardiest).

Use in salads and cooking: Slice broad-leaved types finely if using unblanched; otherwise use as lettuce. Fine-leaved are beautiful colour and shape. Endives also braised, or served in *bagna calda* (see recipes p. 184).

French: *Chicorée scarole, escarole* (broad-leaved); *Chicorée frisée* (curled). Italian: *Indivia scarola* (broad-leaved); *Indivia riccia* (curled).

FLORENCE FENNEL, FINOCCHIO or SWEET FENNEL (*Foeniculum vulgare* var. *dulce*) (see fig. 27): Annual plant with finely-cut feathery foliage, growing over 30–60 cm (2–3 ft) high. Edible part is base of leaf stalks, which overlap and swell to form succulent 'bulb' just above ground level. More widely known and more easily grown on Continent. Do not confuse with the perennial, common or wild fennel (see p. 105).

Soil/situation: Prefers light, sandy, fertile, well-drained soils, rich in organic matter, though will grow on any well-drained

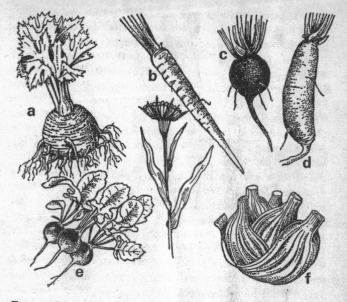

FIG. 27 – ROOT SALAD CROPS
a Celeriac *b* Salsify, root and flower *c* Round winter radish *d* Giant long winter radish *e* Summer radish *f* Sweet fennel

soil. Needs constant moisture when growing and continuously warm weather.

Cultivation: Hitherto not easy to cultivate successfully and form substantial bulb in variable British summer.

Fennel liable to bolt rather than heart up: if sown before the longest day (mid-June); if subjected to spell(s) of cold weather or even draughts; if subjected to dry weather. Problem can be overcome by: using new Swiss-bred varieties which are not susceptible to day-length, so can be sown earlier; keeping well watered throughout growing season; protecting early and late crops with cloches or perforated film, or growing in greenhouse.

Sow at three-week intervals to maintain succession: April to June for July to September harvest; July to first week August for October to November harvest. Can be grown in open or under glass. Sow *in situ* or in blocks or small pots. Thin or plant 30 cm

(12 in) apart. Growth is very rapid. When base starts swelling plants may be earthed up to encourage blanching; cover half the base. Plants normally ready for use fifteen to twenty days later.

Varieties: Florence Fennel (traditional); Zefa Fino (new).

Use in salads and cooking: Stem bases have delicious, fresh, aniseed flavour. Exquisite salad when sliced finely. Also cooked in soups; braised; served with mornay sauce. Leaves can be chopped finely in salads. Seeds used for flavouring many dishes.

Garlic (*Allium sativum*) (see fig. 29): Strongly-flavoured, hardy, Mediterranean bulb of very ancient medicinal and culinary use. White and pink forms.

Soil/situation: Needs open, sunny position. Best bulbs produced in rich, light, well-drained soil. Where grown on heavy soil work a little sand or ashes into bottom of drill. Manure soil for previous crop. Bulbs liable to rot in wet soils or if over-watered; but do need some moisture during summer.

Cultivation: In Britain best to carry out main planting September/October, giving plants time to become established before winter. This will provide early summer crop, which can be thoroughly dried for winter storage. Alternatively, plant as early in year as soil conditions allow (February, March, April). This crop will mature later; in poor summers may not ripen very well.

Planting – split mature garlic bulb into individual cloves (can use ordinary garlic sold in shops). Select firm, large, strong cloves, preferably from outer layers of bulb. Plant about 4 cm (1½ in) deep, with neck of clove just protruding above soil level. (In very light soils can plant deeper; on heavy soils sometimes planted on ridges to improve drainage.) Plant 10 cm (4 in) apart, in rows or blocks, so that weeding can be done without treading on leaves. Keep well weeded during summer months.

Harvesting and storage: Ready for harvesting when foliage has died down, generally end July/August. Wait until dry spell; lift gently. Very important to dry thoroughly in sun. In prolonged sunny weather dry outside, raised off ground. Otherwise dry in greenhouse, plastic tunnel or similar, hanging, or laid on trays. Dry off for up to two weeks until bulbs blanched really white.

Store for winter in dry, frost-free, airy place, hanging in bunches or laid loosely on trays. Remove loose rotten leaves and other debris. Prone to rot if bulbs become damp. Always handle bulbs very gently to minimize bruising and risk of rotting.

(A French lady whose family had grown garlic commercially for thirty years told me to handle it 'like fruit'. It hurt her to see how people threw it about! The same is true of all onions.)

Should keep for ten to eleven months.

Varieties: White varieties most commonly grown; pink varieties traditionally spring planted and reputed to be good keepers.

Use in salads and cooking: Available all the year round if planted in autumn and spring. Strong but unique flavour, use sparingly. Salads improved immeasurably if salad bowl rubbed with clove of garlic. Invaluable in cooking.

GHERKIN see Cucumber.

HORSE RADISH (*Armorocia rusticana*): Hardy, perennial, large-leaved plant, growing up to 60 cm (2 ft) high. Stout fleshy rootstocks and long roots used to make pungently-flavoured sauce. Widely naturalized in Britain. (For wild plant see p. 89.)

Soil/situation: Needs deeply-dug, rich, moisture-retentive soil, ideally with well-rotted manure worked into lower spit. Open, moist position.

Cultivation: Normally raised from root cuttings or pieces of root. Plant about 30 cm (1 ft) apart in February or March. Use pieces of root about .5–1 cm ($\frac{1}{4}$–$\frac{1}{2}$ in) thick, 20–25 cm (8–10 in) long obtained from old plants. Make holes at an angle in the soil, using an iron rod or pole. Insert roots in the holes, broader (top end) uppermost, so that top is about 5 cm (2 in) below soil level.

Keep weed-free and well watered during summer. Some roots can be lifted and stored for winter in damp sand, for use as required. A few pieces left in the bed will multiply and ensure a crop the following year.

Beds should ideally be renewed every three years or roots become fanged and tough. Replant in same or different place in spring. If replanting elsewhere, take care to remove all small pieces of root from original site, as horse radish can become a very troublesome weed.

Use in salads and cooking: Peel just before use as flavour is lost rapidly once cut. Small quantities of grated roots can be used fresh in salad or as garnish for meat. Use to make horseradish sauce.

ICEPLANT (*Mesembryanthemum crystallinum* or *Cryophytum*

crystallinum) (see fig. 26): Perennial, but grown as annual in northern climates. Attractive sprawling plant with small white flowers, thick fleshy leaves covered in tiny membranous bladders which make it look as if covered in dew drops. Used as spinach substitute in hot climates where spinach runs to seed.

Soil/situation: Ordinary soil, full sun; thrives in hot sunny weather. Can be grown in pots or hanging baskets, or ordinary beds. In my (limited) experience, does poorly under plastic.

Cultivation: Sow April (indoors) or May (*in situ* outdoors) thinning or planting 30 cm (12 in) apart. Pick as required during summer months.

Use in salads and cooking: Fleshy leaves surprisingly sweet raw; use whole or cut in salads. Leaves also cooked like spinach.

JAPANESE GREENS see Mizuna.

JAPANESE PARSLEY or MITSUBA (*Cryptotaenia japonica*): (Very closely related to the North American Honewort or Wild Chervil, *Cryptotaenia canadensis*): Hardy, evergreen, perennial woodland plant, with a trifoliate leaf on a long leaf stalk, growing up to 45 cm (18 in) high when flowering.

Soil/situation: Grows on most soils, but thrives in moist shady places and under trees.

Cultivation: Best grown as annual. Traditionally sown spring, but can sow spring until autumn. Sow in rows, thinning or transplanting to 15 cm (6 in) apart; or broadcast more thickly to encourage development of elongated stems.

Japanese blanch leaf stalks like celery in autumn and winter to make them more tender, sweeter and longer. Plants left in ground will seed themselves and seedlings can be thinned or transplanted following year.

Use in salads and cooking: Young leaves and stems used raw in salads; delicate flavour described as blend between celery and angelica. Leaves, leaf stalks and roots cooked by Japanese.

LAMB'S LETTUCE see Corn Salad.

LAND CRESS, AMERICAN or BELLE ISLE CRESS (*Barbarea verna* or *B. praecox*) (see fig. 17): Very hardy, biennial plant, remaining green all winter. Low growing until running to seed, when up to 60 cm (2 ft) high. Leaves deep green, shiny, very indented. Excellent substitute for watercress.

Soil/situation: Tolerates wide range of soils and situations, including fairly wet soil, north-facing borders. Grows best with plenty of organic matter in soil. Light shade is an asset for summer crop. Easily grown as intercrop, or undercropping brassicas.

Cultivation: Sow *in situ*, or in boxes or blocks for transplanting in: March to June for summer crop; July to September for autumn/overwintering/spring crop. Plant or thin to about 15 cm (6 in) apart. Can also broadcast on fertile soil for cut-and-come-again seedling crop.

Young plants may be attacked by flea beetle; control with derris or pyrethrum.

Seedlings, leaves from basal rosette, and leaves from stems of flowering plants can all be used; select the most tender leaves. Generally ready eight weeks after sowing, though seedlings ready sooner. Always best when grown fast; grows most vigorously in spring and autumn. Summer crop benefits from watering. In early summer of second season plants run to seed; leave a few and save the seed or allow them to seed themselves.

Land cress may be difficult to germinate in summer months; sometimes seems to come more easily from self-sown plants. Seedlings easily transplanted if ground well watered. A few seedlings transplanted into greenhouse late autumn or early spring provide very useful early crops. If some left to seed under cover may produce lovely 'broadcast' crop of seedlings following spring. Cloches improve quality of winter crop and encourage early growth in spring.

French: *Cresson de terre*.

Use in salads and cooking: Can be available all the year round if sown twice a year; most useful in winter. Leaves can have slightly hard texture unless used young or grown under cover. Piquant flavour very similar to watercress; use in small quantities in salad or in mixtures calling for watercress. Can also be cooked.

LETTUCE (*Lactuca sativa*) (see fig. 28): Best known of all salad crops; much variation in leaf texture, colour and 'heartiness' of plant. 'Leaf lettuce' grown as cut-and-come-again crop.

Hearted types: Butterhead – Round-headed flattish 'cabbage' lettuce; soft-textured leaves. Can be tasty but tendency to become floppy on picking. Crisphead – Round-headed flattish 'cabbage'

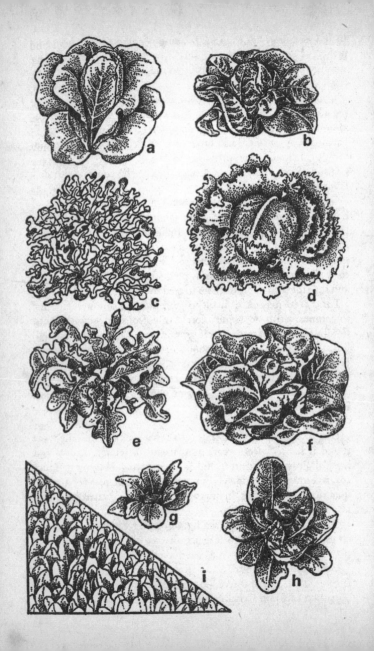

lettuce; crisp-textured leaves. In my view far better flavour and texture, better keeping qualities once cut, than butterheads. American Crisphead varieties relatively slow to bolt. Cos – Tall, straight-leaved, upright lettuces; conical hearts; crisp texture, distinct flavour. Keep well when cut. Sometimes tied to assist blanching. Semi-cos – Smaller forms of cos, excellent flavour, e.g. Little Gem which is exceptionally sweet and crisp.

Non-hearting lettuce: Gathering and cutting lettuces – Mainly 'Salad Bowl' type, in which leaves picked individually or cut for resprouting. Many very pretty and coloured forms.

Rosette types – Entire head cut at once for use, for example small hardy Parella, very frilled Lollo.

Celtuce or Asparagus – Extremely tall-growing Asiatic form. Grown primarily for thick succulent stem, which is peeled and eaten raw like celery. Young leaves used like lettuce.

Soil/situation: Open site; best on light, well-drained, moisture-retentive, fertile soil. Should be rich in organic matter, preferably manured for previous crop, and limed if acid. Important that lettuces should never dry out, especially in summer.

Rotate where possible to avoid build-up of root aphid and fungus diseases. Small-growing types (especially Tom Thumb, also Little Gem) useful for intercropping, intersowing, growing in boxes. Salad Bowl types suitable for growing in flower beds.

Cultivation: Always aim to minimize transplanting of lettuce.

Sow indoors in blocks (ideally) or thinly in boxes for transplanting. Best sown outdoors thinly *in situ* or in seedbed for transplanting. Lettuce germinates at very low temperatures, but some (mainly butterhead) varieties fail to germinate when soil temperature over 25°C (77°F). This may cause poor, erratic germination in late summer/early autumn. Critical period is up to about sixteen hours after sowing in moist soil.

If problem encountered try: sowing in cooler conditions in blocks indoors for transplanting; sowing between two and four in the afternoon (critical period then falls at night); lowering soil

Fig. 28 – Types of lettuce

a Cos *b* Semi-cos var. Little Gem *c* Salad Bowl type *d* Crisphead type *e* Oak-leaved lettuce *f* Butterhead or cabbage type *g* Cut-off stalk of cutting type *h* Parella lettuce *i* Seedling crop temperature by watering beforehand, or covering seedbed or seed box with white reflective material; sowing pre-germinated i.e. chitted seed (see p. 28).

Thin as early as possible to avoid seedlings becoming over-crowded. Thin in stages; thinnings can be used in salads or trans-planted for slightly later crop. Equidistant spacing most logical for lettuce: spring, autumn and winter crops about 23 cm (9 in) apart; summer crops 30 cm (12 in) up to 45 cm (18 in) for large American Crisphead varieties. Plant shallowly with seed leaves just above surface; cos lettuce can be planted slightly deeper.

Protect young seedlings against birds and slugs. In all seasons, important to keep well ventilated to minimize disease.

Remove cloches during the day on spring crop, once tempera-tures warming up. Water as frequently as practical during growth, to obtain good quality, heavy lettuce. If water scarce, give heavy watering seven to ten days before harvesting. Mulch-ing beneficial in summer to prevent drying out.

Can be available almost all the year round with use of cold greenhouses and cloches in winter. Heated greenhouse necessary for mid-winter crop; but these lettuces do not heart well or have good flavour. Once mature, lettuces tend to bolt or deteriorate fairly rapidly. Best to make small successive sowings through-out growing season, using varieties suited to the season.

Early sowings under glass – Mid-February (south) early March (north) for late May/early June crop. Sow *in situ* to crop in cold greenhouse, frames or under cloches. Sow in boxes to transplant outdoors end March/early April in sheltered position or under cloches.

Main sowings in open – Late March to early July for June to October crop. From about mid-June onwards transplanting less successful; advisable to sow *in situ* and thin out unless raising seedlings in blocks. Use mildew-resistant varieties for later sow-ings. If necessary, cloche plants in autumn to improve quality.

Protected winter crop – Late August to early October for November/December, February/March. Sow outdoors or in-doors; plant in cold greenhouse or frame. (In heated green-houses use recommended varieties to obtain crops throughout winter.)

Outdoor overwintered hardy lettuce – August/September for

early May/June. Sow *in situ* and thin in spring. Sow in boxes and transplant in spring. Will be two to three weeks earlier and better quality if cloched.

Likely problems include bolting in hot weather and dry soil. Minimize by avoiding transplanting, using American Crisp varieties, mulching to prevent soil drying out. Soil pests such as wireworm, cutworm, leatherjackets may destroy plants, especially in spring on newly-cultivated land (see p. 22 and fig. 1). Aphids – Lettuce root aphid may attack roots June to August causing plants to wilt and die. Rotate; use resistant varieties; apply diazinon dust or granules around plants in June. Foliage aphids may attack June to October, colonizing underside of leaves and centre of plants. Can spread lettuce virus diseases. Aluminium foil mulch may deter winged aphids from landing on plants. Spray with derris if attacks serious.

Botrytis or grey mould (see fig. 2) causes seedlings to damp off and mature plants to rot at stem shortly before harvested; sometimes leaves become slimy. Worst in cold, damp weather in autumn and early spring. Minimize with strict hygiene and optimum growing conditions. Remove and burn all diseased leaves and debris around plants. Avoid cold, waterlogged soil conditions, overcrowding, deep planting, checks to growth, poor ventilation. Can get some control by spraying with benomyl or thiram when first noticed.

Downy mildew (see fig. 2): First signs pale green and brown angular patches on outer leaves, followed by white downy spores mainly on underside of leaves. Infected areas spread. Worst in late autumn, but ruins appearance of summer crops. Can check by removing and destroying infected leaves. Pay attention to hygiene as for botrytis. Use resistant varieties where available, though if used continually in one garden new resistant strains of fungus may develop.

Salad Bowl types of cutting and gathering lettuce: Far more widely grown on Continent than Britain. Generally non-hearting; though in some small hearts may form.

Leaves either plucked off individually as required or plants cut about 2.5 cm (1 in) above neck and allowed to resprout, which may occur two or three times. Often slower to bolt than conventional lettuce; less prone to mildew. If flower spikes cut off when bolting, may get new growth from base. Some varieties reasonably hardy; can be overwintered with protection. Colours of bronze and red varieties deepen in cold weather. Some soft-leaved; liable to be damaged by hail and severe weather. Sow and plant as for hearted lettuce. Can also be broadcast in patches, and used as seedling crops. Flavour probably poorer than hearted lettuce.

Leaf lettuce: System of growing lettuce very closely together to encourage vigorous growth of upright leaves rather than hearts; most successful with cos lettuce. First cut ready in about two-thirds the time of conventional-hearted lettuce. Yields from small piece of ground several times higher than with conventional crop. Cut leaves off about 1–2.5 cm ($\frac{1}{2}$–1 in) above ground level when 8–13 cm (3–5 in) high. Leave to resprout at least once.

Aim to have seedlings about 5 cm (2 in) apart; or twelve to fifteen seedlings per 30-cm (1-ft) run in rows about 13 cm (5 in) apart. Either: broadcast very thinly; sow very thinly in drills (assuming about 80 per cent germination); transplant to required distance apart. For continuous supply mid-May to mid-October sow as follows: weekly sowings mid-April to mid-May. Ready on average seven and a half weeks after sowing; if cut will give second crop about seven and a half weeks later. Sow weekly first three weeks August to maintain continuity; first cuts will be ready approximately three and a half weeks later; second further four and a half weeks later. A patch about 1 m (1 yd) square is sufficient for average family.

Make sure ground fertile and weed-free initially; keep moist throughout growth.

Note: Many lettuce varieties will resprout from stem after cutting, giving second crop of small leaves, occasionally even forming a second heart. Worth trying, to avoid resowing. Do not try too frequently with one plant or pests and diseases may build up in old stem.

Seedling crops (see p. 175): Most useful for quick, very early spring crop, sown in frames or similar. Some Continental varieties sold especially for the purpose.

Varieties: Early sowings under glass – Hilde (Fortune), Tom Thumb, Unrivalled (Attraction), Little Gem, Winter Density. Main sowings in open – Butterhead: Suzan, Unrivalled,

Sigmaball, Tom Thumb, Buttercrunch (fairly crisp). American Crisphead: Great Lakes, Iceberg, Minetto, Webb's Wonderful, Windermere. Cos: Little Gem. Mildew-resistant (to some extent): Avoncrisp, Avondefiance.

Protected winter crop for cold greenhouse – Butterhead: Unrivalled (Attraction), Kwiek, Kloek, Dandie, Delta, Magnet.

Hardy overwintering lettuce (in all cases quality will be better if protected) – Butterhead: Valdor, Imperial Winter, Verrière Winter, Brown Winter (a French variety), Parella (very hardy, small, rosette, Italian variety, normally broadcast). Cos: Lobjoits Green, Winter Density, Little Gem.

Salad Bowl types: Green Australian Curled, Red American Curled (fairly hardy), American Galaxy, Grand Rapids; Oak leaved; Catalogna (Italian oak-leaved, excellent, very bolt-resistant). Riccio Lollo (very curled beautiful Italian gathering lettuce, virtually bolt- and mildew-resistant, green and red forms, sown in drills or broadcast). Red Italian cutting lettuce (numerous local varieties in Italy). Best sown early spring or in shady position to obtain deepest colourings; liable to bolt in hot weather.

Varieties suitable for leaf lettuce: Paris White Cos, Lobjoits Cos, Valmaine, Crisp Mint, Hilde, Suzan, Borough Wonder, Avoncrisp, Avondefiance.

Seedling crops: Oak-leaved, Blonde à couper.

Use in salads and cooking: Mainly used raw, but can be braised and used in soup, especially when bolted.

MIZUNA, JAPANESE GREENS, POTHERB MUSTARD or KYONA (*Brassica japonica*, or *B. juncea* var. *japonica*) (see fig. 24): Beautiful mustard of Japanese origin, widely grown in East. Finely dissected, dark green, feathery leaves with narrow white stalks. Plants spread to about 30 cm (1 ft) across, generally about 15 cm (6 in) high.

Soil/situation: One of the most tolerant of plants; grows successfully in very cold, very wet and very dry conditions on wide range of soils. Useful for intercropping and undercropping (if plants kept small by constant cutting). Also useful as spring bedding plant, forming dark green foil for flowering plants.

Cultivation: Extraordinarily easy to grow; can be sown all the year round, certainly February to October. Sow *in situ* or in seed boxes or blocks.

Plant about 23 cm (9 in) apart; or thin to this distance in stages using thinnings. Can be ready in less than a month, but generally about five weeks, after sowing. Cut or pick individual leaves, or cut complete plant about 5 cm (2 in) above ground level and leave to resprout. (A crop planted under sweet corn in late May 1979 was cut five times at weekly intervals before the majority of plants showed signs of flowering and becoming tougher. This was in extremely dry conditions. When flower spikes were cut off, many plants started growing from base again.)

Withstands very cold weather, but heavy snow lying on plants causes rotting. Plants in open in severe 1978/79 winter eventually succumbed when temperature was − 15 °C (5 °F). Worth making late September/October sowing for planting in greenhouses or cloches in winter. Plants in cold plastic tunnel planted mid-December 1978 survived − 10 °C (14 °F), providing very useful crop March and April.

Use in salads and cooking: Available all the year round if several sowings made. Use smaller and middle-sized leaves in salads; very decorative. Mild fresh taste, useful in winter and spring to offset sharpness of chicories and endives.

Also used cooked, frying lightly in oil for few minutes only, or in Chinese stir-fry dishes mixed with other vegetables, or as last-minute addition to soups, or as basis for soup. Cooked flavour quite different from fresh – very 'Chinese'.

In the East, mizuna is also pickled and salted. Flowering shoots and flowers can be used cooked or raw while still tender; but they toughen on maturity.

MUSTARD, ABYSSINIAN or ABYSSINIAN CABBAGE (*Brassica carinata*) (see fig. 24): Rapidly growing brassica, in appearance much like young cabbage plants. Grows up to about 60 cm (2 ft) high.

Karate is new variety now available in Britain. (See Appendix III for suppliers.)

Soil/situation: Grows in any reasonably fertile soil. Sow outdoors March to early September. Sow under cloches or in cold greenhouses: October for overwintering early crop, ready March/April; February for April/May crop.

Cultivation: Sow in rows no more than 15 cm (6 in) apart, thinning to 5 cm (2 in) apart; or station-sow individual seeds 8–10 cm (3–4 in) apart. Spring and summer crops ready thirty to forty days after sowing. Very useful for catch cropping, inter-cropping. Can use in salads from stage when seedlings 10–13 cm (4–5 in) high; or as spring greens when 25–30 cm (10–12 in) high. Not totally hardy, but withstands fairly low temperatures.

Use in salads and cooking: Can be available all the year round from successive sowings, but undoubtedly best value in early spring and late autumn. Seedlings and young plants (stems and leaves) all tender and can be used in salads whole or broken into pieces about 5 cm (2 in) long. Very pleasant, fresh, mild taste, with traces of cabbage and mustard.

Can also be cooked by boiling leaves, whole or in small pieces, for three to four minutes.

MUSTARDS, ORIENTAL (see fig. 24): PAK CHOI, MUSTARD GREENS or BROWN MUSTARD (*Brassica chinensis*): There are numerous types of annual and biennial oriental mustards, mainly of Chinese origin, widely grown in China, Japan, and other parts of Far East, which are gradually being introduced into Europe. Relatively little first-hand experience of growing them in this country. All the signs indicate that they adapt well to the British climate, give quick returns, are relatively trouble-free and well worth trying.

Used mainly as cooked greens in Chinese cookery but very tender. Leaves, stems and flowers, depending on variety, can be used in salads. Probably relatively easy to save seed of all open pollinated (non F_1) varieties.

Characteristics: Succulent glossy leaves, often rounded-blade shape; ivory-white leaf stalks and often thick mid-ribs; not unlike Swiss chard in appearance. Generally no hearting. Fast growing, mostly cool-weather, short-day plants, growing best in early spring and autumn. Tendency in many varieties to bolt in summer.

Soil/situation: Prefer cool, moist, reasonably fertile soils.

Cultivation: Can generally sow most of year; for majority late summer best. Sow *in situ* or transplant, thinning or planting usually 15–20 cm (6–8 in) apart. Can be treated as broadcast seedling crops, cutting off young seedlings 8–10 cm (3–4 in) high for salads.

Take precautions against slugs at seedling stage; my limited trials, sown in a wet autumn, were badly affected by slugs. Many

Pak Choi ready six to eight weeks after sowing. Keep picking young growths to encourage further sprouting. Keep well watered in dry weather.

Varieties grown for leaf: Japanese White Celery Mustard; Japanese Giant White Celery Mustard, Chinese Pak Choi. These are cold-resistant; cultivate and use as suggested above, sowing primarily late summer.

Varieties grown for flowers: Chinese Tsai Shim (*Brassica chinensis* var. *parachinensis*). Flowering stalks used instead of leaves. Sow spring to summer; in temperate regions grows well late spring to early autumn. Allow 25 cm (10 in) between plants. Matures forty to sixty days after sowing. Highly resistant to heat and will not bolt readily. Start picking as soon as flower stalks develop, leaving at least three young leaves on plant. For continuous harvesting it is recommended to keep well watered and give fertilizer after each picking.

Stalks can be fried or boiled with other vegetables or meat.

FLOWERING PURPLE PAK CHOI: HON TSAI TAI (*Brassica campestris* var. *purpurea*): Pretty plant with purplish leaves and leaf stalks, yellow flowers. In regions with mild winters, sow early autumn for use in winter and early spring. In regions with cool summers, sow in spring for summer use. Plant or thin 40 cm (16 in) apart.

Harvest shoots when just flowering and about 20–30 cm (8–12 in) long. Keep ground well watered; Japanese recommended top dressing of fertilizer just before flowering. Use flowers and stalks in salads. Can be cut into 5 cm (2 in) pieces and fried in Chinese dishes.

MUSTARD SPINACH or TENDERGREEN (*Brassica rapa*): Another deep green mustard species; noted for extreme hardiness. Will grow and can be sown practically all the year round. Very hardy in cold winters, bursting into vigorous growth following spring. Strong 'Chinese' flavour, but tender enough to use in salads in moderation, leaves cut into strips.

MUSTARD, WHITE (*Brassica alba*) and MUSTARD, BLACK (*B. nigra*) (see fig. 17): Very rapidly-growing annuals, used as seedling crops in salads for many centuries. Seeds of both species used in making mustard.

White mustard is 'mustard and cress' mustard; black mustard has hotter, more 'mustardy' flavour. Both most useful in winter and spring.

(The following cultural notes also apply to cress.)

Soil/situation: For window-sill cultivation see p. 81. Grows on any soil, but fastest on light, well-drained soil.

Cultivation: Sow outdoors, March to September; under glass or cloches, September, October and February; and in any winter months if temperature of 10°C (50°F) can be maintained. Good subject for sowing on spent growing bags. Ideally, work little peat or sand into soil surface. Broadcast seed on surface fairly thickly but not touching. Press or rake into the soil; water gently with rose on can. Cover with newspaper until germinated. Germinates in three to four days (longer in winter months).

Seed leaves yellow at first; start cutting for use when seed leaves open and have turned green, usually eight to ten days after sowing. Cut with scissors just above ground leve'. Likely to resprout to give second and third crop. Faster growing than cress; sow three days after cress if wanted together. Sowing at fortnightly intervals ensures succession. In summer, sow in slightly shaded position and keep watered, or liable to bolt.

Once seedling stage is passed larger leaves can be picked off stem and used in salads; but slightly bristly texture. Can also grow in boxes and seed pans in soil or spent compost. Quick method of resowing in boxes is to scrape off stalks after cutting, sprinkle with fresh soil, and resow on top of old crop. Relatively easy to save seed.

Use in salads and cooking: Available all the year round if sown frequently. Seedlings make spicy and decorative addition to salads.

ONION (*Allium cepa*) (see fig. 29): Large family of strongly-flavoured, mainly biennial plants, usually with narrow leaves in early stages, and developing large solid swollen bulbs when mature. Mature bulbs, immature bulbs and leaves all used in salad. Aim to produce continuous supply of main types.

Soil/situation: Open site; fertile, well-drained, thoroughly-dug and well-prepared soil. Sensitive to acidity; lime if acid. Should ideally be manured several months before sowing or planting (onions should never be grown on freshly-manured land). Advisable to rotate crops of onions to prevent build-up of eelworm, onion fly and white rot disease.

Cultivation: Onions require long growing season to develop to full size. Can be raised from seeds or sets (specially-produced tiny onion bulbs). For all the year round supply, two sowings (and/or plantings) recommended.

Early spring for maincrop onions ready between late August and October and for onions for winter storage, which will keep until the following April or May.

Summer (August) sowings of the new, hardy, overwintering Japanese varieties. These mature June, July and August of the following year.

Seed-raised crop: Prepare seedbed with very fine tilth. Avoid sowing when the soil is very cold; warm with cloches beforehand if necessary or sow under cloches. Use seed treated with fungicide against neck rot and white rot. Sow thinly, between February and April, as early as soil conditions allow. Thin in stages so that plants eventually 4–5 cm (1½–2 in) apart. Can also sow in heat in January for planting out late March or April. Use thinnings as spring onions. Water in early stages until crop established. Keep weed-free, particularly six to eight weeks after seedlings have appeared, or development will be retarded. No need to water onions in later stages of growth.

Onions from sets have the advantage that they are easier to plant, especially under poor growing conditions; give earlier, sometimes higher yields than spring-sown crop; onion has 'head start', compared to seed-raised onion, so better chance of maturing in regions where growing season short.

Disadvantages are: more prone to bolting (select smallest sets, or heat-treated sets which are less likely to bolt and only plant firm sets); more expensive; not available for all varieties. Plant ordinary sets February to early April 5 cm (2 in) apart. (In very mild areas can plant in autumn, but some risk of bolting.) Heat-treated sets must not be planted before late March or early April. Plant with tips at or just below surface level to prevent birds pulling them out. Protect with black cotton where birds are a problem.

Summer-sown Japanese onions: Very useful crop, maturing

June to August when bought onions expensive. Choose well-drained site; prepare as for spring onions, working in base fertilizer dressing unless soil very rich. May need to water bottoms of seed drills before sowing.

Sowing time critical: aim to have onions well established, that is about 15–20 cm (6–8 in) high by October; they will then survive winter conditions but are not so advanced that they bolt in spring.

Recommended sowing times: North England and Scotland, early August; South West and South Wales, end August; rest of England, second and third weeks August.

Sow seed 2·5 cm (1 in) apart. Top dressing of nitro chalk 70–100 g per sq m (2–3 oz per sq yd) recommended in January to get top quality crop. This crop continues growing in mild spells during the winter. Thin in spring to 5 cm (2 in) apart; no need to transplant; use thinnings in salads. (Japanese onions are far more likely to survive the winter than traditional English overwintering onions such as Ailsa Craig.)

Harvesting all bulb onions: Ready when foliage starts to die down and tops bend over. Nothing achieved by bending tops over artificially! Ease bulbs gently from ground, spread to dry on sacks or trays outdoors if weather good. Aim to dry as fast and thoroughly as possible. If in period of prolonged wet weather, bring in after three days and dry off in warmth indoors.

Always handle bulbs for storage very gently; tiny cuts and bruises are starting points for rots which ruin onions in store. Hang bulbs to store, or spread on trays in cool dry place, or knot in suspended nylon stockings.

Varieties: Maincrop – Ailsa Craig, Rijnsburger Robusta; storage – Giant Zittau, F_1 Hygro, Sturon; summer-sown Japanese – F_1 Express Yellow, Imai Yellow, Senshyu Semi Globe Yellow.

SALAD, SPRING or BUNCHING ONIONS: Grown for tender green leaf; either use thinnings from maincrop onions, or grow special varieties, some straight stemmed, some with slightly swollen bulbs.

Cultivation: Prepare seedbed as for maincrop onions; use treated seed.

Sow: March to June in succession for summer supplies; July (north), August (south) for overwintered crop for use following March to May, using hardy varieties.

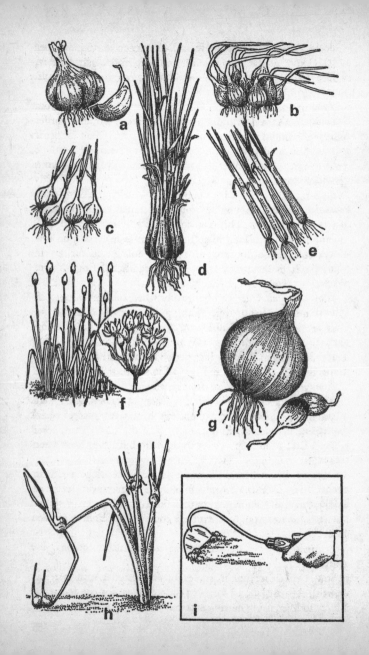

Ideal spacing, approximately 300 plants per sq m (30 plants per sq ft). Sow 2–2.5 cm ($\frac{3}{4}$–1 in) apart, in rows 10 cm (4 in) apart, or in 8-cm (3-in) wide bands, with 23 cm (9 in) between bands. No need to thin further; pull as required for use.

Water if soil becomes dry. Cloche protection beneficial from September onwards in cold areas. Overwintered crop may suffer from botrytis and white rot disease in cold damp conditions; if so, rely in future on evergreen forms of onion (see below).

Varieties: White Lisbon, Japanese bunching onions (vigorous growing, very strong flavour). In both cases there are hardy forms.

PICKLING ONIONS: Tiny bulbs grown specially for pickling; mostly white but some reddish brown.

Cultivation: Can be grown on fertile or poor dry soils. Sow March or April, thickly, about 1 cm ($\frac{1}{2}$ in) deep, seeds about 1 cm ($\frac{1}{2}$ in) apart in rows, or bands 23 cm (9 in) wide. No need to thin; competition keeps the bulbs small. Normally ready August.

Allow foliage to die down and harvest as for bulb onions. Lift and store until required for pickling.

Varieties: Paris Silver Skin, Barla, Barletta (Cocktail), Brunswick (reddish brown).

TREE, EGYPTIAN or BULB-BEARING ONION (*Allium cepa*): Extremely hardy, perennial onion, growing up to 130 cm (4 ft) high. Curious in that clusters of tiny, hazel-nut-like aerial bulbs or bulblets are formed instead of seed after flowering. Main stem of plant then puts out further growth, producing further aerial clusters of bulblets, and eventually bends over to ground level where bulblets root of their own accord (unless they have been picked!).

Cultivation: Prefers rich, well-drained soil, but succeeds in almost any soil. Plant large bulbs, single bulblets, or cluster of bulblets about 2.5 cm (1 in) apart in spring or autumn. (Bulblets put out green shoots when still in the air, and can be picked off at this stage for planting.)

FIG. 29 – ONIONS
a Garlic, showing mature bulb and individual clove *b* Shallot *c* Pickling onion *d* Welsh onion *e* Spring onion *f* Chinese chives with inset of edible flower *g* Maincrop onion and small sets for planting *h* Tree onion *i* Onion hoe

Protect against birds with black cotton; planting whole clusters said to prevent some bird damage. Plants may need staking. Large bulbs produce bulblets in first season, or second season if autumn planted. Bulblets produce large basal bulb in first year; aerial bulblets in second year. Leave plants in ground for further season as they become stronger and more prolific.

A patch will perpetuate itself, but thin out when becoming overcrowded.

Use in salads and cooking: Bulblets can be picked all the year round; best used when fully grown before skins harden; use fresh or in pickles. All parts of plant edible; use young shoots like green onions. Use large basal bulbs when thinning out.

WELSH ONION or CIBOULE (*Allium fistulosum*): Hollow-leaved, relatively hardy, perennial onion, growing about 60 cm (2 ft) high. Base of leaf stems thickened, but not forming true bulb. Grown all over world; widely cultivated in the East. All-the-year-round substitute for spring onions as leaves remain green all winter.

Cultivation: Does best in full sun, fertile, well-prepared soil, but tolerates ordinary soil. Useful edging for kitchen garden. Often grown as annual or biennial in very severe climates, as seed-raised plants are said to be hardier than those raised by division.

Sow *in situ* February to May, or in August. Thin in stages to about 20 cm (8 in) apart. Plant grows into clumps which thicken every year. Divide clumps every two or three years in spring or autumn, replanting young parts.

In Far East plants are earthed up to blanch stems.

Use green leaves whenever required; flavour is fairly strong. If thicker onion required, pull off few basal growths, leaving rest of clump to multiply.

EVERLASTING ONION (*Allium perutile*): Hardy onion, forming clumps rather like large chives, 15–20 cm (6–8 in) high. Leaves remain green all winter. Grow and use like Welsh onion; propagation must be by division as plant does not produce seed.

PEPPER, SWEET or CAPSICUM (*Capsicum annum*) (see fig. 25): Tender plants native to tropical America. Grown for delicious fruits, used immature or mature. Generally green when immature, turning red, yellow or even blackish purple on maturity; some yellow varieties turn red on maturity. Tremendous variation in fruit shape and type: upright and pendulous; square, rectangular, tomato-shaped, long and straight, long with ends curled like a goat's horn.

Soil/situation: Reasonably fertile but not over-rich soil; avoid fresh manure but work in well-rotted compost beforehand. Appreciative of warm, sheltered position; always better with protection. In milder parts of country can grow unprotected in open; in colder regions advisable to grow in cold greenhouses, frames or under cloches. Heated greenhouses only necessary for out-of-season crop. Can also be grown in pots or growing bags. Peppers like high light intensity, good ventilation and not too dry an atmosphere.

Cultivation: Aim to grow without any severe check. Sow indoors in blocks, small pots (two seeds per pot, pulling out weakest seedling later), or in seed trays: February to March for indoor crop; March to early April for outdoor crop. Plants get off to better start if sown in gentle heat.

At about the three-leaf stage, prick out into 5–8 cm (2–3 in) pots. If being grown permanently in pots, move eventually into at least 20-cm (8-in) pots. Can be planted out once 8–10 cm (3–4 in) high; plant about 38 cm (15 in) apart. Plant outdoors after thorough hardening off when all risk of frost is past, generally mid-May to early June, depending on district. Cloche protection invaluable for outdoor crop; when cloches outgrown, turn on their sides to shield plants from wind (see fig. 12).

Aim to obtain strong bushy plant. Advisable to nip out growing point when plants about 45 cm (18 in) high outdoors; about 75 cm (2½ ft) high indoors. Where growth very weak and spindly remove first flowers. Plants may need support if growth is very vigorous; use single stakes, or wires or string on either side of plants about 30–45 cm (12–18 in) above ground level. Important not to let roots dry out; mulching beneficial.

Daily syringing with water in hot weather advisable; relatively humid atmosphere encourages fruit set and discourages red spider. In greenhouse, red spider and aphids main pests; spray with liquid derris or systemic insecticide. Once fruits start swell-

157

ing can give liquid feed every week or fortnight. Once fruits about tennis-ball size, start picking to encourage production of more fruit.

Harvesting: Outdoor crop unlikely to turn red or yellow in average British summer, though may do so occasionally. Immature fruits normally ready mid-July to November in greenhouses, late August until frost outdoors. Can uproot before frosted and hang in frost-free shed. Fruits will keep reasonably firm and sound for several months.

Varieties: Rectangular fruit – early cropping F_1 varieties Early Prolific, Canapé and New Ace highly recommended for indoors or outdoors. Tomato or Bonnet Shaped – Pedro, Wondertop (protection advisable). Yellow – Tweeny, Twiggy (protection advisable).

Use in salads and cooking: Fresh peppers available July until November. Mature and immature peppers excellent raw, sliced thinly in salads. Flavour is different cooked; superb cold dishes made from cooked peppers. Worth growing peppers of various colours and shapes to create interesting effect in salads and cooked dishes. Peppers freeze very well, whole, in strips or in pre-cooked dishes.

(Chili peppers are a much spicier perennial form of capsicum, requiring slightly warmer conditions. Then can be grown successfully in cold greenhouses. Well-ripened pods can be kept for several years if hung in a dry place.)

PURSLANE (*Portulaca oleracea*) (see fig. 18): Low-growing, half-hardy, succulent plant with rounded fleshy leaves. Green and golden varieties. Used all over the world.

Soil/situation: Prefers well-drained, light, sandy soil, but will grow on heavier soil. Sunny, sheltered position advisable; grows profusely in warm conditions. Good subject for odd corners in greenhouses, frames, or under cloches.

Cultivation: Sow in April in cold greenhouse or frame; May to June (July in mild districts) in succession outside, in rows or broadcast. Thin or plant 15 cm (6 in) apart.

Keep well watered to encourage rapid growth; mulching advisable. Gold varieties said to be brighter in colour if watered in full sunshine. First leaves ready to pick within two months of sowing. Pick young growths of leaves and stems; Evelyn recommended 'leaves of middling size'. Always leave two leaves at base of stem for regrowth. Do not allow plants to flower, or leaves become coarse.

In cold summers plants look dejected, leaves drop off, slug attacks likely. Cloche protection serves as 'pick-me-up'! Gold forms not so hardy and robust as green, but very decorative.

Varieties: Green, Large Leaved Golden.

French: *Pourpier vert* (green), *à large feuille doré* (golden).

Use in salads and cooking: Available mid-June until frost. Use leaves and stems raw; pleasant flavour, crunchy succulent texture. Leaves and stems can also be pickled. Leaves also used in soup, or cooked like spinach.

RADISH (*Raphanus sativus*) (see fig. 27): Very rapidly-growing vegetable with swollen roots of varying sizes, shapes and colour, characterized by hot flavour and crisp texture, of very ancient culinary use. Roots, seedlings, mature leaves and seed pods all edible, both raw and cooked. Available all the year round if different types grown.

SUMMER RADISH: Forms – round and long; red, white, red and white.

Soil/situation: Do best in warm, light, fertile soils, manured for previous crop. Rich sandy soils ideal. Essential to have adequate supplies of water during growing period. In very poor or dry soils radishes become very hot flavoured.

Very useful crop for intersowing or intercropping, for example broadcast with early carrots; sown on top of early-planted potatoes; sown between widely-spaced brassicas, rows of peas, beans or lettuce. Will be ready to pull before the main crop would be disturbed.

Cultivation: Must be grown fast or they become woody outside, puffy inside. Sow little and often, say at two-week intervals, for continuous supply. In most seasons ready three to four weeks after sowing.

Sow: Outdoors February (if soil light and situation warm) until September; in greenhouse soil indoors or under cloches, September to early November; February to April, protecting from frost if necessary. Sow shallowly in drills or broadcast, thinning to 2·5 cm (1 in) apart. (It may sound absurd, but it really does pay to sow seeds 2·5 cm (1 in) apart; countless radish failures stem from thick sowing and, because they grow so fast, failing to thin.) Overcrowded seedlings become leggy, matted and never form useful radishes. Flea beetle may attack seedling leaves, nibbling holes; dust with derris.

Summer sowings run to seed rapidly in hot weather. In mid-summer sow in a lightly-shaded situation; but not too shaded or plants become drawn. Water drills very thoroughly before sowing, and whenever necessary to prevent soil drying out. Summer sowings and sowings in greenhouses particularly vulnerable to drying out. Pull for use as soon as ready; some modern varieties stand better than older varieties without deteriorating.

Varieties: Numerous varieties available, some especially adapted to sowing at certain seasons. Be guided by catalogues. Early sowing – Saxerre, Saxa (Red Forcing), Red Prince, Inca. Long-standing summer varieties – Red Prince, Cherry Belle, Revosa, Inca. Autumn sowing under cover – Saxa.

Use in salads and cooking: Young seedling leaves used in salads in old days. Broadcast in spring or autumn. Tender leaves of mature plants, and tender tops also used in salads.

Seed pods widely used in East, where special varieties, for example Rat's Tail Radish (*Raphanus caudatus*), grown for the purpose. In Europe, pods of ordinary radishes and Bavarian radishes used. Allow a few plants to go to seed; pick pods while still tender. Radish pods are recommended in sandwiches of finely-sliced brown bread and butter. Also popular all over the world when pickled.

Bavarian radish: Sow in spring, allowing for fact that they will grow over 90 cm (3 ft) high; thin to 15–23 cm (6–9 in) apart. WINTER RADISH: Huge, fast-growing hardy radishes; black, red, and white skinned; round, cylindrical and long and tapered in shape. Weights range from 1–18 kg (2–40 lb) with some Japanese varieties, without becoming tough; can be nearly 60 cm (2 ft) long if grown in suitable soil. Valuable source of winter/early spring radish.

Soil/situation: Light, well-drained, deeply-dug, fertile soil, not freshly manured. Tolerates heavier soil than ordinary radish.

Cultivation: Sow July/early August *in situ*. Most important to sow thinly, or thin early to 10–15 cm (4–6 in). Keep moist during growing season.

Spray with derris if signs of flea beetle damage. Can lift in winter and store in boxes of sand under cover, or in clamps. Flavour best if left in ground protected with straw or litter, though may need to lift if being severely damaged by slugs. Can give supplies from October until April.

Varieties: Chinese Rose, Black Spanish, Violet de Gournay, Mino Early.

Use in salads and cooking: Use sliced or grated in salads; keep root wrapped in cool place once it has been started. Also used cooked – boiled like turnips, in stews, curried or in soups. Can be pickled. Leafy tops can be boiled in spring.

ROCKET or ITALIAN CRESS (*Eruca sativa*) (see fig. 18): Annual or overwintering Mediterranean plant; fairly hardy. Low-growing normally, but over 60 cm (2 ft) high when seeding. Naturalized in parts of Great Britain.

Soil/situation: Tolerates most soils and situations. Mid-summer crop best in light shade. In cold areas sheltered position advisable for winter crop. Grown undercropping brassicas on Continent.

Cultivation: Can be broadcast as a patch crop, or grown in rows. Normally ready six to eight weeks after sowing; very easy crop to grow.

Sow: February/early March as patch in greenhouse for very useful spring crop; March to June outdoors for summer crop; August to October for autumn, overwintering and early spring crop. Plant 15 cm (6 in) apart. Cutting can start when seedlings about 5 cm (2 in) high. Plant can resprout about five times; in summer, cut flower spikes back to basal tuft. Leaves can be stripped off stems of mature plants. Growth is best early spring and autumn; tendency to run to seed in summer.

Frequent watering advisable in summer to keep plants tender, and to moderate flavour, which becomes stronger with mature plants and under dry conditions. Very easy to save seed; leave a few of best plants in late spring, and collect seed pods when dry. Small plants more likely to survive cold winter than large; cloche protection beneficial in winter.

French: *Roquette*. Italian: *Rucola*.

Use in salads and cooking: Can be available all the year round if several sowings made and winter crop protected. Delicious spicy flavour; leaves and flowers edible. Leaves also used in sauces and cooked like spinach; in France cooked with peas.

SALSIFY, SALSAFY, OYSTER PLANT or VEGETABLE OYSTER (*Trago-pogon porrifolius*) (see fig. 27): Hardy biennial plant, growing over 90 cm (3 ft) high, with long tapering roots, narrow leaves and purple daisy-like flowers. Roots, shoots (known as chards), buds and flowers can all be used in salads. (For wild salsify see p. 91.)

Soil/situation: Any position. Roots develop best on deep, light, stone-free soil, manured well for previous crop.

Cultivation: Sow March to May *in situ*. If growing primarily for roots, thin to 10 cm (4 in) apart. If growing for shoots or flowers can sow groups of three to four seeds at about 15-cm (6-in) intervals, leaving plants unthinned. Germination tends to be erratic. (Use fresh seed as viability deteriorates fairly rapidly.) Keep weeded and watered during summer; mulching beneficial.

Roots ready for use October onwards. In very cold areas, or for convenience, lift and store for winter in boxes of sand. Otherwise, leave in soil; cover with straw or bracken to facilitate lifting when ground is frosty.

Production of chards: There are two alternatives: Cut off old leaves about 2·5 cm (1 in) above ground in autumn, and earth up roots with 12–15 cm (5–6 in) of soil. This will produce well-blanched chards in early spring; or cover plants with at least 10 cm (4 in) straw or dry leaves when growth starts in spring. These growths will be less blanched but very clean and tasty in salads. Cut chards when about 10–12 cm (4–5 in) long. They are most tender at the base. Stumps will resprout several times, providing several cuts. During late spring and early summer the green leaves are tender enough to use in salads. Allow some plants to flower and pick buds just before opening.

Use in salads and cooking: Delicately-flavoured roots available October to May. Cook and serve hot or cold with dressing. Chards ready February to May. Sweet flavoured. Use raw in salads or lightly cooked. Flowering season June and July. Use flowers raw or pickled. Cook buds lightly; serve hot or cold with butter or dressing.

SCORZONERA or VIPER'S GRASS (*Scorzonera hispanica*): Hardy perennial plant, appearance and use much like salsify, except broader leaves, black-skinned root, yellow flowers.

Soil/situation: As for salsify.

Cultivation: As for salsify, except that being perennial it can be left in the soil for second season. Lift one or two sample roots in autumn; if only finger thickness leave in ground until following autumn; they will thicken without toughening. Can also sow in August for use following autumn.

Besides raising from seed, old gardening books suggest propagation from roots: by cutting or breaking roots into pieces; by planting cut-off tops of roots in good moist ground when roots are lifted.

Use in salads and cooking: As for salsify. Flower buds form fair-sized clusters and are exceptionally tasty and succulent, almost like asparagus. Boil lightly and eat hot or cold.

FRENCH SCORZONERA (*Scorzonera picroides*): Annual form growing in rosette shape, mentioned in old gardening books. It was sown in drills like chives and cut several times during season, the young leaves being used raw in salads. Has, unfortunately, disappeared from modern catalogues.

SEAKALE (*Crambe maritima*) (see fig. 26): Perennial seashore plant of ancient usage, grown for blanched young leaf stalks in spring. Large attractive plant with broad, frilled and twisted, glaucous blue-green leaves, sometimes tinged pink when young. Grows up to 60 cm (2 ft) high. Not cultivated until early 19th century (for wild plant see p. 91).

Soil/situation: Good, well-manured soil; sunny position which will not dry out in summer.

Cultivation: Once established seakale plantation lasts eight to ten years. Allow 30 cm (1 ft) between plants. Can be raised from seed, 'thongs' (root cuttings) or by division.

Seed: Sow in seedbed or *in situ* March to April (or even during winter months). Use fresh seed, as viability falls off in second year. Seed has hard outer coat, and may take a long time to break down and germinate; ensure ground kept moist during germination period. (Not recommended to scrape off outer shell as is sometimes advocated.) Best to defer blanching until plants two years old.

Thongs: Thongs can be purchased for autumn or spring planting.

To prepare thongs, lift old plant in autumn; select roots of finger thickness, cut into pieces 10–15 cm (4–6 in) long; trim flat across top end, diagonally across lower end, to avoid planting upside down! Store upright in moist sand until early March, when buds form on thongs. Rub out all but central strongest bud.

Plant outdoors spring.

Lift old plants in autumn or spring and split roots carefully. Keep plants weeded and well watered until established. If many feeble shoots produced, thin out to encourage strong ones. Keep old rootstocks covered with soil so they are not bare.

Forcing: Plants may be forced *in situ* or can be brought indoors.

In situ – When plants die down in autumn remove all decaying foliage. In January cover crowns with large boxes, pots, old-fashioned clay seakale pots (if available) or structure made of frame covered with black polythene. Allow for 45 cm (18 in) growth. Complete darkness essential to develop best flavour. Boxes can be covered additionally with old leaves or manure to encourage earlier development. Young blanched shoots ready for use between March and May. Remove cover after cutting; allow plant to grow again, and blanch again following year.

Indoors – Widely practised in past to get earlier crop. Plants lifted November, side roots trimmed, potted up close together in boxes, pots or darkened area under greenhouse staging, and forced in warm temperature. Artificially-forced plants have to be discarded after use.

Harvesting: Cut shoots below soil level with portion of root attached. Cut just before use, as they toughen up on exposure to light. Leave small shoots to come into leaf during summer.

Varieties: Common (slightly pink tinge when young), Lilywhite (purer white).

Use in salads and cooking: Unique, delicate, nutty flavour; crisp texture. Slice young blanched leaf stalks finely into salads. Young leaves can be used during spring and summer while still tender. Seakale also cooked like asparagus, served with melted butter, grated cheese or sauces.

SHALLOT (*Allium ascalonicum*) (see fig. 29): Well-flavoured bulb which rapidly multiplies into cluster of bulbs. Useful substitute for onions as easily grown, mature faster and keep better. Red and yellow forms.

Soil/situation: Open site; deeply-worked, well-drained, light soils best. Rotate as for onions; do not plant on freshly-manured soil.

Cultivation: Grown from sets. Plant sets as early as possible: December to January in very mild areas; February to March elsewhere. Plant small sets 15 cm (6 in) apart; large sets 20 cm (8 in) apart. Small sets are less likely to bolt. Remove loose scales before planting, plant firmly, burying sets to half their depth.

Protect against birds with black cotton; lift and replant carefully any uprooted sets. Keep weed-free. Shoots can be used sparingly as green onion. Harvest as for bulb onions; stored bulbs will keep until following May or June. Provided sets are perfectly healthy, reserve a few small ones to plant following season. (Some strains of shallots are virused – be suspicious of very cheap offers!)

Varieties: Long Keeping Yellow, Long Keeping Red, Hative de Niort.

Use in salads and cooking: Use as bulb onions; superb pickled.

SORREL, COMMON (*Rumex acetosa*); FRENCH and BUCKLER-LEAVED (*Rumex scutatus*) (see fig. 18): Vigorously-growing, hardy, perennial plants, with arrow-shaped leaves characterized by superb, sharp, lemon flavour. Common sorrel almost ground-cover plant, but growing up to 60 cm (2 ft) in height. Buckler-leaved sorrel lower growing ground-cover plant; large-leaved French sorrel up to 90 cm (3 ft) high. French sorrel reputed to be better flavoured and more acid than common. Both species found wild in England (see p. 91).

Soil/situation: Very easily grown; useful to establish bed in out-of-way corner.

Cultivation: Can treat as annual, sowing *in situ* March, thinning to 10 cm (4 in) apart, and pulling whole plant for use. Alternatively, treat as perennial, renewing beds every three or four years.

To start new patch: sow in spring *in situ*, thinning to about 25 cm (10 in) apart; divide mature roots in autumn or early spring (preferably when still dormant); leave few plants to seed, and shake seeds on to new ground when ripe.

Can usually start picking two to three months after sowing, when 3–4 leaves on plant. Pick small individual leaves initially; once plant well-established can cut across neck, treating as cut-and-come-again crop. Remove flowering spikes as they form. In summer, leaves are apt to become hard and extremely bitter if grown in exposed position; it is worth having a few plants in a shadier site to maintain a good-quality supply.

Sorrel is one of last plants to die back in autumn; it appears very early in spring, often in February. In mild winters or very sheltered position may be able to pick few leaves all winter, especially if plants cloched or protected. Cloche protection early in the year brings on early growth dramatically, at a time when salad extremely scarce. Can also lift few roots in late autumn, plant in boxes, and move into greenhouse for winter; or plant direct in greenhouse soil. Alternatively, sow seed in pots in July for winter use indoors.

Varieties: Few named varieties in this country, but several in France, for example Large de Belleville (Chambourcy), a very large-leaved form of French sorrel with slightly pink-tinged leaf stalks.

French: *Oseille*.

Use in salads and cooking: Can be available almost all the year round. Young leaves delicious in salad, whole or chopped. Also used in green mayonnaise. Cooked in many ways, for example soup, sauces, cooked like spinach (often mixed with spinach to moderate the acidity) and in stews.

Tomato (*Lycopersicon esculentum*) (see fig. 25): Half-hardy South American plant with red or yellow fruits, originally introduced as ornamental greenhouse climber.

Climbing types: 'Indeterminate' varieties, which grow almost *ad infinitum*, that is over 3·6 m (12 ft) in suitable conditions; side shoots in leaf axils can develop into branches several feet long. Usually grown as cordons trained up canes or string, with side shoots nipped out regularly and growing point stopped when sufficiently tall. With skill, can be trained in many ways.

Bush types: 'Determinate' varieties which stop growing naturally, remaining dwarf bush shape, sprawling on ground. Re-

Fig. 30

a Side-shooting tomatoes   *b* Male cucumber flower   *c* Female cucumber flower

quire no side shooting or stopping. Tend to have earlier and shorter productive season; useful for culture outdoors, especially under cloches.

Both types can be grown indoors or outside.

Climate: The more heat and protection tomatoes have the better the quality and yield of the crop and the longer the season, but the higher the costs, and more difficult and demanding the cultivation. For outdoor crop protection is essential in northern and colder parts of the country; protection beneficial in average summer in south to obtain satisfactory crop.

Alternative growing methods and cropping season: Heated greenhouse – May/June onwards; cold greenhouse – end June/early July onwards. Greenhouse crops are grown either in border soil, or in pots, boxes, growing bags or bottomless pots (ring culture); frames or cloches – July/early August, using bush

varieties or cordons trained horizontally; outdoors – August/
September; or mid-July onwards using pre-germinated seed (see
below). Tomatoes can be grown outdoors in the ground, or in
pots, boxes, or growing bags which can b placed anywhere.

Soil sickness (see p. 22): Where tomatoes grown for more than
two or three years consecutively in same soil, especially in greenhouses, soil pests and diseases build up, resulting in crop failure.
Specialized systems have to be adopted. Outdoors, rotation is advisable over four- or five-year period.

(For specialized systems o tomato culture in greenhouses
consult specialist books. The following text mainly concerns outdoor and cloched crop, but basically applies also to cold greenhouse crop.)

Soil/situation: Outdoor crop needs sunny site sheltered from
cold winds and draughts; against south-facing wall is ideal.
Avoid growing near potatoes; potato blight commonest serious
disease on outdoor tomatoes. Well-drained fertile soil essential,
limed if acid. Prepare soil beforehand by working in very well-
rotted compost or manure; water well and apply general fertilizer ten days before planting. If growing in pots use John Innes
potting compost 3 or equivalent compost.

Cultivation: For cold greenhouse and outdoor crop sow in
gentle heat, 18°C (65°F), mid-March to early April. (Allow six to
eight weeks from sowing to planting.) Early sowings require heat
to germinate, but seedlings withstand surprisingly low temperatures once small roots develop.

Sow singly in blocks; or two to three seeds per small pot, thinning later to one seedling; or in pans, pricking out into boxes or
into 5–8-cm (2–3-in) pots at three-leaf stage.

Alternatively, buy plants when required, choosing short sturdy
plants, preferably grown in individual pots rather than boxes.

Space out plants as they grow so individual plants not touching. Do not coddle – the sturdier and hardier they are the better !
Usually planted when 18–20 cm (7–8 in) high and first flowers
showing. With outdoor bush crops, research indicates that planting when first truss just visible gives best combination of earliness and high yield.

Plant: mid/late April (cold greenhouse); early/mid May

(frames or cloches); early June or after last frost expected (unprotected outdoor crop; but some protection preferable at least in early stages). Harden off well before planting outdoors. Plant cordons 45 cm (18 in) apart; bush varieties 60 cm (2 ft) apart.

Outdoor tomatoes can also be protected with perforated plastic film, used flat for bush varieties, or as upright 'bags' for cordons. Remove in August (see fig. 13).

With cordons nip out side shoots (see fig. 30) and any shoots from base as growth proceeds. Tie main stem to cane or support, allowing room for stem to thicken. Water regularly; tomatoes require plenty of water, but many problems stem from faulty watering, especially under glass. Plants should neither be overwatered nor allowed to dry out. Mulching is beneficial.

Subsequent treatment of outdoor crop: Normally requires no supplementary feed, except when grown in pots or growing bags, unless plants appear starved after second truss has set. In wet humid conditions or 'blight prone' areas, spray against potato blight with Bordeaux mixture or copper fungicide, in July and August. Late July/early August stop plants by nipping out growing point two leaves above top truss; this generally leaves three trusses in north; four or five in south. Remove and burn withered and yellow leaves. Pick fruit from plant as ripe as possible.

In September, cut down plants from support, lay on straw or plastic, cover with cloches to ripen; or pull up completely and hang in greenhouse or indoors. Alternatively, pick off fruits and ripen in cupboards (flavour never as good as fresh picked).

Research has shown that using suitable varieties and pregerminated seed outdoor crops can be grown to fruit mid/late July. For full details of varieties and methods consult NVRS Practical Guides.

Subsequent treatment of indoor crop: Give weekly feed with tomato fertilizer. Keep house very well ventilated, as far higher risk of disease with indoor crop. Sprinkle or damp down house and plants during day in hot weather. Remove yellow and dead leaves, and leaves below first truss to improve air circulation. Stop plants at seven or eight trusses; fruiting may continue into November.

Varieties: Huge choice. Many modern varieties bred mainly

169

for glasshouse use; have considerable resistance to many diseases and give high yields, but generally felt that flavour has been sacrificed.

Cordon: Widely grown for use indoors and out – Ailsa Craig, Alicante, Best of All, Harbinger, Moneymaker, Outdoor Girl (mainly grown outdoors).

Small, sweet-fruited cordon: Gardener's Delight (Sugarplum), F_1 Sweet 100.

Marmande: Large, fleshy Continental tomatoes, often misshapen, but excellent texture and flavour. Most are determinate, but some forms taller and grown as cordons – Marmande, Super Marmande.

Bush: Sleaford Abundance, Sigmabush.

Yellow: Add lovely colour to salads; some very sweet, fleshy, and well-flavoured – Golden Sunrise commonest variety.

Plum shaped: Roma – grown for canning in Italy, but tend to be late ripening in Britain.

Ornamental: Decorative, usually small-fruited types, tasty and attractive in salads, in which often used whole. Examples include cherry, currant and pear tomato (all have red and yellow forms); oxheart tomato (pink and yellow forms); white tomato. Unfortunately seed not easily obtained in this country.

Use in salads and cooking: Used raw and cooked. Made into purées, sauces, juice, red and green chutney. Also preserved by bottling or freezing, whole or as purée.

WATERCRESS (*Nasturtium officinale* or *Rorippa nasturtium aquaticum*) (see fig. 18): Hardy perennial aquatic plant, native of Europe. Long stems creep or float on surface, readily producing roots. Leaves have spicy, pungent flavour, very rich in vitamins and minerals. For many centuries used in salads, as cooked vegetable, and for medicinal purposes.

Soil/situation: Grows naturally in springs or fresh-running streams in chalk or limestone situations. Prefers constant water temperature of about 10°C (50°F). Requires bright light but not full sun; typical 'stream' conditions.

Cultivation: Not easy to cultivate successfully outdoors under amateur conditions.

Aim to reproduce conditions as similar as possible to natural situation, that is: running, very clean, uncontaminated, slightly alkaline water; sheltered site with bright light but not full sun; water enriched through decayed organic matter.

To cultivate in running water – grow in flowing alkaline stream, or ponds or trenches fed with clean water which can be emptied periodically. In spring, plant young rooted pieces from old plants, dipped into soil of pond or stream edges about 15 cm (6 in) apart.

In garden – dig sunken beds few inches below ground level. Plant end March with tops of old plants 15 cm (6 in) apart. Alternatively, sow in drills thinning to 15 cm (6 in) apart. Keep well supplied with water (perhaps twice daily), pinch out top growths, remove all flower heads, give regular top dressings of fertilizer. Should give supplies until autumn.

For winter supplies – make similar bed either in greenhouse, or in frame which can be covered in winter, or plant up in pots or pans in a greenhouse (see below).

To cultivate in pots – recommended position: porch in summer, north-facing kitchen window in winter. Put layer of gravel or moss in bottom of a 20-cm (8-in) pot (to prevent soil being washed out). Cover with rich potting soil or compost, to which a little ground limestone is added. Stand pot in pan of fresh cool water. This must be changed daily in summer, alternate days in winter.

Take cuttings from old plants (can use watercress being sold in shops). Cut stems into pieces with joint at top. Drop these in water or soil to root; roots normally form within few days. Plant rooted cuttings in pot with portion sticking out of pot.

Alternatively, raise from seed sown in moist soil (spring to late summer). Add a little fresh ground limestone about once a month. Feed occasionally (liquid seaweed recommended). Do not allow plants to flower. This system will provide watercress all the year round; maintain a continuous supply by taking cuttings from your own plants.

Varieties: Brown – larger-leaved, hardier variety; Green – easier to grow; more susceptible to frost.

Use in salads and cooking: Young shoots and leaves used raw. Also used as cooked vegetable (cooked like spinach) in many parts of the world.

WINTER PURSLANE see Claytonia.

'SECONDARY VEGETABLES': These are very brief notes on vegetables which are normally grown for use cooked, but which are also very valuable salad vegetables, sometimes eaten raw, but more frequently cooked and allowed to cool. For full cultural details it is best to consult a general book on vegetable growing.

ARTICHOKES, GLOBE: Thistle-like plants grown for flowering heads. Best to raise from offsets planted in spring about 90 cm (3 ft) apart. Protect with straw in winter. 'Chokes' (the central part) of very small heads are eaten raw and pickled; larger heads make excellent salad after cooking.

ASPARAGUS: Perennial crop grown in well-drained fertile soil. Buy one-year-old crowns for spring planting, or raise from seed. Do not start cutting until plants are in their third year. Used cooked and cooled.

ASPARAGUS PEA: Very pretty plant with triangular-shaped pods used young, when no more than 2·5 cm (1 in) long. Sow outdoors 15 cm (6 in) apart end April, early May. Used raw and cooked.

BEANS, FRENCH: Dwarf and climbing forms; tremendous variation in shape, colour and form of both pods and beans. Fresh and dried beans both make excellent salads. All beans can be dried, but some varieties recommended for the purpose. Beans like a warm climate. Failures usually stem from sowing in cold wet conditions. Best to sow indoors April, for transplanting in May; or sow directly outside May. Sow or plant about 15 cm (6 in) apart. Cloche at beginning and end of season if possible. Early sowing in greenhouse for early crop very valuable. Keep picking to encourage further production. Water well once flowering has started. For dried beans leave pods unpicked until turning brown; then pull up plants, hang in airy shed. Shell when perfectly dry. Yellow waxpod varieties have excellent flavour; Chevrier Vert grown for dried bean.

BEAN, RUNNER: Sliced green pods good in salads. Grow as for French beans, but most varieties vigorous climbers and need strong supports.

CABBAGE: Useful all the year round both for cole slaw and in mixed salad. If sliced finely, virtually any variety can be used raw; but varieties listed below especially recommended for sweetness, crispness and suitability for salads. Raw red cabbage adds superb colour and flavour to salads; it is also pickled. Always plant cabbage firmly. Following sowings would ensure all-the-year-round supply:

For early spring (April to May): sow July/August, plant September 45 cm (18 in) apart. Varieties: Avoncrest, F_1 Prospera.

For early summer (May/June): sow in frame September, plant out March/April 35-45 cm (14-18 in) apart. Varieties: F_1 Minicole; red cabbage Langedijker St Pancras. Sow in frame or open February/March, plant April. Varieties: F_1 Hispi, Greyhound, Darkri; red cabbage Langedijker St Pancras.

For mid-summer to autumn (July to October): sow March to May, plant June/July 35-45 cm (14-18 in) apart. Varieties: F_1 Minicole; red cabbage Norma and F_1 Ruby Ball.

For use fresh all winter (November to March): sow April/May, plant June/July 45 cm (18 in) apart. Varieties: F_1 Celtic, January King, Savoy.

To lift and store for winter: grow as hardy varieties. Store in clamps or hang in dry sheds.

Varieties: Dutch Winter White; red cabbage Kwanta.

CARROTS: Grated raw carrot makes excellent salad. For all-the-year-round supply sow short types February/March (in frames or cloches); March to May outdoors; and again in August/September, covering with cloches towards end of season, for late crop. Sow intermediate maincrop varieties outdoors from April until June; use thinnings during season, lift roots in autumn to store in sand or ashes for winter. Always sow thinly (see radish) to minimize need for thinning and risk of carrot fly attack.

GOOD KING HENRY: Useful perennial plant with leaves like spinach, and tasty shoots which appear early in spring; both generally cooked but also used raw in salads. Raise by dividing old plants, or sowing seed spring (preferably in gentle heat), planting in humus-rich soil April/May, 38 cm (15 in) apart. Use leaves first season; shoots from second season onwards. Cover plants with litter in spring to bring on shoots. Renew clumps every five to six years. (For wild plant see p. 89.)

KOHL RABI: Hardy, fast-growing member of cabbage family in which stem swells into knobbly ball just above ground level. Excellent subtle flavour. Grows fast in rich moist soil. Sow *in situ* March to June for summer supply, July for winter supply; thin to 10–15 cm (4–6 in) apart. Can leave in soil for winter or lift and store in sand. Must eat when no larger than tennis ball. Grate raw into salads, or use cooked: stuffed, in stews, served hot or cold with sauce.

ORACH or MOUNTAIN SPINACH: Handsome plants like giant docks, over 1·5 m (5 ft) high, once widely grown as spinach substitute. Sow *in situ* March to July, preferably in rich, moisture-retentive soil. Apt to run to seed in dry conditions. Pinch out flower heads to encourage foliage. Select tender young leaves for cooking or use in salads. Pale (known as white), green and red forms are found, the red being especially decorative in salads and appreciated by flower arrangers. A few plants left to flower will seed themselves.

POTATOES: For good potato crops disease-free fertile soil, plenty of moisture, and a long growing season are needed. To extend the growing season early potatoes, in particular, are started by sprouting indoors. Plant potatoes March onwards, starting with earlies. All potatoes can be used in salads, but generally closer-textured first and second earlies, and yellow-fleshed nutty-flavoured Continental varieties considered best. Especially recommended for salads: Fir Apple, Red Craig's Royal, Kipfler. (See Appendix II for suppliers.)

SPINACH BEET or PERPETUAL SPINACH: Spinach used in salads in United States, and here, in the past, as a seedling crop. Many types of spinach cultivated; most reliable type for all-the-year-round supply is spinach beet (perpetual spinach). Sow March/April *in situ*, thinning to about 15 cm (6 in) apart. This will give supplies in summer and autumn and will frequently stand until late following spring, especially if protected during winter. Also sow July/August for supplementary crop during winter (if protected), lasting until following summer.

SUGAR or MANGETOUT PEAS: Varieties of peas in which pods are tender and used whole when peas inside still tiny. Some can also be used shelled in later stages. Excellent flavour; easier to prepare and grow than ordinary peas. Sow March to June in fertile soil, placing peas 5–7 cm (2–3 in) apart. Protect from birds. Taller varieties need support. Can be used raw, or cooked and cooled, but only cook briefly. Good varieties: Tezieravenir, Sugar Snap, Snow Pea.

SEEDLING CROPS: A very productive means of raising salad material quickly in limited space. Almost any salad crop can be used, as most are tender and succulent when very young. In 17th and 18th century cresses, spinach, radish, turnip, mustard, rape, lettuce, orange and lemon seedlings were all grown for salads; other possibilities include chicories, alfalfa, claytonia, land cress, corn salad, kale, oriental mustards, Japanese greens and mixtures (see below).

Could be good means of utilizing old packets of salad crops, where germination of the seed is in doubt!

Soil/situation: Reasonably fertile, weed-free soil, kept moist if successive crops required. Open position spring and autumn; light shade in summer. Useful for intercropping, catch-cropping, utilizing spare corners in greenhouses and frames, especially early and late in the year. Small patches can give tremendous returns.

Cultivation: Seed broadcast (preferably) or sown in drills. For time of sowing and position, the advice given by Richard Bradley in 1720 still holds good: mid-February to end March under glass or frames; until May in open; while hot, in shady places; September/October as in February/March; frosty weather on hot beds. (He also suggested that if seedlings were frosted, they should be steeped in hot water for two hours to revive them.)

Start cutting seedlings when 2–5 cm (1–2 in) high, sometimes seven to ten days after sowing. Many crops will regrow several times.

Remove any loose leaves after cutting, or they may cause rotting. Keep patches well watered. Apply foliar feed if patch seems to be flagging and further use required.

Mixtures: Packets of mixed seed for use as broadcast seedling crop are sold on the Continent. My only trial has been with an Italian mixture. Sown in March under plastic was very useful early crop, though rather too much rocket germinated as temperatures still very low. Sown in late May in open proved very valuable during summer, slower to run to seed than many other salad crops, providing varied, interesting salad material from July onwards over several months. Mixture contained cos and cutting lettuce, rocket, broad and curled endive, corn salad, red, cutting and Catalogna chicory.

Once seedling stage is past a proportion of the plants can be left to mature.

Italian: *Misticanza (miscuglio di semi)*.

French: *Salade en mélange (Mesclum)*.

German: *Salatsamenmischung*.

Part III
Recipes

A Wise man should gather the Herbs
An Avaricious man fling in ye salt and vinegar
A Prodigal the Oyle
(Ancient ditty on salad making, quoted with approbation by John Evelyn in 1669.)

Recipes for salads are almost unnecessary; in few culinary fields is there such scope for intuitive imaginative use of whatever happens to be in season, blended, dressed and decorated as the cook fancies: so all I have tried to do here is to give a few hints on preparing and using salad vegetables, some recipes for salad dressings, traditional salads, and a few favourite combinations, plus recipes for pickling, stir-frying, and braising – alternative methods of using many of the vegetables covered in this book. (See also main vegetable entries in Part II for suggestions on using salad vegetables.)

SALAD BOWL: A wooden salad bowl is infinitely the best, especially for green salads. Wipe it, never wash it. Oil and garlic seep into the wood over the years, imparting a wonderful 'something' to the salad.

PICKING AND PREPARING SALAD PLANTS: Gather flowers in the morning before the sun is on them; otherwise gather salad material as shortly before use as possible.

Wash leafy salad material in cold water; shake dry immediately in salad basket or cloth. Avoid bruising or crushing leaves. Leafy salad material is traditionally broken, rather than cut, into pieces of a convenient size.

If necessary, keep leafy salads in plastic bags in a fridge; roots such as radish in cold water in fridge. Where no fridge is available hang lettuce in a muslin cloth in a cold, dark place, dipping in cool water twice daily. Crisp up leafy salad just before use by tossing leaves in a bowl with ice cubes.

Peel and grate roots just before use, as most discolour on exposure to air.

TYPES OF SALAD:

Crudités: French name for small quantities of very fresh, crisp, top quality raw salad, delicately presented, usually served as part of the hors d'œuvre. Typical *crudités* would be: spring onions, grated carrot, very finely shredded white cabbage, finely sliced cucumber and more thickly-sliced tomatoes, both dressed with a light vinaigrette, cauliflowers broken into individual florets, matchsticks of fennel or celeriac, lettuce leaves.

Simple salads: Salads made from only one or two ingredients, served with a dressing.

Mixed fresh salads: The 'saladini' idea. Any salad plants can be mixed together to create constantly varying salads all the year round.

Aim for a greater proportion of sweeter leaves, that is, lettuce in summer, lamb's lettuce and inner leaves of Sugar Loaf chicories in winter. Shred the more bitter leafy ingredients, such as endives and chicories, to soften their astringency, though sharpness is largely lost in a mixture, simply becoming another element. Aim for as much diversity in colour, texture and flavour as possible.

Rub the salad bowl with garlic and/or lovage before putting in the salad. Toss the whole salad in a French dressing just before serving (chopsticks are a wonderful tool for tossing salads if you can handle them!) Add whole flowers or petals after the salad has been dressed.

Mixtures using rice: Wonderful salads can be made using a basis of cooked rice and cold cooked meats, fish, poultry, vegetables, or any left-overs dressed with some type of mayonnaise. Many different types of ingredients can be added: raisins, sultanas, sliced dates, prunes, nuts, sunflower seeds; grapes, apples or pears (grated, sliced or cubed); pieces of orange or pineapple; orange and lemon peel; yogurt, hard-boiled eggs, grated cheese; root and leafy salad material; herbs, pickles and marigold petals.

SALAD DRESSINGS:

Oils: Olive and walnut oils are strongest flavoured; less dominating ground nut oil widely used in Mediterranean; corn oil, other vegetable oils and mixed oils can also be used. The finer the oil, the better.

Vinegars: Use the best quality possible of wine, cider or any other white vinegar; tarragon or other herb vinegars; or juice from making pickles.

Tarragon vinegar: To make, gather dry tarragon in July before it flowers; remove leaves from stalks, put in a bottle and pour in wine vinegar, allowing 110 g (4 oz) leaves per 1·2 l (2 pints) vinegar. Cork well; leave for two weeks, strain, rebottle and cork again. Use same method with basil, chervil or elder flower. (Gather elder sprays when almost fully open.)

Shallot vinegar: Cut up eight shallots, put into a bottle, fill with good wine vinegar and cork. Ready in four weeks.

Vinegars can be flavoured by infusing with mixed herbs, or by standing sprigs of tarragon, thyme, rosemary, marjoram or other herbs in them.

Basic French dressing or 'vinaigrette': Essentially oil blended with vinegar in ratio of one part vinegar to three or four parts oil, plus salt, pepper, and if liked a little sugar. Mix seasoning and vinegar in a bowl or large spoon. Add the oil gradually, blending carefully. Pour over the salad just before serving, toss the salad gently until thoroughly 'dressed'. Can substitute lemon juice for the vinegar.

Common additions: chopped garlic (or rub bowl with garlic); Dijon mustard, say 1 tbsp per ½ cup oil (this makes a thicker vinaigrette); chopped herbs; onions; spoonful mayonnaise.

Mayonnaise: Heavier than a vinaigrette. Suitable for the more substantial salad vegetables, potatoes and eggs. Mayonnaise will keep in a screwtop jar in a fridge for several days.

Basic mayonnaise: 1 tbsp Dijon mustard, 4 egg yolks, 280 ml (½ pint) oil, salt, pepper, 1 tbsp vinegar or lemon juice. (Generally allow 1 or 2 eggs per 140 ml (¼ pint) oil; the higher the proportion of egg yolks used, the richer the mayonnaise.) Place mustard and egg yolks in a large bowl; mix in salt and pepper. Divide off 140 ml (¼ pint) oil. Whatever quantities of mayonnaise being made, add the first 140 ml (¼ pint) oil to the eggs drop by drop, beating continuously with a balloon whisk. The mixture emulsifies. Then add the rest of the oil in larger quantities, still beating.

The mixture then thickens. Finally, whip in the vinegar and thin to whatever consistency required with warm water. (Can omit the mustard, but it adds a valuable piquancy, especially where a bland oil is used.)

Note: If the mayonnaise curdles, beat the curdled mixture into another egg yolk in a fresh bowl.

Mayonnaise may also be made very successfully in a blender, using whole eggs.

Mayonnaise variations: Mousseline – Add crushed garlic, whip in handful finely-chopped chives and parsley, and one or two egg whites, previously whipped until thick. Very light dressing for green salads.

Green mayonnaise – (a) Blanch some chervil, tarragon, spinach and watercress for about five minutes. Dry, pound, sieve through a mouli and add to the mayonnaise. Anchovies are sometimes added to the herbs before they are moulied. (b) Add mixture of very finely-chopped fresh herbs to the mayonnaise.

Aioli – Blend crushed garlic with mayonnaise.

Tomato purée – Add fresh tomato purée, garlic and little Worcester sauce to the mayonnaise. Good on potato salad.

Yogurt dressing: Mix 1 standard pot of natural yogurt with $\frac{1}{2}$ tbsp vinegar, 1 tbsp chopped onion, salt and pepper. Use with green salads, cucumber, beetroot.

Roquefort dressing: Blend 50 g (2 oz) Roquefort or blue cheese with 3 tbsp wine vinegar. Add $\frac{1}{4}$ tsp dry mustard, salt and dash of Tabasco sauce. Stir in one cup sour cream and $\frac{1}{2}$ cup mayonnaise. Beat until blended.

Egg yolk dressing: Pound hard-boiled egg yolks to a purée. Mix in pepper, salt, drop of vinegar or lemon juice and olive oil until a creamy consistency is obtained. Use with grated vegetables, tomatoes or cucumber.

(Consult standard recipe books for other traditional sauces and dressings such as Hollandaise, Béarnaise, Rémoulade, 1000 Island dressing.)

Dressing cooked vegetables: Cooked vegetables destined to be eaten cold should, wherever possible, be mixed with the dressing when still warm, so the flavour is absorbed while cooling.

SALAD RECIPES:

Artichokes: Trim off stalk, tough leaves at base, and top third of bracts. Cook in salted water about twenty minutes, until bracts can be pulled off easily. Drain well. Serve hot or cold, dipping bracts into melted butter, vinaigrette, herb-flavoured mayonnaise or hollandaise sauce. Very young artichoke hearts can be eaten raw or pickled.

Asparagus: Very young tender spears can be eaten raw. Otherwise serve cooked asparagus hot or cold with mayonnaise or vinaigrette. Tarragon goes well with cold asparagus.

Asparagus Pea: Recommended raw with a mayonnaise dressing.

Beans, French: Italian French bean salad. ½ kg (1 lb) green beans, lettuce, chopped hard-boiled egg, grated Parmesan cheese, 1 minced onion, 4 tbsp oil, 2 tbsp vinegar, seasoning. Boil chopped beans for six to eight minutes. Drain. Mix with oil, vinegar, onion and seasoning. Cover and leave to cool. Serve piled on lettuce leaves, sprinkled with Parmesan cheese, garnished with egg.

Cooked, cooled French beans can be combined with any of the following: finely-chopped onion and pieces of tinned tuna; raw sliced sweet peppers and tomatoes cut into strips; equal quantities of cooke. young peas, half the quantity of cooked haricot beans, chopped chives. Dress with vinaigrette. Garnish with hard-boiled egg and/or cress. Season with tarragon or other herbs.

Beans, Dried: Turkish dried bean or dried pea salad. 200 g (½ lb) dried beans or peas (haricot or kidney beans, chick peas), 2 crushed garlic cloves, 2 tbsp olive oil, 1 tbsp vinegar, sugar, seasoning, lemon, parsley. Soak and cook beans or peas in usual way until soft but not mushy. Drain and mix thoroughly while still hot with garlic, oil, vinegar, sugar and seasoning. Leave to cool. Garnish with finely-chopped parsley and black olives, sliced tomatoes, sliced peppers if available. Squeeze lemon over beans before serving.

Beetroot: Turkish beetroot and yogurt salad. 4 beets, 280 ml (½ pint) yogurt, 2 cloves garlic, few caraway seeds, paprika, seasoning. Boil or bake beets until tender. Cool and rub off skins carefully. Slice or dice, season, arrange in dish. Beat yogurt with crushed garlic, little salt and caraway seeds. Pour over beetroot. Garnish with paprika.

Beet has better flavour fresh than pickled. Suggestions for cooked cold beet: sliced, dressed with vinaigrette to which grated horse radish added; sliced thin, served with little oil, lots of chopped parsley; diced, served with mayonnaise; diced, combined with carrots, celery and apples, dressed with thin mayonnaise, garnished with parsley and finely-chopped hard-boiled egg; small whole beets, dressed with olive oil and seasoning, served with land cress; diced, mixed with thinly-sliced celery and corn salad leaves, dressed with vinaigrette.

Cabbage: Cole slaw – white (or red) cabbage shredded finely, and mixed with any of infinite variety of ingredients according to taste. (See Mixed Salads, p. 178.) Dress with vinaigrette, mustardy mayonnaise, Roquefort dressing, or similar.

Red cabbage and mushroom salad – 1 red cabbage, 110–225 g ($\frac{1}{4}$–$\frac{1}{2}$ lb) mushrooms, watercress, vinaigrette. Slice mushrooms thinly, mix with vinaigrette. Slice cabbage thinly; just before serving mix with mushrooms, adding enough watercress to enliven without dominating.

Scandinavian red cabbage salad – shred 225 g (8 oz) red cabbage; mix with 2 coarsely-grated apples and chopped onion (optional). Toss in vinaigrette made with chopped dill or parsley.

Cabbage core – slice thinly, serve with almost any dressing.

Carrots: Carrot *crudités* – grate old or young raw carrots very finely, either almost to a purée or into large 'matchsticks'. Discard the core of older carrots. Serve with a vinaigrette; flavoured with chopped chervil, chives, parsley, or fennel, salt and sugar; mixed with grated celeriac, winter radish or kohl rabi, dressed with garlic-flavoured mayonnaise; mixed with finely-chopped onion or shallot, a little oil, lemon juice, seasoning and pinch of sugar; dressed with orange juice; garnished with chopped chervil or parsley.

Celeriac: Preparation – scrub rough knobbly root; cut into 1 cm ($\frac{1}{2}$ in) slices; peel each individually, then grate, or cut into cubes or matchsticks. Use raw, or blanched, or cooked and cooled. To avoid discoloration, put into acidulated water when cut.

Celeriac Waldorf salad – mix equal quantities grated celeriac (and/or chopped celery) and apple. Sprinkle with lemon juice and seasoning; add chopped walnuts or hazelnuts. Dress with mayonnaise or eat as it is.

Other suggestions for serving: raw with mayonnaise; cut into matchsticks, marinated in oil with seasoning; grated raw into mixed green salads, or mixed with red cabbage and carrots; raw or blanched, dressed with sharp rémoulade; matchsticks, blanched briefly, dressed with mayonnaise mixed with chopped anchovies and capers.

Celery: Chill before serving by standing whole or cut stems in icy water. Suggestions for serving – in Waldorf salad (see above); sliced thinly, mixed with sliced fennel, dressed with vinaigrette to which 2 tbsp blue cheese added; chilled, drained and dried, mixed with vinaigrette and chopped hard-boiled eggs, sprinkled with finely-chopped herbs; cut into fine strips, dressed with oil, salt and lemon; chilled and dressed with Béarnaise sauce.

Chicory, Witloof: Preparation – remove green or discoloured outer leaves from blanched heads. Washing is unnecessary. Slice across head, either finely or in 2·5 cm (1 in) slices.

Suggestions for use – sliced finely, dressed with mayonnaise flavoured with horse radish, garnished with chopped parsley, chervil, or winter savory; combined with diced cooked beetroot, dressed with vinaigrette; mixed with any or all of: endive, watercress, nuts, pieces of orange, thin rounds red or green peppers and dressed with vinaigrette made, preferably, with lemon juice.

Witloof and red Italian chicories can be cooked in many ways, including braising. Chopped raw into mixed salads, they add white and red colour respectively.

Chinese Cabbage: Cole slaw – 1 Chinese cabbage, small piece fresh ginger sliced finely, soy sauce, sesame oil, rice, wine vinegar, pinch sugar. Shred cabbage finely, mix all ingredients together, add sugar just before serving.

Sweet and sour dressing for Oriental vegetables – make syrup by warming 1 tbsp sugar in ½ cup water. Cool. Add lemon juice and salt until sweet/sour balance obtained. Add tarragon.

Corn Salad: Serve alone or in green salad mixtures, with vinaigrette or 1000 Island dressing; or as Caesar's salad. (See p. 184.)

Cucumber: Peel or not as you please; slice, dice or cut in strips.

Suggestions for use – peeled and sliced, served very cold with yogurt beaten with little salt, few drops of vinegar (or lemon juice) and oil (chopped mint optional extra); mixed with buttermilk, sliced peppers, chopped onion, tomatoes, salt; sliced thinly, marinated for three hours in oil, lemon juice and chopped dill, served with fresh tarragon; mixed with cubed melon, dressed with oil and mixture of chopped dill, mint and tarragon, and pinch of sugar; sliced thinly, marinated for three hours in a vinaigrette, garnished with nasturtium flowers and leaves; mixed with sliced fennel and radish, dressed with lemon juice vinaigrette, crushed garlic and chopped mint.

Dandelion: Use blanched or green. Tastiest parts are lower leaves and tops of roots. Dress with vinaigrette, crushed garlic and/or olives.

Salade aux lardons – prepare dandelion and put in salad bowl rubbed with garlic. Cut streaky bacon into cubes, fry until fat runs, and pour over dandelions while still hot. Add 2–3 tbsp wine vinegar to fat in frying pan, let it bubble, pour over salad, mix and eat immediately.

Endive, Broad and Curled: Piedmontese *bagna calda* – warm together 300 g (10½ oz) each of crushed garlic and anchovy, 200 g (7 oz) each olive oil and butter. Shred endive very finely. Pour *bagna calda* over endive. Cover tightly. Eat ten minutes later, when cooled.

Other suggestions – *aux lardons* (see above) with croutons rubbed with garlic added; mixed with celery and apple, dressed with mayonnaise; mixed with Witloof chicory, shelled and halved walnuts, chopped shallot and dressed with vinaigrette made with lemon juice to which 1 tbsp orange juice added; with 1000 Island dressing; Caesar's salad (see below).

Fennel: Crisp heads before slicing by putting in iced water for half an hour. Slice thinly, dress with vinaigrette made with lemon. Ideally leave two to three hours before serving. Can mix with seasoned sliced tomatoes and/or radishes before being dressed.

Land Cress: Suggestions for use – add small quantities to mixed salads; mix with radish and celery, dressed with vinaigrette to which plenty of ground black pepper and a teaspoon soy sauce added; use as garnish and as watercress substitute.

Lettuce: Caesar's salad – cut cos lettuce into quarters. Sprinkle with 1½ tsp salt, ¼ tsp dry mustard, ground black pepper, vinaigrette. Boil an egg for 1½ minutes, drop from its shell on to salad. Add garlic croutons (see p. 190), grated Parmesan cheese, toss together and serve at once.

Cos lettuce with cream sauce – make dressing with small cup cream, tsp each mustard, sugar and tarragon vinegar plus yolk of one hard-boiled egg. Sprinkle with squeezed garlic (optional), chopped egg white and chives.

Other suggestions – *aux lardons* (see p. 184); 1000 Island dressing; vinaigrette; mayonnaise, etc.

Mustard, Cress and Apple Layers: Cut peeled apples into matchsticks and arrange on a plate. Squeeze lemon juice over them; season lightly. Cover with layer of mustard and cress, similarly dressed, and a further layer of dressed apple. Finish with layer of mustard and cress garnished with nasturtium flowers.

Peppers: Marinated peppers – put peppers in hot oven until skins start to crinkle and blacken. (Or put under a grill, turning frequently.) Remove from heat, wrap in paper and leave ten minutes. Outer skin then peels off easily. Cut into thin strips, remove seeds, and marinate in vinaigrette plus chopped garlic, seasoning and chopped herbs. Leave twenty-four hours if possible. Serve chilled.

Note: Ratatouille, made by stewing prepared green peppers, onions, aubergines, tomatoes and sometimes courgettes in olive oil, is superb served cold.

Potato: Use new potatoes or recommended salad varieties. Scrub, boil in skins. (Do not overcook.) Drain, peel as soon as cool enough, slice. Season while still warm with vinaigrette and plenty of chopped herbs (parsley, chervil, chives) or with mayonnaise. An infinite number of ingredients – apples, anchovies, pickles – can be added.

Some variations – *cressonière*, potatoes mixed with watercress, chopped parsley, chervil, garnished with hard-boiled egg; summer tourangelle – cooked potatoes cut in thick julienne strips, mixed with cooked French beans, sliced apple and thin mayonnaise; winter tourangelle – French beans substituted with celery or blanched celeriac; potatoes mixed with crisp celery, whipping in cream and juice of half lemon before serving, garnishing with cooked ham or spiced sausage and chopped parsley.

Radish: Some suggestions – use as appetizer dipped in salt; dice and mix with cucumber, cottage cheese, and chives or spring onions; grate and mix with grated carrot and mayonnaise; cut winter radishes in thin slices and marinate in vinaigrette for two hours before use.

Seakale: Tie in bundles, cook in boiled salted water until just tender. Sprinkle with chervil, dress with creamy mayonnaise, serve hot or cold.

Sorrel: Sorrel and celeriac salad – 1 large celeriac, peeled and diced, 1½ tbsp lemon juice, 4–6 tbsp mayonnaise, 170 g (6 oz) chopped raw sorrel, 6 tbsp finely-chopped celery, 200-g (7-oz) tin tuna, 1 or 2 chopped hard-boiled eggs.

Boil diced celeriac in small quantity salted water, with 1 tbsp lemon juice for 2 mins. Drain, steam off moisture, cool. Toss with all remaining ingredients. Add seasoning and mild vinaigrette if moistening needed. Garnish with parsley.

Sorrel purée – cook in minimum water. Put through mouli. Add sour cream and lemon. Chill.

Spinach: Some suggestions – use tender leaves as salad; combine with endive; serve *aux lardons* (see p. 184); toss with sliced raw mushrooms in well-seasoned vinaigrette and garnish with crispy fried bacon; serve with vinaigrette made with garlic and mustard, garnish with hard-boiled egg and sliced onion.

Tomato: Basic tomato salad – slice thickly, sprinkle with salt, black pepper, vinaigrette made with lemon and chopped herbs. Leave to marinate as long as possible. Herbs can be parsley, chives, basil, marjoram, cumin, coriander or tarragon.

Hungarian tomato salad – skin tomatoes (drop first into hot water for a minute). Make mayonnaise seasoned with grated horse radish and paprika; fold into it an equal quantity of whipped cream. Place tomatoes on lettuce, cover with sauce, garnish with paprika and chives.

Provençal salad – pound large bunch of parsley with salt, 2 cloves garlic, olive oil and basil. Cut tops off large tomatoes, spoon out the pulp, sprinkle insides with salt, turn upside down to drain. Fill with mixture of parsley, garlic, basil and pulp. Serve after an hour or so.

Gazpacho salad – use diced tomatoes, thinly-sliced green peppers, chopped cucumber, peeled and chopped onions. Arrange vegetables in thin layers (ideally in a clear glass bowl), sprinkling each layer with seasoning. Dress with vinaigrette to which crushed garlic cloves, a pinch of cumin, chopped parsley and chopped shallots have been added.

Niçoise salad – line salad bowl with tomato cut into chunks, chopped onions, sliced green peppers, black olives, cooked chilled French beans, handful cooked haricot beans. Dress with anchovy fillets, tuna, good vinaigrette made with chopped garlic. Garnish with sliced hard-boiled eggs.

Watercress: Sour cream dressing – 1 cup sour cream, 1 tbsp wine vinegar or lemon juice, $\frac{1}{2}$ tsp salt, freshly-ground black pepper, $\frac{1}{2}$ tsp celery seeds. Chill watercress. Cut off coarse stems and mix with dressing just before serving.

Watercress and mushroom salad – put watercress in salad bowl. Slice mushrooms (including stems) and drop immediately into vinaigrette. Stir occasionally. Just before serving place in midst of watercress with little of mushroom/vinaigrette juice.

Root Vegetables: Mint, carrot, Hamburg parsley and onion salad – pound finely (or grate) one small sliced onion with 100 g (4 oz) fresh mint leaves. Add 2 heaped tbsp each grated raw carrot and Hamburg parsley root. Mix well. Add lemon juice, salt and pepper.

Parsnip and cheese salad – skin cooked cold parsnip and core. Cut into small cubes; cut cheese cubes of same size. Toss together in good salad dressing. Serve on lettuce. (Also suitable for celeriac.)

Cooked, cold roots (kohl rabi, salsify, scorzonera, celeriac) – serve cooked, chilled roots with purée made from boiled onions; or with Hollandaise or Béarnaise sauce.

Turnip stalks – in old days stalks which were running to seed were cooked, chilled, and served as salad with vinegar. (Cabbage stalks were treated similarly.)

Left-over vegetables – Almost any cooked, cold, left-over vegetables can be served in a salad, alone or in mixtures. Sprinkle with mixed chopped herbs, dress with mayonnaise. Cheese and nuts can be added. Can serve piled attractively on a flan case.

Sprouted Seeds: Sprouted seed salad – 1 cup alfalfa or bean sprouts, 3–4 cups salad greens, 6 sliced radishes, $\frac{1}{2}$ cucumber (sliced), $\frac{1}{4}-\frac{1}{2}$ cup toasted sunflower seeds. (Toast by stirring over medium heat for about three minutes in dry skillet.) Combine all together; dress with French dressing; garnish with sliced hard-boiled egg.

Adzuki bean salad – fry beans lightly. Mix with sliced raw cabbage and yoghurt. Add nuts or ground almonds.

Sprouted seed combinations: Most sprouted seeds blend well together; or with cole slaw, grated red cabbage, *crudités*, potato salad, nuts, raisins, currants, diced or shredded apple, pineapple, pears, grated cheese. Can dress with sour cream or yoghurt.

Flowers: Stuffed nasturtium flowers – 12 fresh flowers, ¼ cup nasturtium leaves, 4 hard-boiled eggs, 1 tbsp finely-chopped parsley, 2 tbsp mayonnaise, dressing made from 2 tbsp oil, 1 tbsp vinegar. Mix mashed eggs, parsley, mayonnaise, seasoning. Fill flowers with mixture. Line salad bowl with leaves sprinkled with dressing. Arrange flowers on top. (Flowers can also be stuffed with cream cheese and pineapple mixture.)

Nasturtium leaves and flowers – Add chopped to: cucumbers dressed with dill and chives; French bean and spring onion salad; white salads such as shredded cabbage or celeriac; green salads.

Pickling: Early gardening books mention many plants which were pickled for use in winter salads, including artichokes, beet, French beans, cucumbers, leeks, melon, mushrooms, onions, purslane, radish pods, turnips, walnuts, the herbs summer savory and tarragon, flowers such as broom buds, chicory, cowslip, elder flowers and buds, goat's beard, salsify, clove-scented pinks and nasturtium buds, flowers and seeds.

In pickling, vinegar acts as the preservative; use the best quality vinegar available. Malt vinegar gives the best flavour. Pickle in glass or pottery containers.

Spiced vinegar For every 1 litre (2 pints) vinegar allow either 50 g (2 oz) whole pickling spice or 7 g (¼ oz) each of allspice, cloves and cinnamon bark, ¼ blade mace, 6 peppercorns. Bring to the boil in a pan. Cover. Leave to cool for two hours. Strain before use. (Vinegar can also be spiced by leaving spices to stand in unheated vinegar for two months.)

To pickle flowers: Lay down layers of flowers in container, covering each layer with sugar. Pack down fairly firmly. Boil up cider or wine vinegar to cover. Allow to cool and pour over flowers. They are ready for use in four days. (This is very successful with salsify, scorzonera and chicory flowers.)

Pickled radish pods: Make brine by dissolving 50 g (2 oz) salt in 0·5 litre (1 pint) water. Boil. Drop radish pods into hot brine, leave them there until cool. Drain and pack into jars. Fill with white vinegar and close jars. Add spices if required.

Pickled nasturtium seeds: A 1-lb jam jar of nasturtium seeds, 2 bay leaves, 1 tsp dill seed; 1 tbsp chopped horse radish; 0·5 litre (1 pint) vinegar; 1 small onion; 20 g ($\frac{3}{4}$ oz) peppercorns.

Pick nasturtium seeds three to seven days after flowers have dropped. Wash and dry seeds. Put in layers in jar, mixed with pieces of bay leaf, horse radish and dill seed. Bring to the boil sliced onion, peppercorns, salt and vinegar. Simmer for ten minutes. Cool. When cold, pour over seeds, covering completely. Cover jar with lid. Store in cool dark place for two months.

American dill pickles: Sterilize 1-litre (2-pint) jars. Place in each jar 1 clove garlic, 6 peppercorns, 1 clove, sprig of dill with seeds. Scrub thoroughly and dry 8-cm (3-in) long cucumbers or gherkins, or larger cucumbers cut into pieces. Pack closely into the jars. Bring to the boil 1 litre (2 pints) cider vinegar, 0·5 litre (1 pint) water, 50 g (2 oz) coarse salt. Cool. Fill jars to cover cucumbers. Leave at least five days before using.

Pickled onions or shallots: Place onions in brine made from 450 g (1 lb) salt dissolved in 4·5 litres (1 gal) water. Leave for twelve hours. Remove, peel and cover with fresh brine. Leave for further two to three days. Remove from brine, drain well, pack into jars and cover with cold spiced vinegar.

Pickled beet: Wash carefully. Bake in foil in moderate oven, or boil in salted water until tender. Peel. Leave whole or slice. Cover with spiced vinegar. If baked, add 14 g ($\frac{1}{2}$ oz) salt per 0·5 litre (1 pint).

Short-term pickle: Dilute malt vinegar 50 per cent with water; boil; add pepper and sugar. Use to marinate artichoke hearts overnight.

Horse Radish Sauce: Traditional – for 4 tbsp grated horse radish allow $\frac{1}{2}$ cup thick cream, $1\frac{1}{2}$ tbsp vinegar, $\frac{1}{2}$ tsp salt. Grate horse radish just before required. Mix with vinegar and salt, then add cream, beaten stiff.

Made with yogurt – whip grated horse radish with plain yoghurt, adding seasoning and a little sugar.

GENERAL RECIPES

Stir-frying – quick, nutritious way of cooking many vegetables, alone or in mixtures. Widely used for oriental vegetables. Use deep-frying pan or, preferably, a wok.

Cut vegetables into 2·5–5-cm (1–2-in) lengths. Heat small quantity of oil or fat in pan. When moderately hot add vegetables, putting in thicker vegetables (such as midribs of Chinese cabbage) first. Cover for first minute or two to cut down on splash and smoke, but not too long or vegetables lose colour. Remove lid; then add a little water if cooking firm vegetables (such as peas or beans) or add sauce, such as soy, where recipe calls for it. Leafy vegetables such as spinach, mustard or cabbage require no additional liquid. Cook for further three to five minutes, stirring continuously.

Braising: Method for cooking vegetables in a closed pot. Conserves delicate flavour and nutritive value.

First put knob of butter or little oil in dish. Warm. Cut vegetables into medium-sized pieces. Put into fat and turn until well coated. Add very small amount of water or stock (about $\frac{1}{2}$ cup to 1 kg (2 lb) cabbage), appropriate herbs and seasoning, cover and simmer very gently until tender. Suitable for carrots, celery, all types of chicory, Chinese cabbage, cucumber, endive, fennel, lettuce, onions, peas, peppers, salsify, seakale, spinach.

To make croutons: cut bread into 0·5–1-cm ($\frac{1}{4}$–$\frac{1}{2}$-in) cubes, fry quickly in lard or oil until crisp and golden. Alternatively, cut slices of toast into 0·5–1-cm ($\frac{1}{4}$–$\frac{1}{2}$-in) dices. Can rub garlic into bread first, or crush garlic into oil used for frying. Use mixed with grated raw salads, in green salads mixed with fried bacon, or in the bottom of the salad bowl.

APPENDIX I

SOWING GUIDE

Rough guide to main sowing periods for salads. Consult main text for appropriate variety to sow in each season. Sow early and late outdoors only where soil conditions suitable. 'Protection' indicates sowing in cold greenhouse, frame or under cloches. Asterisk indicates advisable to sow in gentle heat, such as propagator.

JANUARY
Protected: chicory (hardy cutting types), endive (Golda).
FEBRUARY
Alfalfa, chicories (hardy cutting types), Chinese chives, garlic, horse radish, onion (maincrop and Welsh), radish, seakale, shallot.
Protected: beetroot, celeriac,* celery,* chicories (hardy cutting types), chop suey greens, cress, endive (Golda), lettuce, mizuna greens, mustard (Karate and white), peppers,* radish, rocket.
MARCH
Alfalfa, chicory (grumolo, red and green for cutting), Chinese chives, chop suey greens, corn salad, cress, dandelion, garlic, horse radish, Japanese parsley, land cress, mizuna greens, mustard (all types), onion (all types), radish, rocket, salsify, scorzonera, seakale, shallots, sorrel.
Protected: beet, celeriac,* celery,* endive (all types), lettuce, mustard (Karate and white), peppers, radish, rocket, tomatoes.*
APRIL
Alfalfa, beet, celeriac, celery, Chinese chives, chop suey greens, claytonia, corn salad, chicory (as March), cress, dandelion, endive (all types), garlic, Japanese parsley, land cress, lettuce, mizuna greens, mustard (all types), onion (all types), radish, rocket, salsify, scorzonera, seakale, sorrel.
Protected: cucumber,* fennel, gherkin,* iceplant, pepper, purslane.

MAY

Alfalfa, beet, chicory (all types), Chinese chives, chop suey greens, claytonia, corn salad, cress, dandelion, endive (all types), fennel, iceplant, Japanese parsley, land cress, lettuce, mizuna greens, mustard (all types), onion (spring and Welsh), purslane, radish, rocket, salsify, scorzonera.

Protected: cucumber, gherkin.

JUNE

Beet, chicories (all types), chop suey greens, corn salad, cress, cucumber, dandelion, endive (all types), fennel, land cress, lettuce, mizuna greens, mustard (Karate, Oriental, white), onion (spring), purslane, radish, rocket.

JULY

Beet, chicory (cutting, grumolo, red, Sugar Loaf), Chinese cabbage, chop suey greens, claytonia, corn salad, cress, endive (all types), fennel, land cress, lettuce, mizuna greens, mustard (Karate, Oriental, white), onion (spring), radish (summer and winter), rocket, sorrel.

AUGUST

Chicory (grumolo, red for cutting, spadona, Sugar Loaf), Chinese cabbage, chop suey greens, claytonia, corn salad, cress, endive (broad), fennel, land cress, lettuce, mizuna greens, mustard (all types), onion (Japanese, spring and Welsh), radish (summer and winter), rocket, scorzonera.

SEPTEMBER

Alfalfa, chicory (grumolo, red for cutting, spadona), Chinese cabbage, chop suey greens, claytonia, corn salad, cress, garlic, land cress, lettuce, mizuna greens, mustard (all types), radish, rocket.

Protected: cress, endive (broad), mustard.

OCTOBER

Chicory (grumolo, spadona), garlic, lettuce, mizuna greens, rocket.

Protected: corn salad, cress, endive (broad), lettuce, mustard (Karate, white), radish.

NOVEMBER

Protected: chicory (spadona), corn salad, endive (Golda).

APPENDIX II

SUPPLIERS OF SEED, PLANTS AND EQUIPMENT

MAIL ORDER SEED FIRMS: with a good range of both the traditional and less common vegetables used in salads: J. W. Boyce, Soham, Ely, Cambridge CB7 5ED; Thomas Butcher Ltd, 60 Wickham Road, Shirley, Croydon, Surrey; Samuel Dobie and Sons Ltd, Upper Dee Mills, Llangollen, Clwyd LL20 8SD; Hillside Nurseries, West Road, Pointon, Sleaford, Lincolnshire; S. E. Marshall and Co. Ltd, Regal Road, Wisbech, Cambridge; Suttons Seeds Ltd, Hele Road, Torquay, Devon TH2 7QJ; Thompson and Morgan, London Road, Ipswich IP2 OBA.

SPECIALIST MAIL ORDER SEED FIRMS: Chiltern Seeds, Sunymede Avenue, Chesham, Buckinghamshire (Oriental and uncommon vegetables, ice plant, herbs); M. Holtzhausen, 14 High Cross Street, St Austell, Cornwall (uncommon vegetables, unusual varieties); Mommersteeg International, Station Road, Finedon, Wellingborough, Northamptonshire (Abyssinian mustard Karate, wild plant seeds); W. Robinson and Sons Ltd, Sunnybank, Forton, Nr Preston, Lancashire PR3 0BN (unusual tomatoes, onions, celery); Suffolk Herbs, Sawyers Farm, Little Cornard, Sudbury, Suffolk (wide range herb seed, salad, Oriental and wild plant seed); Wells and Winter, Mereworth, Maidstone, Kent (culinary and salad herbs – seed and plants).

PLANT/ROOT SUPPLIERS: A. R. Paske, Regal Lodge, Newmarket, Suffolk CB8 7QB (asparagus, seakale, globe artichokes); Donald MacLean, Dornoch Farm, Crieff, Perthshire (wide range of potato varieties – send s.a.e. in October for current list); Thornby Herbs Garden Centre, Thornby, Northampton (salad herbs and flowers – Chinese chives, fennel, garlic, Good King Henry, horse radish, orach, sorrel. No mail order).

Sprouting seeds (mail order): G. R. Lane Health Products Ltd, Sisson Road, Gloucester GL1 3QB; Tangent Marketing, Tangent House, 9 Arnison Road, East Molesey, Surrey KT8 9JF.

Equipment: Gardening equipment is available from garden centres and hardware shops. Members of garden and allotment societies can often obtain equipment at discount prices through bulk buying. Some useful items for salad growing are also available direct from manufacturers or distributors. Addresses as follows: Anderson Engineering Ltd, Albert Road, Crowthorne, Berkshire RG11 7LT (Jiffy Soil Heating Unit); Erme Wood Forge, Woodlands, Ivybridge, South Devon PL21 9HF (Devon cloche); Essex Garden Products Ltd, Robjohns Road, Chelmsford, Essex CM1 3TA (Essex cloche; Sprouter); LBS Polythene, Whiteholme Mill, Trawden, Nr Colne BB8 8RA (polythene tunnels, polythene sheeting and hoops for low tunnels); Rumsey Clips, 20 Beacon Down Avenue, Plymouth (clips for assembling glass cloches); Rutland (M.O.) Products Co. Ltd, Manor Lane, Langham, Rutland (Correx cloches and sheeting); Tangent Marketing, Tangent House, 9 Arnison Road, East Molesey, Surrey KT8 9JF (Sproutakit); Westray Cloches, 15 Church Road, Upper Boddington, Daventry, Northampton NN11 6DL (cloches).

Suppliers of predators: Natural Pest Control (Amateur), Watermead, Yapton Road, Barnham, Bognor Regis, Sussex PO22 0BQ; Perifleur Ltd, Hangleton Lane, Ferring, Sussex BN12 6PP.

APPENDIX III

FURTHER READING

The following books I have found very useful and can recommend for further reading and reference.

The Observer's Book of Vegetables, Allan A. Jackson (Frederick Warne, 1977).

The Vegetable Garden, Vilmorin-Andrieux (Frederick Warne, 1885, reprinted 1977).

Know and Grow Vegetables, edited by P. J. Salter and J. K. A. Bleasdale (Oxford University Press, 1979).

Rare Vegetables, John Organ (Faber & Faber, 1960).

Tomato Growing, Louis N. Flawn (Foyles Handbooks, 3rd edition, 1975).

Grow Your Own Chinese Vegetables, Geri Harrington (Collier Macmillan, 1978).

Culinary and Salad Herbs, Eleanour Sinclair Rohde (Dover Publications, 1972).

Culinary Herbs, Mary Page and William T. Stearn (Royal Horticultural Society, 1974).

Herb Gardening, Claire Loewenfeld (Faber & Faber, 1964).

The Edible Ornamental Garden, John E. Bryan and Coralie Castle (Pitman Publishing, 1976).

Cooking with Flowers, Greet Buchner (Thorsons Publishers, 1978).

Food for Free, Richard Mabey (Fontana Collins, 1972).

Free for All, Ceres (Thorsons Publishers, 1977).

Successful Sprouting, Frank Wilson (Thorsons Publishers, 1978).

Wild Flowers of Britain, Roger Phillips (Pan Books & Ward Lock, 1977).

Concise British Flora in Colour, W. Keble Martin (George Rainbird, 3rd edition, 1974).

LEAFLETS

National Vegetable Research Station Gardeners' Guides. The following are relevant to salad growing: No. 2 Early Bulb

Onions; No. 5 Fluid Sowing of Pre-germinated Seed; No. 7 Water in the Vegetable Garden; No. 8 Aphids; No. 10 Weeds; No. 11 Lettuce Sowing; No. 13 Outdoor Bush Tomatoes; No. 14 Lettuce Mildew. (For current list send s.a.e. to The Librarian, NVRS, Wellesbourne, Warwick.)

Horticultural books can be obtained by mail order from: Landsman's Bookshop, Buckenhill, Bromyard, Herefordshire.

APPENDIX IV

TERMS NOT EXPLAINED IN TEXT

ANNUAL – plant which germinates, flowers and dies within twelve months.

BASE DRESSING – fertilizer worked into the soil prior to sowing or planting.

BIENNIAL – plant which germinates, flowers and dies within two years.

BLANCHING (horticultural) – excluding light from plants to render them white and tender; (culinary) immersing briefly in boiling water.

BOLTING – flowering prematurely.

BRASSICA – large genus of plants including cabbages, turnips, swedes, mustards.

CHECK – growth being halted through adverse conditions such as drought, cold, starvation, failure to plant out.

CORDON – plant growing up single stem.

CULTIVAR – a variety raised in cultivation.

EARTHING UP – drawing up soil around the base and stem of a plant.

F_1 HYBRID – see p. 27.

GROWING POINT – tip of a plant.

HALF-HARDY – plant unable to survive British winter conditions without protection.

HARD-WOOD CUTTING – cutting taken from matured growth at end of growing season.

HARDY – plant capable of surviving British winter conditions without portection.

In situ SOWING – sowing where plant is to grow, so avoiding transplanting.

LEAF AXIL – angle between leaf and stem.

LEGUMES – plants which produce pods.

MARINATE (culinary) – to leave soaking in oil and vinegar (and possibly herbs) for a few hours.

Off-set – plant produced at base of parent plant.

Open-pollinated – seed produced from natural, random pollination.

Perennial – plant which lives for several years.

Seed leaves – the first leaf or leaves produced by a seedling when it germinates.

Short- and long-day plants – plants in which flowering is governed by day length, that is, plants which flower naturally before (short-day plant) or after (long-day plant) the longest day is passed in mid-June.

Soft-wood cuttings – cuttings taken from young growths early in the season.

Species – grouping of plants which differ only in minor details, and will freely cross with each other. Fairly closely related species are grouped together in a genus.

Stopping – removing the growing point of a plant.

Tender – plants which are injured by frost or cold weather.

Top dressing – fertilizer application to growing plants.

Viable seed – living seed, capable of germination.

INDEX

202

Prices and postage and packing rates shown below were correct at the time of going to press.

FICTION

All prices shown are exclusive of postage and packing.

GENERAL FICTION

☐ THE AFFAIR OF NINA B.	Simmel	£1.20
☐ H.M.S. BOUNTY	John Maxwell	£1.00
☐ TY-SHAN BAY	R. T. Aundrews	95p
☐ A SEA CHANGE	Lois Gould	80p
☐ THE PLAYERS	Gary Brandner	95p
☐ MR. FITTON'S COMMISSION	Showell Styles	85p
☐ CRASH LANDING	Mark Regan	95p
☐ SUMMER LIGHTNING	Judith Richards	£1.00
☐ THE HALO JUMP	Alistair Hamilton	£1.00
☐ SUMMERBLOOD	Anne Rudeen	£1.25
☐ PLACE OF THE DAWN	Gordon Taylor	90p
☐ EARTHLY POSSESSIONS	Anne Tyler	95p
☐ THE MASTER MECHANIC	I. G. Broat	£1.50
☐ THE MEXICAN PROPOSITION (Western)	Matt Chisholm	75p

CRIME/THRILLER

☐ THE TREMOR OF FORGERY	Patricia Highsmith	80p
☐ STRAIGHT	Steve Knickmeyer	80p
☐ THE COOL COTTONTAIL	John Ball	80p
☐ JOHNNY GET YOUR GUN	John Ball	85p
☐ CONFESS, FLETCH	Gregory Mcdonald	90p
☐ THE TRIPOLI DOCUMENTS	Henry Kane	95p
☐ THE EXECUTION	Oliver Crawford	90p
☐ TIME BOMB	James D. Atwater	90p
☐ THE SPECIALIST	Jasper Smith	85p
☐ KILLFACTOR FIVE	Peter Maxwell	85p
☐ ROUGH DEAL	Walter Winward	85p
☐ THE SONORA MUTATION	Albert J. Elias	85p
☐ THE RANSOM COMMANDO	James Grant	95p
☐ THE DESPERATE HOURS	Joseph Hayes	90p
☐ THE MOLE	Dan Sherman	95p

(H13A:10–12:79)

NON-FICTION

☐ THE HAMLYN BOOK OF CROSSWORDS 1		60p
☐ THE HAMLYN BOOK OF CROSSWORDS 2		60p
☐ THE HAMLYN BOOK OF CROSSWORDS 3		60p
☐ THE HAMLYN BOOK OF CROSSWORDS 4		60p
☐ THE HAMLYN FAMILY GAMES		
BOOK	Gyles Brandreth	75p
☐ LONELY WARRIOR (War)	Victor Houart	85p
☐ BLACK ANGELS (War)	Rupert Butler	£1.00
☐ THE SUNDAY TELEGRAPH PATIO		
GARDENING BOOK	Robert Pearson	80p
☐ THE COMPLETE TRAVELLER	Joan Bakewell	£1.50
☐ RESTORING OLD JUNK	Michèle Brown	75p
☐ FAT IS A FEMINIST ISSUE	Susie Orbach	85p
☐ AMAZING MAZES 1	Michael Lye	75p
☐ GUIDE TO THE CHANNEL ISLANDS	Janice Anderson and	
	Edmund Swinglehurst	90p
☐ THE STRESS FACTOR	Donald Norfolk	90p
☐ WOMAN × TWO	Mary Kenny	90p
☐ THE HAMLYN BOOK OF		
BRAINTEASERS AND		
MINDBENDERS	Ben Hamilton	85p
☐ THE HAMLYN CARTOON		
COLLECTION 2		70p
☐ WORLD WAR 3	edited by Shelford Bidwell	£1.25
☐ THE HAMLYN BOOK OF		
AMAZING INFORMATION		80p
☐ IN PRAISE OF YOUNGER MEN	Sandy Fawkes	85p
☐ THE HAMLYN FAMILY QUIZ BOOK		85p
☐ BONEY M	John Shearlaw and	
	David Brown	90p
☐ KISS	John Swenson	90p
☐ CARING FOR CATS AND KITTENS	John Montgomery	95p
☐ PUDDINGS AND DESSERTS		
(500 Recipes)	Monica Mawson	85p
☐ THE HAMLYN PRESSURE COOKBOOK	Jane Todd	85p
☐ HINTS FOR MODERN COOKS	Audrey Ellis	£1.00

COOKERY

☐ MIXER AND BLENDER COOKBOOK	Myra Street	80p
☐ HOME BAKED BREADS AND CAKES	Mary Norwak	75p
☐ EASY ICING	Marguerite Patten	85p
☐ HOME MADE COUNTRY WINES		40p
☐ COMPREHENSIVE GUIDE TO DEEP		
FREEZING		40p
☐ COUNTRY FARE	Doreen Fulleylove	80p
☐ HOME PRESERVING AND BOTTLING	Gladys Mann	80p
☐ WINE MAKING AT HOME	Francis Pinnegar	80p

All these books are available at your local bookshop or newsagent, or can be ordered direct from the publisher. Just tick the titles you want and fill in the form below.

NAME..

ADDRESS...

....

Write to Hamlyn Paperbacks Cash Sales, PO Box 11, Falmouth, Cornwall TR10 9EN
Please enclose remittance to the value of the cover price plus:

UK: 25p for the first book plus 10p per copy for each additional book ordered to a maximum charge of £1.05.

BFPO and EIRE: 25p for the first book plus 10p per copy for the next 8 books, thereafter 4p per book.

OVERSEAS: 40p for the first book and 12p for each additional book.

Whilst every effort is made to keep prices low it is sometimes necessary to increase cover prices and also postage and packing rates at short notice. Hamlyn Paperbacks reserve the right to show new retail prices on covers which may differ from those previously advertised in the text or elsewhere.

(H14:10–12:79)